Consequentialism

Blackwell Readings in Philosophy
Series Editor: Steven M. Cahn

Blackwell Readings in Philosophy are concise, chronologically arranged collections of primary readings from classical and contemporary sources. They represent core positions and important developments with respect to key philosophical concepts. Edited and introduced by leading philosophers, these volumes provide valuable resources for teachers and students of philosophy, and for all those interested in gaining a solid understanding of central topics in philosophy.

Consequentialism

Edited by

Stephen Darwall

Blackwell Publishing

Editorial material and organization © 2003 by Stephen Darwall

350 Main Street, Malden, MA 02148-5018, USA
108 Cowley Road, Oxford OX4 1JF, UK
550 Swanston Street, Carlton, Victoria 3053, Australia
Kurfürstendamm 57, 10707 Berlin, Germany

The right of Stephen Darwall to be identified as the Author of the Editorial
Material in this Work has been asserted in accordance with the UK Copyright,
Designs, and Patents Act 1988.

First published 2003 by Blackwell Publishers Ltd, a Blackwell Publishing
company

Library of Congress Cataloging-in-Publication Data

Consequentialism/edited by Stephen Darwall.
p. cm. – (Blackwell readings in philosophy; 7)
Includes bibliographical references and index.
ISBN 0-631-23107-2 (alk. paper) – ISBN 0-631-23108-0 (pbk. : alk. paper)
1. Consequentialism (Ethics)   I. Darwall, Stephen L., 1946–   II. Series.

BJ1031 .C594 2002
171'.5 – dc21
2002066425

A catalogue record for this title is available from the British Library.

Set in 10/12½ Palatino
by SNP Best-set Typesetter Ltd., Hong Kong
Printed and bound in the United Kingdom
by TJ International Ltd, Padstow, Cornwall

For further information on
Blackwell Publishing, visit our website:
http://www.blackwellpublishing.com

Contents

Acknowledgments

I am indebted to Steven Cahn for initially suggesting the idea of this anthology, to Jeff Dean for patiently shepherding me through the production process, to Blackwell's anonymous referees for very helpful comments, to Anthony Grahame for expert copy-editing, and to Sue London for yeoman work in copying.

The editor and publisher gratefully acknowledge the following for permission to reproduce copyright material:

Chapter 1: Jeremy Bentham, © University of London 1970. Reprinted by permission of Oxford University Press from Jeremy Bentham, *An Introduction to the Principles of Morals and Legislation*, an authoritative edition by J. H. Burns and H. L. A. Hart (1996);

Chapter 2: John Stuart Mill, *Utilitarianism*, edited by George Sher. Copyright © Hackett Publishing Company, Inc. Reproduced by permission of Hackett Publishing Company, Inc. 1979. All rights reserved;

Chapter 3: John Stuart Mill, "Dr Whewell on Moral Philosophy" was first published as "Whewell on Moral Philosophy' in the *Westminster Review*, October 1852. The text printed here is taken from *Dissertations and Discussions: Political, Philosophical and Historical*, first published by John W. Parker, London, 1859;

Chapter 4: Henry Sidgwick, from *The Method of Ethics*, seventh edition (London: Macmillan, 1967);

Chapter 5: G. E. Moore, from *Principia Ethica* (1993). Reproduced by permission of Cambridge University Press;

Chapter 6: Philip Pettit, "Consequentialism" from *A Companion to Ethics*, edited by Peter Singer (1991). Reproduced by permission of Blackwell Publishing;

Chapter 7: Samuel Scheffler, reprinted by permission of Oxford University Press from *The Rejection of Consequentialism: A Philosophical Investigation of the Considerations Underlying Rival Moral Conceptions* by Samuel Scheffler (revised edition, 1994);

Chapter 8: Derek Parfit, © Derek Parfit 1984. Reprinted from *Reasons and Persons* by Derek Parfit (1984) by permission of Oxford University Press;

Chapter 9: Peter Railton, "Alienation, Consequentialism, and the Demands of Morality" from *Philosophy and Public Affairs* 13 (1984). Copyright © 1984 by Princeton University Press. Reprinted by permission of Princeton University Press.

Chapter 10: John C. Harsanyi, "Bayesian Decision Theory and Utilitarian Ethics" from *The American Economic Review* 68 (1978);

Chapter 11: Richard B. Brandt, reprinted from "Toward a Credible Form of Rule-Utilitarianism" in *Morality and the Language of Conduct*, edited by Hector-Neri Castañeda and George Nahnikian (1965). Reproduced by permission of Wayne State University Press;

Chapter 12: Robert Adams, "Motive Utilitarianism" from *The Journal of Philosophy* 73 (1976). Reproduced by permission of The Journal of Philosophy and the author;

Chapter 13: John Rawls, "Classical Utilitarianism" reprinted by permission of the publisher from *A Theory of Justice* by John Rawls, pp. 23–7. Cambridge, Mass.: The Belknap Press of Harvard University Press. Copyright © 1971, 1999 by the President and Fellows of Harvard College;

Chapter 14: Amartya Sen, "Utilitarianism and Welfarism" from *The Journal of Philosophy* 76 (1979). Reproduced by permission of The Journal of Philosophy and the author.

The publisher apologizes for any errors or omissions in the above list and would be grateful if notified of any corrections that should be incorporated in future reprints or editions of this book.

Introduction

Consequentialism begins with the idea that there are values that are prior to morality. Even if there were no moral right and wrong, some things would still be good and others bad. The pain and suffering caused by a cataclysmic earthquake, for example, are bad things, regardless of any relation to vice or misconduct. They are bad things *to happen*, bad states of the world. Actually there are two different ideas here. First, and most obviously, pain and suffering are bad *for* those who experience them; they have "agent-relative" disvalue.[1] But it can also seem a bad thing *period*, and not *just* for them, when people's lives are bad for them in this way. Unlike the agent-relative disvalue involved in the very idea of harm, this value is non-relative or "agent-neutral." It can seem a bad thing agent-neutrally, that is, that agent-relative disvalues, like pain and suffering, occur. Both the agent-relative and the agent-neutral disvalue of pain are independent of morality, however, so both are called "nonmoral."

Consequentialist moral theories are standardly based on a theory of nonmoral, agent-neutral value: a normative theory of which states of the world (hence, possible consequences of action) have intrinsic (non-relative) value, which have intrinsic disvalue, and some account of how these values compare, either in an ordinal ranking or with some cardinal measure. What makes the values nonmoral, again, is that they involve evaluations of outcomes or states rather than distinctively moral evaluations of agency or character. Of course, such states might include agency and character. But even here the evaluation of the state can be distinguished from the moral evaluation of the act or character trait that is a constituent of it. Thus one might consistently think it would have been a good thing if Hitler had been assassinated, say because of the lives it would have saved, even if such an assassination would, perhaps, have been morally wrong. As we will see, a consequentialist might deny that assassinating Hitler would have been wrong, but the point is that there would be no inconsistency in holding it to be wrong and, at the same time, thinking that the state of the world following Hitler's being assassinated would, on balance, have been a good thing to have occurred.

Again, the relevant nonmoral evaluations concern the agent-neutral value of possible outcomes or states. These states may, of course, include agent-relative values and disvalues, benefits or harms *to* particular individuals. However, according to the most familiar forms of consequentialism, at least, what makes these benefits or harms morally relevant is that it is a good or bad thing from an agent-neutral perspective, say, from the moral point of view, or, as Sidgwick put it, "from the point of view of the Universe," that these agent-relative goods and evils occur.

A fundamental tenet on which all consequentialist moral theories agree is that the moral rightness and wrongness of acts is determined by the *nonmoral value* of *relevant consequences*. There are, however, two kinds of issues on which consequentialist theories divide. First, and most obviously, they can disagree by being based on different theories of nonmoral value. A consequentialist with a hedonist value theory, according to which pleasure is the only intrinsic good, will disagree, for example, with one who holds that the preservation of species or, perhaps, historical or cultural treasures can be a good thing in itself. Second, consequentialist theories can also disagree by holding that consequences of different sorts are relevant to determining moral right and wrong. *Act-consequentialism* holds that whether a given act is right depends on the value of the consequences of the specific act in question, compared with those of anything else the agent is able to do in the circumstances. According to *rule-consequentialism*, on the other hand, the rightness of acts does not depend on the consequences of the act in question; it depends rather on the consequences of the social acceptance of rules that either require, forbid, or permit the act, compared with the consequences of accepting other possible rules for acts and circumstances of that kind. If, for example, accepting a rule requiring an act of that kind would have the best consequences, then the act is morally required. And consequentialism can also take other forms, for example, motive-consequentialism, trait-consequentialism, and so on.

Consequentialists agree, however, in understanding moral evaluation to be most fundamentally an assessment of *instrumental* or *extrinsic* value. All [i.e. all consequentialists] are based on theories of the intrinsic, nonmoral value of outcomes, and all assess the moral status of acts and character by determining which acts, social rules, or traits of character are the best instruments for promoting the most valuable states. According to act-consequentialism, a morally right act is the best instrument available to the agent for producing nonmoral value in the situation in which she finds herself. And rule-consequentialism judges the rightness of acts by the verdicts of socially realizable rules that are, via their participation in social practices of moral reasoning and criticism, the best instruments of their kind for producing nonmoral value.

In principle, virtually any theory of nonmoral, outcome-value can be harnessed to a consequentialist moral theory. Historically, however, consequentialism has been advanced most frequently by philosophers who have thought that a valuable outcome must somehow involve agent-relative value, value *to* some conscious being.[2] *Welfare consequentialism* is the view that valuable states always concern the good or welfare of some being, and that moral assessment must ultimately be based on this. This does not, however, commit welfare consequentialists to holding that valuable states always involve an effect on subjective consciousness. It is possible to believe that something can benefit or harm a being by affecting something other than the quality of experience or what is related to a conscious mental state. For example, perfectionists sometimes assert that a being's realizing an ideal for its kind is intrinsically beneficial to it. This is what leads to the conclusion of Aristotle's famous "function" argument that human good or flourishing consists in excellent, distinctively human activity.[3] By and large, however, welfare consequentialists have tended to hold that individuals can be benefited or harmed only by things that are appropriately related to their consciousness, either by affecting the quality of their experience or by affecting the objects of such mental states as desire. Welfare consequentialists, in other words, have generally held either *hedonistic* or *desire-based* forms of consequentialism.

The most popular form historically has been *utilitarianism*, which is distinguished by three features. First, utilitarians are welfare consequentialists who hold either hedonistic or desire-based conceptions of welfare. Second, utilitarians hold that the nonmoral value of outcomes is determined by summing the benefits and costs (in pleasure or desire-satisfaction) to all affected parties. And, third, utilitarians believe that the moral rightness of action or the moral goodness of character traits depends on what would produce the greatest overall value, determined by such a sum. The classical *hedonistic* utilitarian formulation, in Bentham for example, holds that happiness is an experienced state and that people can be benefited only by the intrinsic qualities of their conscious lives, the degree of pleasure that they experience compared with their pain or suffering.[4] Another classical formulation, John Stuart Mill's, allows for the possibility of higher forms of pleasure and takes the informed desires of experienced judges as evidence for these.[5] And yet another kind of utilitarianism, especially popular with economists, holds that an individual's welfare is determined by his actual desires and preferences, whatever these might be. Such a view sometimes seems to be grounded in autonomy as a free-standing value. Since people can have preferences for things other than the intrinsic qualities of their own conscious states, this *desire-satisfaction* form of utilitarianism has rather different implications than a hedonist version. For example, someone might strongly desire the survival of a certain wilderness area for its own sake. A desire-satisfaction form of utilitarianism would weigh this fact in favor of saving the area even if saving it made no contribution to the quality of any being's experience (say, if the individual in question knew nothing of the area's survival).

Although consequentialists have usually been utilitarians or welfare consequentialists of some sort, there is nothing in the logic of consequentialism that restricts it to these versions. Philosophers have frequently argued that such things as knowledge, understanding, friendship, love, beauty, and artistic and other cultural activity and creation have intrinsic values that cannot be reduced to the benefits they bring to human (or other sentient) life. After all, some of our deepest satisfactions seem themselves to involve the *appreciation* of these values, so the values cannot wholly consist in these satisfactions. When it comes to controversial issues, for example, in environmental or medical ethics, it is open to consequentialists to argue that relevant values include such things as the existence of a species or of a relationship of a certain kind between doctors and patients. The consequentialist's test for moral relevance will simply be whether a given state of affairs' existence makes a positive contribution to the value instantiated in the world, whether it is a good or bad thing that it exist or happen.

This structure enables consequentialism to take account, in principle, of a wider range of considerations than can contractarianism or contractualism. Most notably, there is nothing in the consequentialist conception of morality that ties it specially to the condition of other members of the moral community, or that restricts its consideration to human beings in any way. If pain or suffering is a bad thing then, it seems, it would be bad whether the being that suffers is capable of moral agency or not. For this reason, advocates for the interests of animals frequently cite Bentham's dictum: "The question is not, can they reason? . . . but, can they suffer?"[6] And consequentialists who believe that intrinsically valuable states are not restricted to welfare or agent-relative value can take advantage of a wider array of considerations yet. Of course, moral reasoning is not simply a matter of deploying rhetorical resources. Any moral conception will face the burden of defending the relevance of the considerations it advances and, in the end, anyone who adopts that conception will need to think through how the moral relevance of such considerations can be situated in a philosophically adequate conception of moral obligation.

The agent-neutrality of its fundamental values is an important feature of consequentialism. Since agent-neutral values attach simply to the existence of the relevant states, they justify whatever actions, policies, or practices might bring the states into existence, irrespective of *the agent's* relation to them. An example will clarify this idea and its relevance. Suppose you think that among the intrinsically bad things that can happen is someone's being betrayed by a friend. The thought here is not that it is wrong to betray friends, or even that this is a bad thing to do, but that someone's being betrayed by a friend is a bad thing to happen. And again, it is not just that this is bad for the person being betrayed (bad in agent-relative terms), but that it is a bad thing period (agent-neutrally) for someone to be hurt in this way. If you think this is a bad thing to happen, you should also think that it would be good, other things being equal, for actions, policies, and practices to be taken that would prevent this. Suppose that there are two people, A and B, who are contemplating betraying their friends. Suppose also that circumstances are such that if you betray *your* friend, A and B will be so horrified that they will not betray theirs, although they would have otherwise. We can now put the idea of agent-neutrality this way. From the point of view of the intrinsic (agent-neutral) badness of friends' being betrayed, in this situation you would seem to have reason to betray your friend since it would go farther to minimizing the intrinsically disvaluable states of betrayals than would your not betraying your friend. Of course, this runs against moral common sense. We commonly believe that friends have duties to each other that are *agent-relative* rather than *agent-neutral*, that a moral agent has a duty not to betray *his or her* friends that is not reducible to preventing the (agent-neutral) evil of friends' being betrayed.

The idea that there are moral obligations that are agent-relative in this way is a hallmark of *deontological* moral theories, which are frequently contrasted with consequentialism. According to deontologists, agency and action are not simply instruments for producing valuable states. Rather actions are based on reasons and principles, and some important moral principles hold that the agent's relation to various persons (or other beings) in the outcomes she affects is critically relevant. It is commonly thought to be a wrong-making feature of an action, for example, that it will involve *one's* (that is, *the agent's*) harming *others*, betraying *her* friend, breaking *her* promise, and so on.

Some consequentialist theories, although not all, can agree with these aspects of moral common sense. Rule-consequentialism will agree if, and only if, it produces the greatest overall value (assessed agent-neutrally) for there to exist social practices of moral criticism and psychological patterns of moral reasoning that are themselves guided by agent-relative rules. If this is so, then rule-consequentialism will hold that whether an act is morally right or wrong depends on the verdicts of these socially beneficial rules. Moreover, it is widely agreed among consequentialists that this is in fact the case. Consequentialists generally agree that the most effective way to produce the greatest overall value is *indirectly*. Were everyone to be guided by act-consequentialism in their deliberations and moral criticism, the results would be much worse for many different reasons. Shared rules, many of them agent-relative, are necessary, consequentialists generally agree, to coordinate complex cooperation, establish reliable expectations, diminish self-serving rationalizing and special pleading when the long-run effects of particular actions are unclear, and so on. In the end, however, even rule-consequentialists will agree that the fundamental reason for accepting such agent-relative rules and principles is that this is instrumentally useful in promoting states whose value is agent-neutral. And act-consequentialists will argue that even if there are good consequentialist reasons for *accepting* agent-relative rules as deliberative or social guides, that doesn't make them *true*. What is true, the act-consequentialist believes, is that moral right and wrong are determined in every instance by what would promote the greatest overall, agent-neutral value.

The readings that follow fall into three main categories: classical sources, contemporary expressions, and contemporary discussion. In the first category, there is a further division between philosophers like Jeremy Bentham and John Stuart Mill, who situate consequentialism within a thoroughgoing empiricism, and Henry Sidgwick and G. E. Moore, who reject empiricism but accept consequentialism nonetheless as the result of rational intuition. The selections from contemporary consequentialists range from discussing the fundamental rationale for consequentialism in comparison with its rivals (Philip Pettit and Samuel Scheffler), to defending consequentialism against influential contemporary criticisms (Derek Parfit and Peter Railton), to showing how utilitarianism might be justified by plausible constraints on moral reasoning (John C. Harsanyi), to developing versions of utilitarianism that adequately account for the significance of moral rules (rule-utilitarianism) and motives (motive util-itarianism) (Richard B. Brandt and Robert Adams). Finally, third, there are two important discussions of consequentialism in the writings of John Rawls and Amartya Sen.

Notes

1 A more appropriate qualifier in this context would be "patient-" or "subject-relative," but I will follow the more standard philosophical usage "agent-relative." A more fine-grained analysis might distinguish between more properly *agent*-relative value – what is good from the agent's point of view – and what is good for someone in the sense of their good, interest, benefit, or welfare. On this point, see my "Self-Interest and Self-Concern," in Ellen F. Paul, ed., *Self-Interest* (Cambridge: Cambridge University Press, 1997); and *Social Philosophy & Policy* 14 (1997): 158–78.

2 Again, "subject-relative" might be more appropriate than "agent-relative," since a welfare consequentialist need not hold that only agents can be bene-fited or harmed (or even that benefits or harms to subjects who are agents is identical with what is good or bad from the deliberative point of view).

3 Aristotle, *Nicomachean Ethics*, Bk. I, ch. 7.

4 Jeremy Bentham, *Introduction to the Principles of Morals and Legislation* (origi-nally published in 1789).

5 John Stuart Mill, *Utilitarianism* (originally published in 1861). I provide an extended discussion of Mill's ethical philosophy in *Philosophical Ethics* (Boulder, CO: Westview Press, 1998), pp. 109–38.

6 *Introduction to the Principles of Morals and Legislation*, Ch. XVII, § 4, note b.

Part I

Classical Sources

1

From *An Introduction to the Principles of Morals and Legislation*

Jeremy Bentham

CHAPTER I
Of the Principle of Utility

1.   Nature has placed mankind under the governance of two sovereign masters, *pain* and *pleasure*. It is for them alone to point out what we ought to do, as well as to determine what we shall do. On the one hand the standard of right and wrong, on the other the chain of causes and effects, are fastened to their throne. They govern us in all we do, in all we say, in all we think: every effort we can make to throw off our subjection, will serve but to demonstrate and confirm it. In words a man may pretend to abjure their empire: but in reality he will remain subject to it all the while. The *principle of utility*[1] recognises this subjection, and assumes it for the foundation of that system, the object of which is to rear the fabric of felicity by the hands of reason and of law. Systems which attempt to question it, deal in sounds instead of sense, in caprice instead of reason, in darkness instead of light.

But enough of metaphor and declamation: it is not by such means that moral science is to be improved.

2.   The principle of utility is the foundation of the present work: it will be proper therefore at the outset to give an explicit and determinate account of what is meant by it. By the principle[2] of utility is meant that principle which approves or disapproves of every action whatsoever,

Jeremy Bentham, *An Introduction to the Principles of Morals and Legislation*, J. H. Burns, ed. (Oxford: Clarendon Press, 1996), pp. 11–16, 38–50, 100–2.

according to the tendency which it appears to have to augment or diminish the happiness of the party whose interest is in question: or, what is the same thing in other words, to promote or to oppose that happiness. I say of every action whatsoever; and therefore not only of every action of a private individual, but of every measure of government.

3.   By utility is meant that property in any object, whereby it tends to produce benefit, advantage, pleasure, good, or happiness, (all this in the present case comes to the same thing) or (what comes again to the same thing) to prevent the happening of mischief, pain, evil, or unhappiness to the party whose interest is considered: if that party be the community in general, then the happiness of the community: if a particular individual, then the happiness of that individual.

4.   The interest of the community is one of the most general expressions that can occur in the phraseology of morals: no wonder that the meaning of it is often lost. When it has a meaning, it is this. The community is a fictitious *body*, composed of the individual persons who are considered as constituting as it were its *members*. The interest of the community then is, what? – the sum of the interests of the several members who compose it.

5.   It is in vain to talk of the interest of the community, without understanding what is the interest of the individual.[3] A thing is said to promote the interest, or to be *for* the interest, of an individual, when it tends to add to the sum total of his pleasures: or, what comes to the same thing, to diminish the sum total of his pains.

6.   An action then may be said to be conformable to the principle of utility, or, for shortness sake, to utility, (meaning with respect to the community at large) when the tendency it has to augment the happiness of the community is greater than any it has to diminish it.

7.   A measure of government (which is but a particular kind of action, performed by a particular person or persons) may be said to be conformable to or dictated by the principle of utility, when in like manner the tendency which it has to augment the happiness of the community is greater than any which it has to diminish it.

8.   When an action, or in particular a measure of government, is supposed by a man to be conformable to the principle of utility, it may be convenient, for the purposes of discourse, to imagine a kind of law or dictate, called a law or dictate of utility: and to speak of the action in question, as being conformable to such law or dictate.

9.   A man may be said to be a partisan of the principle of utility, when the approbation or disapprobation he annexes to any action, or to any measure, is determined by, and proportioned to the tendency which he

conceives it to have to augment or to diminish the happiness of the community: or in other words, to its conformity or unconformity to the laws or dictates of utility.

10.   Of an action that is conformable to the principle of utility, one may always say either that it is one that ought to be done, or at least that it is not one that ought not to be done. One may say also, that it is right it should be done; at least that it is not wrong it should be done: that it is a right action; at least that it is not a wrong action. When thus interpreted, the words *ought*, and *right* and *wrong*, and others of that stamp, have a meaning: when otherwise, they have none.

11.   Has the rectitude of this principle been ever formally contested? It should seem that it had, by those who have not known what they have been meaning. Is it susceptible of any direct proof? it should seem not: for that which is used to prove every thing else, cannot itself be proved: a chain of proofs must have their commencement somewhere. To give such proof is as impossible as it is needless.

12.   Not that there is or ever has been that human creature breathing, however stupid or perverse, who has not on many, perhaps on most occasions of his life, deferred to it. By the natural constitution of the human frame, on most occasions of their lives men in general embrace this principle, without thinking of it: if not for the ordering of their own actions, yet for the trying of their own actions, as well as of those of other men. There have been, at the same time, not many, perhaps, even of the most intelligent, who have been disposed to embrace it purely and without reserve. There are even few who have not taken some occasion or other to quarrel with it, either on account of their not understanding always how to apply it, or on account of some prejudice or other which they were afraid to examine into, or could not bear to part with. For such is the stuff that man is made of: in principle and in practice, in a right track and in a wrong one, the rarest of all human qualities is consistency.

13.   When a man attempts to combat the principle of utility, it is with reasons drawn, without his being aware of it, from that very principle itself.[4] His arguments, if they prove any thing, prove not that the principle is *wrong*, but that, according to the applications he supposes to be made of it, it is *misapplied*. Is it possible for a man to move the earth? Yes; but he must first find out another earth to stand upon.

14.   To disprove the propriety of it by arguments is impossible; but, from the causes that have been mentioned, or from some confused or partial view of it, a man may happen to be disposed not to relish it. Where this is the case, if he thinks the settling of his opinions on such a subject worth the trouble, let him take the following steps, and at length, perhaps, he may come to reconcile himself to it.

(1)   Let him settle with himself, whether he would wish to discard this principle altogether; if so, let him consider what it is that all his reasonings (in matters of politics especially) can amount to?

(2)   If he would, let him settle with himself, whether he would judge and act without any principle, or whether there is any other he would judge and act by?

(3)   If there be, let him examine and satisfy himself whether the principle he thinks he has found is really any separate intelligible principle; or whether it be not a mere principle in words, a kind of phrase, which at bottom expresses neither more nor less than the mere averment of his own unfounded sentiments; that is, what in another person he might be apt to call *caprice*?

(4)   If he is inclined to think that his own approbation or disapprobation, annexed to the idea of an act, without any regard to its consequences, is a sufficient foundation for him to judge and act upon, let him ask himself whether his sentiment is to be a standard of right and wrong, with respect to every other man, or whether every man's sentiment has the same privilege of being a standard to itself?

(5)   In the first case, let him ask himself whether his principle is not despotical, and hostile to all the rest of human race?

(6)   In the second case, whether it is not anarchical, and whether at this rate there are not as many different standards of right and wrong as there are men? and whether even to the same man, the same thing, which is right today, may not (without the least change in its nature) be wrong to-morrow? and whether the same thing is not right and wrong in the same place at the same time? and in either case, whether all argument is not at an end? and whether, when two men have said, 'I like this', and 'I don't like it', they can (upon such a principle) have any thing more to say?

(7)   If he should have said to himself, No: for that the sentiment which he proposes as a standard must be grounded on reflection, let him say on what particulars the reflection is to turn? if on particulars having relation to the utility of the act, then let him say whether this is not deserting his own principle, and borrowing assistance from that very one in opposition to which he sets it up: or if not on those particulars, on what other particulars?

(8)   If he should be for compounding the matter, and adopting his own principle in part, and the principle of utility in part, let him say how far he will adopt it?

(9)   When he has settled with himself where he will stop, then let him ask himself how he justifies to himself the adopting it so far? and why he will not adopt it any farther?

(10)   Admitting any other principle than the principle of utility to be a right principle, a principle that it is right for a man to pursue; admitting (what is not true) that the word *right* can have a meaning without reference to utility, let him say whether there is any such thing as a *motive* that a man can have to pursue the dictates of it: if there is, let him say what that motive is, and how it is to be distinguished from those which enforce the dictates of utility: if not, then lastly let him say what it is this other principle can be good for?

Notes

1   Note by the Author, July 1822.
   To this denomination has of late been added, or substituted, the *greatest happiness* or *greatest felicity* principle: this for shortness, instead of saying at length *that principle* which states the greatest happiness of all those whose interest is in question, as being the right and proper, and only right and proper and universally desirable, end of human action: of human action in every situation, and in particular in that of a functionary or set of functionaries exercising the powers of Government. The word *utility* does not so clearly point to the ideas of *pleasure* and *pain* as the words *happiness* and *felicity* do: nor does it lead us to the consideration of the *number*, of the interests affected; to the *number*, as being the circumstance, which contributes, in the largest proportion, to the formation of the standard here in question; the *standard of right and wrong*, by which alone the propriety of human conduct, in every situation, can with propriety be tried. This want of a sufficiently manifest connexion between the ideas of *happiness* and *pleasure* on the one hand, and the idea of *utility* on the other, I have every now and then found operating, and with but too much efficiency, as a bar to the acceptance, that might otherwise have been given, to this principle.

2   (Principle) The word principle is derived from the Latin *principium*: which seems to be compounded of the two words *primus*, first, or chief, and *cipium*, a termination which seems to be derived from *capio*, to take, as in *mancipium*, *municipium*; to which are analogous *auceps*, *forceps*, and others. It is a term of very vague and very extensive signification: it is applied to any thing which is conceived to serve as a foundation or beginning to any series of operations: in some cases, of physical operations; but of mental operations in the present case.
   The principle here in question may be taken for an act of the mind; a sentiment; a sentiment of approbation; a sentiment which, when applied to an

action, approves of its utility, as that quality of it by which the measure of approbation or disapprobation bestowed upon it ought to be governed.

3   (Interest, &c.) Interest is one of those words, which not having any superior *genus*, cannot in the ordinary way be defined.

4   'The principle of utility, (I have heard it said) is a dangerous principle: it is dangerous on certain occasions to consult it.' This is as much as to say, what? that it is not consonant to utility, to consult utility: in short, that it is *not* consulting it, to consult it.

Addition by the author, July 1822.

Not long after the publication of the Fragment on Government, anno 1776, in which, in the character of an all-comprehensive and all-commanding principle, the principle of *utility* was brought to view, one person by whom observation to the above effect was made was *Alexander Wedderburn*, at that time Attorney or Solicitor General, afterwards successively Chief Justice of the Common Pleas, and Chancellor of England, under the successive titles of Lord Loughborough and Earl of Rosslyn. It was made – not indeed in my hearing, but in the hearing of a person by whom it was almost immediately communicated to me. So far from being self-contradictory, it was a shrewd and perfectly true one. By that distinguished functionary, the state of the Government was thoroughly understood: by the obscure individual, at that time not so much as supposed to be so: his disquisitions had not been as yet applied, with any thing like a comprehensive view, to the field of Constitutional Law, nor therefore to those features of the English Government, by which the greatest happiness of the ruling *one* with or without that of a favoured few, are now so plainly seen to be the only ends to which the course of it has at any time been directed. The *principle of utility* was an appellative, at that time employed – employed by me, as it had been by others, to designate that which, in a more perspicuous and instructive manner, may, as above, be designated by the name of the *greatest happiness principle*. 'This principle (said Wedderburn) is a dangerous one.' Saying so, he said that which, to a certain extent, is strictly true: a principle, which lays down, as the only *right* and justifiable end of Government, the greatest happiness of the greatest number – how can it be denied to be a dangerous one? dangerous it unquestionably is, to every government which has for its *actual* end or object, the greatest happiness of a certain *one*, with or without the addition of some comparatively small number of others, whom it is matter of pleasure or accommodation to him to admit, each of them, to a share in the concern, on the footing of so many junior partners. *Dangerous* it therefore really was, to the interest – the sinister interest – of all those functionaries, himself included, whose interest it was, to maximize delay, vexation, and expense, in judicial and other modes of procedure, for the sake of the profit, extractable out of the expense. In a Government which had for its end in view the greatest happiness of the greatest number, Alexander Wedderburn might have been Attorney General and then Chancellor: but he would not have been Attorney General with £15,000 a year, nor Chancellor, with a peerage, with a veto upon all justice, with £25,000 a year, and with 500 sinecures at his disposal, under the name of Ecclesiastical Benefices, besides *et ceteras*.

CHAPTER IV
Value of a Lot of Pleasure or Pain, How to be Measured

1.   Pleasures then, and the avoidance of pains, are the *ends* which the legislator has in view: it behoves him therefore to understand their *value*. Pleasures and pains are the *instruments* he has to work with: it behoves him therefore to understand their force, which is again, in another point of view, their value.

2.   To a person considered *by himself*, the value of a pleasure or pain considered *by itself*, will be greater or less, according to the four following circumstances:[1]

1.   Its *intensity*.
2.   Its *duration*.
3.   Its *certainty* or *uncertainty*.
4.   Its *propinquity* or *remoteness*.

3.   These are the circumstances which are to be considered in estimating a pleasure or a pain considered each of them by itself. But when the value of any pleasure or pain is considered for the purpose of estimating the tendency of any *act* by which it is produced, there are two other circumstances to be taken into the account; these are,

5.   Its *fecundity*, or the chance it has of being followed by sensations of the *same* kind: that is, pleasures, if it be a pleasure: pains, if it be a pain.
6.   Its *purity*, or the chance it has of *not* being followed by sensations of the *opposite* kind: that is, pains, if it be a pleasure: pleasures, if it be a pain.

These two last, however, are in strictness scarcely to be deemed properties of the pleasure or the pain itself; they are not, therefore, in strictness to be taken into the account of the value of that pleasure or that pain. They are in strictness to be deemed properties only of the act, or other event, by which such pleasure or pain has been produced; and accordingly are only to be taken into the account of the tendency of such act or such event.

4. To a *number* of persons, with reference to each of whom the value of a pleasure or a pain is considered, it will be greater or less, according to seven circumstances: to wit, the six preceding ones; viz.

1. Its *intensity*.
2. Its *duration*.
3. Its *certainty* or *uncertainty*.
4. Its *propinquity* or *remoteness*.
5. Its *fecundity*.
6. Its *purity*.

And one other; to wit:

7. Its *extent*; that is, the number of persons to whom it *extends*; or (in other words) who are affected by it.

5. To take an exact account then of the general tendency of any act, by which the interests of a community are affected, proceed as follows. Begin with any one person of those whose interests seem most immediately to be affected by it: and take an account,

1. Of the value of each distinguishable *pleasure* which appears to be produced by it in the *first* instance.
2. Of the value of each *pain* which appears to be produced by it in the *first* instance.
3. Of the value of each pleasure which appears to be produced by it *after* the first. This constitutes the *fecundity* of the first *pleasure* and the *impurity* of the first *pain*.
4. Of the value of each *pain* which appears to be produced by it after the first. This constitutes the *fecundity* of the first *pain*, and the *impurity* of the first pleasure.
5. Sum up all the values of all the *pleasures* on the one side, and those of all the *pains* on the other. The balance, if it be on the side of pleasure, will give the *good* tendency of the act upon the whole, with respect to the interests of that *individual* person; if on the side of pain, the *bad* tendency of it upon the whole.
6. Take an account of the *number* of persons whose interests appear to be concerned; and repeat the above process with respect to each. *Sum up* the numbers expressive of the degrees of *good* tendency, which the act has, with respect to each individual, in regard to whom the tendency of it is *good* upon the whole: do this again with respect to each individual, in regard to whom the tendency of it is *bad* upon the

whole. Take the *balance*; which, if on the side of *pleasure*, will give the general *good tendency* of the act, with respect to the total number or community of individuals concerned; if on the side of pain, the general *evil tendency*, with respect to the same community.

6. It is not to be expected that this process should be strictly pursued previously to every moral judgment, or to every legislative or judicial operation. It may, however, be always kept in view: and as near as the process actually pursued on these occasions approaches to it, so near will such process approach to the character of an exact one.

7. The same process is alike applicable to pleasure and pain, in whatever shape they appear: and by whatever denomination they are distinguished: to pleasure, whether it be called *good* (which is properly the cause or instrument of pleasure) or *profit* (which is distant pleasure, or the cause or instrument of distant pleasure,) or *convenience*, or *advantage*, *benefit*, *emolument*, *happiness*, and so forth: to pain, whether it be called *evil*, (which corresponds to *good*) or *mischief*, or *inconvenience*, or *disadvantage*, or *loss*, or *unhappiness*, and so forth.

8. Nor is this a novel and unwarranted, any more than it is a useless theory. In all this there is nothing but what the practice of mankind, wheresoever they have a clear view of their own interest, is perfectly conformable to. An article of property, an estate in land, for instance, is valuable, on what account? On account of the pleasures of all kinds which it enables a man to produce, and what comes to the same thing the pains of all kinds which it enables him to avert. But the value of such an article of property is universally understood to rise or fall according to the length or shortness of the time which a man has in it: the certainty or uncertainty of its coming into possession: and the nearness or remoteness of the time at which, if at all, it is to come into possession. As to the *intensity* of the pleasures which a man may derive from it, this is never thought of, because it depends upon the use which each particular person may come to make of it; which cannot be estimated till the particular pleasures he may come to derive from it, or the particular pains he may come to exclude by means of it, are brought to view. For the same reason, neither does he think of the *fecundity* or *purity* of those pleasures.

Thus much for pleasure and pain, happiness and unhappiness, in *general*. We come now to consider the several particular kinds of pain and pleasure.

Note

1 These circumstances have since been denominated *elements* or *dimensions* of *value* in a pleasure or a pain.

   Not long after the publication of the first edition, the following memoriter verses were framed, in the view of lodging more effectually, in the memory, these points, on which the whole fabric of morals and legislation may be seen to rest.

> *Intense, long, certain, speedy, fruitful, pure –*
> Such marks in *pleasures* and in *pains* endure.
> Such pleasures seek, if *private* be thy end:
> If it be *public*, wide let them *extend*.
> Such *pains* avoid, whichever be thy view:
> If pains *must* come, let them *extend* to few.

CHAPTER V
Pleasures and Pains, Their Kinds

1. Having represented what belongs to all sorts of pleasures and pains alike, we come now to exhibit, each by itself, the several sorts of pains and pleasures. Pains and pleasures may be called by one general word, interesting perceptions. Interesting perceptions are either simple or complex. The simple ones are those which cannot any one of them be resolved into more: complex are those which are resolvable into divers simple ones. A complex interesting perception may accordingly be composed either, 1. Of pleasures alone: 2. Of pains alone: or, 3. Of a pleasure or pleasures, and a pain or pains together. What determines a lot of pleasure, for example, to be regarded as one complex pleasure, rather than as divers simple ones, is the nature of the exciting cause. Whatever pleasures are excited all at once by the action of the same cause, are apt to be looked upon as constituting all together but one pleasure.

2. The several simple pleasures of which human nature is susceptible, seem to be as follows: 1. The pleasures of sense. 2. The pleasures of wealth. 3. The pleasures of skill. 4. The pleasures of amity. 5. The pleasures of a good name. 6. The pleasures of power. 7. The pleasures of piety. 8. The pleasures of benevolence. 9. The pleasures of malevolence. 10. The pleasures of memory. 11. The pleasures of imagination. 12. The pleasures of expectation. 13. The pleasures dependent on association. 14. The pleasures of relief.

3. The several simple pains seem to be as follows: 1. The pains of privation. 2. The pains of the senses. 3. The pains of awkwardness. 4. The pains of enmity. 5. The pains of an ill name. 6. The pains of piety. 7. The pains of benevolence. 8. The pains of malevolence. 9. The pains of the memory. 10. The pains of the imagination. 11. The pains of expectation. 12. The pains dependent on association.[1]

4. (1) The pleasures of sense seem to be as follows: 1. The pleasures of the taste or palate; including whatever pleasures are experienced in satisfying the appetites of hunger and thirst. 2. The pleasure of intoxication. 3. The pleasures of the organ of smelling. 4. The pleasures of the touch. 5. The simple pleasures of the ear; independent of association. 6. The simple pleasures of the eye; independent of association. 7. The pleasure of the sexual sense. 8. The pleasure of health: or, the internal pleasurable feeling or flow of spirits (as it is called,) which accompanies a state of full health and vigour; especially at times of moderate bodily exertion. 9. The pleasures of novelty: or, the pleasures derived from the gratification of the appetite of curiosity, by the application of new objects to any of the senses.[2]

5. (2) By the pleasures of wealth may be meant those pleasures which a man is apt to derive from the consciousness of possessing any article or articles which stand in the list of instruments of enjoyment or security, and more particularly at the time of his first acquiring them; at which time the pleasure may be styled a pleasure of gain or a pleasure of acquisition: at other times a pleasure of possession.

(3) The pleasures of skill, as exercised upon particular objects, are those which accompany the application of such particular instruments of enjoyment to their uses, as cannot be so applied without a greater or less share of difficulty or exertion.[3]

6. (4) The pleasures of amity, or self-recommendation, are the pleasures that may accompany the persuasion of a man's being in the acquisition or the possession of the good-will of such or such assignable person or persons in particular: or, as the phrase is, of being upon good terms with him or them: and as a fruit of it, of his being in a way to have the benefit of their spontaneous and gratuitous services.

7. (5) The pleasures of a good name are the pleasures that accompany the persuasion of a man's being in the acquisition or the possession of the good-will of the world about him; that is, of such members of society as he is likely to have concerns with; and as a means of it, either their love or their esteem, or both: and as a fruit of it, of his being in the way to have the benefit of their spontaneous and gratuitous services. These may likewise be called the pleasures of good repute, the pleasures of honour, or the pleasures of the moral sanction.

8. (6) The pleasures of power are the pleasures that accompany the persuasion of a man's being in a condition to dispose people, by means of their hopes and fears, to give him the benefit of their services: that is, by the hope of some service, or by the fear of some disservice, that he may be in the way to render them.

9. (7) The pleasures of piety are the pleasures that accompany the belief of a man's being in the acquisition or in possession of the good-will or favour of the Supreme Being: and as a fruit of it, of his being in a way of enjoying pleasures to be received by God's special appointment, either in this life, or in a life to come. These may also be called the pleasures of religion, the pleasures of a religious disposition, or the pleasures of the religious sanction.

10. (8) The pleasures of benevolence are the pleasures resulting from the view of any pleasures supposed to be possessed by the beings who may be the objects of benevolence; to wit, the sensitive beings we are acquainted with; under which are commonly included, 1. The Supreme Being. 2. Human beings. 3. Other animals. These may also be called the pleasures of good-will, the pleasures of sympathy, or the pleasures of the benevolent or social affections.

11. (9) The pleasures of malevolence are the pleasures resulting from the view of any pain supposed to be suffered by the beings who may become the objects of malevolence: to wit, 1. Human beings. 2. Other animals. These may also be styled the pleasures of ill-will, the pleasures of the irascible appetite, the pleasures of antipathy, or the pleasures of the malevolent or dissocial affections.

12. (10) The pleasures of the memory are the pleasures which, after having enjoyed such and such pleasures, or even in some case after having suffered such and such pains, a man will now and then experience, at recollecting them exactly in the order and in the circumstances in which they were actually enjoyed or suffered. These derivative pleasures may of course be distinguished into as many species as there are of original perceptions, from whence they may be copied. They may also be styled pleasures of simple recollection.

13. (11) The pleasures of the imagination are the pleasures which may be derived from the contemplation of any such pleasures as may happen to be suggested by the memory, but in a different order, and accompanied by different groups of circumstances. These may accordingly be referred to any one of the three cardinal points of time, present, past, or future. It is evident they may admit of as many distinctions as those of the former class.

14.   (12)   The pleasures of expectation are the pleasures that result from the contemplation of any sort of pleasure, referred to time *future*, and accompanied with the sentiment of *belief*. These also may admit of the same distinctions.[4]

15.   (13)   The pleasures of association are the pleasures which certain objects or incidents may happen to afford, not of themselves, but merely in virtue of some association they have contracted in the mind with certain objects or incidents which are in themselves pleasurable. Such is the case, for instance, with the pleasure of skill, when afforded by such a set of incidents as compose a game of chess. This derives its pleasurable quality from its association partly with the pleasures of skill, as exercised in the production of incidents pleasurable of themselves: partly from its association with the pleasures of power. Such is the case also with the pleasure of good luck, when afforded by such incidents as compose the game of hazard, or any other game of chance, when played at for nothing. This derives its pleasurable quality from its association with one of the pleasures of wealth; to wit, with the pleasure of acquiring it.

16.   (14)   Farther on we shall see pains grounded upon pleasures; in like manner may we now see pleasures grounded upon pains. To the catalogue of pleasures may accordingly be added the pleasures of *relief*: or, the pleasures which a man experiences when, after he has been enduring a pain of any kind for a certain time, it comes to cease, or to abate. These may of course be distinguished into as many species as there are of pains: and may give rise to so many pleasures of memory, of imagination, and of expectation.

17.   (1)   Pains of privation are the pains that may result from the thought of not possessing in the time present any of the several kinds of pleasures. Pains of privation may accordingly be resolved into as many kinds as there are of pleasures to which they may correspond, and from the absence whereof they may be derived.

18.   There are three sorts of pains which are only so many modifications of the several pains of privation. When the enjoyment of any particular pleasure happens to be particularly desired, but without any expectation approaching to assurance, the pain of privation which thereupon results takes a particular name, and is called the pain of *desire*, or of unsatisfied desire.

19.   Where the enjoyment happens to have been looked for with a degree of expectation approaching to assurance, and that expectation is made suddenly to cease, it is called a pain of disappointment.

20. A pain of privation takes the name of a pain of regret in two cases: 1. Where it is grounded on the memory of a pleasure, which having been once enjoyed, appears not likely to be enjoyed again: 2. Where it is grounded on the idea of a pleasure, which was never actually enjoyed, nor perhaps so much as expected, but which might have been enjoyed (it is supposed,) had such or such a contingency happened, which, in fact, did not happen.

21. (2)   The several pains of the senses seem to be as follows: 1. The pains of hunger and thirst: or the disagreeable sensations produced by the want of suitable substances which need at times to be applied to the alimentary canal. 2. The pains of the taste: or the disagreeable sensations produced by the application of various substances to the palate, and other superior parts of the same canal. 3. The pains of the organ of smell: or the disagreeable sensations produced by the effluvia of various substances when applied to that organ. 4. The pains of the touch: or the disagreeable sensations produced by the application of various substances to the skin. 5. The simple pains of the hearing: or the disagreeable sensations excited in the organ of that sense by various kinds of sounds: independently (as before,) of association. 6. The simple pains of the sight: or the disagreeable sensations if any such there be, that may be excited in the organ of that sense by visible images, independent of the principle of association. 7.[5] The pains resulting from excessive heat or cold, unless these be referable to the touch. 8. The pains of disease: or the acute and uneasy sensations resulting from the several diseases and indispositions to which human nature is liable. 9. The pain of exertion, whether bodily or mental: or the uneasy sensation which is apt to accompany any intense effort, whether of mind or body.

22. (3)[6]   The pains of awkwardness are the pains which sometimes result from the unsuccessful endeavour to apply any particular instruments of enjoyment or security to their uses, or from the difficulty a man experiences in applying them.[7]

23. (4)   The pains of enmity are the pains that may accompany the persuasion of a man's being obnoxious to the ill-will of such or such an assignable person or persons in particular: or, as the phrase is, of being upon ill terms with him or them: and, in consequence, of being obnoxious to certain pains of some sort or other, of which he may be the cause.

24. (5)   The pains of an ill-name, are the pains that accompany the persuasion of a man's being obnoxious, or in a way to be obnoxious to the ill-will of the world about him. These may likewise be called the pains of ill-repute, the pains of dishonour, or the pains of the moral sanction.[8]

25. (6)[9] The pains of piety are the pains that accompany the belief of a man's being obnoxious to the displeasure of the Supreme Being: and in consequence to certain pains to be inflicted by his especial appointment, either in this life or in a life to come. These may also be called the pains of religion; the pains of a religious disposition; or the pains of the religious sanction. When the belief is looked upon as well-grounded, these pains are commonly called religious terrors; when looked upon as ill-grounded, superstitious terrors.

26. (7) The pains of benevolence are the pains resulting from the view of any pains supposed to be endured by other beings. These may also be called the pains of good-will, of sympathy, or the pains of the benevolent or social affections.

27. (8) The pains of malevolence are the pains resulting from the view of any pleasures supposed to be enjoyed by any beings who happen to be the objects of a man's displeasure. These may also be styled the pains of ill-will, of antipathy, or the pains of the malevolent or dissocial affections.

28. (9) The pains of the memory may be grounded on every one of the above kinds, as well of pains of privation as of positive pains. These correspond exactly to the pleasures of the memory.

29. (10) The pains of the imagination may also be grounded on any one of the above kinds, as well of pains of privation as of positive pains: in other respects they correspond exactly to the pleasures of the imagination.

30. (11) The pains of expectation may be grounded on each one of the above kinds, as well of pains of privation as of positive pains. These may be also termed pains of apprehension.[10]

31. (12) The pains of association correspond exactly to the pleasures of association.

32. Of the above list there are certain pleasures and pains which suppose the existence of some pleasure or pain of some other person, to which the pleasure or pain of the person in question has regard: such pleasures and pains may be termed *extra-regarding*. Others do not suppose any such thing: these may be termed *self-regarding*. The only pleasures and pains of the extra-regarding class are those of benevolence, and those of malevolence: all the rest are self-regarding.[11]

33. Of all these several sorts of pleasures and pains, there is scarce any one which is not liable, on more accounts than one, to come under the consideration of the law. Is an offence committed? it is the tendency which it has to destroy, in such or such persons, some of these pleasures, or to produce some of these pains, that constitutes the mischief of it, and the ground for punishing it. It is the prospect of some of these pleasures, or of security from some of these pains, that constitutes the motive or temptation, it is the attainment of them that constitutes the profit of the offence. Is the offender to be punished? It can be only by the production of one or more of these pains, that the punishment can be inflicted.[12]

Notes

1   The catalogue here given, is what seemed to be a complete list of the several simple pleasures and pains of which human nature is susceptible: insomuch, that if, upon any occasion whatsoever, a man feels pleasure or pain, it is either referable at once to some one or other of these kinds, or resolvable into such as are. It might perhaps have been a satisfaction to the reader, to have seen an analytical view of the subject, taken upon an exhaustive plan, for the purpose of demonstrating the catalogue to be what it purports to be, a complete one. The catalogue is in fact the result of such an analysis; which, however, I thought it better to discard at present, as being of too metaphysical a cast, and not strictly within the limits of this design.
2   There are also pleasures of novelty, excited by the appearance of new ideas: these are pleasures of the imagination. See infra 13.
3   For instance, the pleasure of being able to gratify the sense of hearing, by singing, or performing upon any musical instrument. The pleasure thus obtained, is a thing super-added to, and perfectly distinguishable from, that which a man enjoys from hearing another person perform in the same manner.
4   In contradistinction to these, all other pleasures may be termed pleasures of *enjoyment*.
5   The pleasure of the sexual sense seems to have no positive pain to correspond to it: it has only a pain of privation, or pain of the mental class, the pain of unsatisfied desire. If any positive pain of body result from the want of such indulgence, it belongs to the head of pains of disease.
6   The pleasures of novelty have no positive pains corresponding to them. The pain which a man experiences when he is in the condition of not knowing what to do with himself, that pain, which in French is expressed by a single word *ennui*, is a pain of privation: a pain resulting from the absence, not only of all the pleasures of novelty, but of all kinds of pleasure whatsoever.

   The pleasures of wealth have also no positive pains corresponding to them: the only pains opposed to them are pains of privation. If any positive pains result from the want of wealth, they are referable to some other class of positive pains; principally to those of the senses. From the want of food, for instance, result the pains of hunger; from the want of clothing, the pains of cold; and so forth.

7   It may be a question, perhaps, whether this be a positive pain of itself, or whether it be nothing more than a pain of privation, resulting from the consciousness of a want of skill. It is, however, but a question of words, nor does it matter which way it be determined.

8   In as far as a man's fellow-creatures are supposed to be determined by any event not to regard him with any degree of esteem or *good* will, or to regard him with a less degree of esteem or *good* will than they would otherwise; not to do him any sorts of *good* offices, or not to do him so many *good* offices as they would otherwise; the pain resulting from such consideration may be reckoned a pain of privation: as far as they are supposed to regard him with such a degree of aversion or disesteem as to be disposed to do him positive *ill* offices, it may be reckoned a positive pain. The pain of privation, and the positive pain, in this case run one into another indistinguishably.

9   There seem to be no positive pains to correspond to the pleasures of power. The pains that a man may feel from the want or the loss of power, in as far as power is distinguished from all other sources of pleasure, seem to be nothing more than pains of privation.

10 In contradistinction to these, all other pains may be termed pains of *sufferance*.

11 By this means the pleasures and pains of amity may be the more clearly distinguished from those of benevolence: and on the other hand, those of enmity from those of malevolence. The pleasures and pains of amity and enmity are of the self-regarding cast: those of benevolence and malevolence of the extra-regarding.

12 It would be a matter not only of curiosity, but of some use, to exhibit a catalogue of the several complex pleasures and pains, analyzing them at the same time into the several simple ones, of which they are respectively composed. But such a disquisition would take up too much room to be admitted here. A short specimen, however, for the purpose of illustration, can hardly be dispensed with.

The pleasures taken in at the eye and ear are generally very complex. The pleasures of a country scene, for instance, consist commonly, amongst others, of the following pleasures:

I. Pleasures of the senses
    1. The simple pleasures of sight, excited by the perception of agreeable colours and figures, green fields, waving foliage, glistening water, and the like.
    2. The simple pleasures of the ear, excited by the perceptions of the chirping of birds, the murmuring of waters, the rustling of the wind among the trees.
    3. The pleasures of the smell, excited by the perceptions of the fragrance of flowers, of new-mown hay, or other vegetable substances, in the first stages of fermentation.
    4. The agreeable inward sensation, produced by a brisk circulation of the blood, and the ventilation of it in the lungs by a pure air, such as

that in the country frequently is in comparison of that which is breathed in towns.

II.   Pleasures of the imagination produced by association
1.   The idea of the plenty, resulting from the possession of the objects that are in view, and of the happiness arising from it.
2.   The idea of the innocence and happiness of the birds, sheep, cattle, dogs, and other gentle or domestic animals.
3.   The idea of the constant flow of health, supposed to be enjoyed by all these creatures: a notion which is apt to result from the occasional flow of health enjoyed by the supposed spectator.
4.   The idea of gratitude, excited by the contemplation of the all-powerful and beneficent Being, who is looked up to as the author of these blessings.

These four last are all of them, in some measure at least, pleasures of sympathy.

The depriving a man of this group of pleasures is one of the evils apt to result from imprisonment; whether produced by illegal violence, or in the way of punishment, by appointment of the laws.

CHAPTER X
Of Motives

§ii.   *No motives either constantly good, or constantly bad*

9.   In all this chain of motives, the principal or original link seems to be the last internal motive in prospect; it is to this that all the other motives in prospect owe their materiality: and the immediately acting motive its existence. This motive in prospect, we see, is always some pleasure, or some pain; some pleasure, which the act in question is expected to be a means of continuing or producing: some pain which it is expected to be a means of discontinuing or preventing. A motive is substantially nothing more than pleasure or pain, operating in a certain manner.

10.   Now, pleasure is in *itself* a good: nay, even setting aside immunity from pain, the only good: pain is in itself an evil; and, indeed, without exception, the only evil; or else the words good and evil have no meaning. And this is alike true of every sort of pain, and of every sort of pleasure. It follows, therefore, immediately and incontestibly, that *there is no such thing as any sort of motive that is in itself a bad one.*[1]

11.   It is common, however, to speak of actions as proceeding from *good* or *bad* motives: in which case the motives meant are such as are internal. The expression is far from being an accurate one; and as it is apt to occur in the consideration of almost every kind of offence, it will be requisite to settle the precise meaning of it, and observe how far it quadrates with the truth of things.

12.   With respect to goodness and badness, as it is with every thing else that is not itself either pain or pleasure, so is it with motives. If they are good or bad, it is only on account of their effects: good, on account of their tendency to produce pleasure, or avert pain: bad, on account of their tendency to produce pain, or avert pleasure. Now the case is, that from one and the same motive, and from every kind of motive, may proceed actions that are good, others that are bad, and others that are indifferent. This we shall proceed to shew with respect to all the different kinds of motives, as determined by the various kinds of pleasures and pains.

13.   Such an analysis, useful as it is, will be found to be a matter of no small difficulty; owing, in great measure, to a certain perversity of structure which prevails more or less throughout all languages. To speak of motives, as of any thing else, one must call them by their names. But the misfortune is, that it is rare to meet with a motive of which the name expresses that and nothing more. Commonly along with the very name of the motive, is tacitly involved a proposition imputing to it a certain quality; a quality which, in many cases, will appear to include that very goodness or badness, concerning which we are here inquiring whether, properly speaking, it be or be not imputable to motives. To use the common phrase, in most cases, the name of the motive is a word which is employed either only in a *good sense*, or else only in a *bad sense*. Now, when a word is spoken of as being used in a good sense, all that is necessarily meant is this: that in conjunction with the idea of the object it is put to signify, it conveys an idea of *approbation*: that is, of a pleasure or satisfaction, entertained by the person who employs the term at the thoughts of such object. In like manner, when a word is spoken of as being used in a bad sense, all that is necessarily meant is this: that, in conjunction with the idea of the object it is put to signify, it conveys an idea of *disapprobation*: that is, of a displeasure entertained by the person who employs the term at the thoughts of such object. Now, the circumstance on which such approbation is grounded will, as naturally as any other, be the opinion of the *goodness* of the object in question, as above explained: such, at least, it must be, upon the principle of utility: so, on the other hand, the circumstance on which any such disapprobation is grounded, will, as naturally as any other, be the opinion of the *badness* of the object: such, at least, it must be, in as far as the principle of utility is taken for the standard.

Now there are certain motives which, unless in a few particular cases, have scarcely any other name to be expressed by but such a word as is used only in a good sense. This is the case, for example, with the motives of piety and honour. The consequence of this is, that if, in speaking of such a motive, a man should have occasion to apply the epithet bad to any actions which he mentions as apt to result from it, he must appear to be guilty of a contradiction in terms. But the names of motives which have scarcely any other name to be expressed by, but such a word as is used only in a bad sense, are many more. This is the case, for example, with the motives of lust and avarice. And accordingly, if in speaking of any such motive, a man should have occasion to apply the epithets good or indifferent to any actions which he mentions as apt to result from it, he must here also appear to be guilty of a similar contradiction.[2]

This perverse association of ideas cannot, it is evident, but throw great difficulties in the way of the inquiry now before us. Confining himself to the language most in use, a man can scarce avoid running, in appearance, into perpetual contradictions. His propositions will appear, on the one hand, repugnant to truth; and on the other hand, adverse to utility. As paradoxes, they will excite contempt: as mischievous paradoxes, indignation. For the truths he labours to convey, however important, and however salutary, his reader is never the better: and he himself is much the worse. To obviate this inconvenience, completely, he has but this one unpleasant remedy; to lay aside the old phraseology and invent a new one. Happy the man whose language is ductile enough to permit him this resource. To palliate the inconvenience, where that method of obviating it is impracticable, he has nothing left for it but to enter into a long discussion, to state the whole matter at large, to confess, that for the sake of promoting the purposes, he has violated the established laws of language, and to throw himself upon the mercy of his readers.[3]

Notes

1 Let a man's motive be ill-will; call it even malice, envy, cruelty; it is still a kind of pleasure that is his motive: the pleasure he takes at the thought of the pain which he sees, or expects to see, his adversary undergo. Now even this wretched pleasure, taken by itself, is good: it may be faint; it may be short: it must at any rate be impure: yet while it lasts, and before any bad consequences arrive, it is as good as any other that is not more intense. See Ch. IV (Value).

2 To this imperfection of language, and nothing more, are to be attributed, in great measure, the violent clamours that have from time to time been raised

against those ingenious moralists, who, travelling out of the beaten tract of speculation, have found more or less difficulty in disentangling themselves from the shackles of ordinary language: such as Rochefoucault, Mandeville, and Helvetius. To the unsoundness of their opinions, and, with still greater injustice, to the corruption of their hearts, was often imputed, what was most commonly owing either to a want of skill, in matters of language on the part of the author, or a want of discernment, possibly now and then in some instances a want of probity, on the part of the commentator.

3   Happily, language is not always so intractable, but that by making use of two words instead of one, a man may avoid the inconvenience of fabricating words that are absolutely new. Thus instead of the word lust, by putting together two words in common use, he may frame the neutral expression, sexual desire: instead of the word avarice, by putting together two other words also in common use, he may frame the neutral expression, pecuniary interest. This, accordingly, is the course which I have taken. In these instances, indeed, even the combination is not novel: the only novelty there is consists in the steady adherence to the one neutral expression, rejecting altogether the terms, of which the import is infected by adventitious and unsuitable ideas.

In the catalogue of motives, corresponding to the several sorts of pains and pleasures, I have inserted such as have occurred to me. I cannot pretend to warrant it complete. To make sure of rendering it so, the only way would be, to turn over the dictionary from beginning to end: an operation which, in a view to perfection, would be necessary for more purposes than this.

2

From *Utilitarianism*

John Stuart Mill

CHAPTER II
What Utilitarianism Is

A passing remark is all that needs be given to the ignorant blunder of supposing that those who stand up for utility as the test of right and wrong
use the term in that restricted and merely colloquial sense in which utility
is opposed to pleasure. An apology is due to the philosophical opponents
of utilitarianism for even the momentary appearance of confounding
them with anyone capable of so absurd a misconception; which is the
more extraordinary, inasmuch as the contrary accusation, of referring
everything to pleasure, and that, too, in its grossest form, is another of
the common charges against utilitarianism: and, as has been pointedly remarked by an able writer, the same sort of persons, and often the very
same persons, denounce the theory "as impracticably dry when the word
'utility' precedes the word 'pleasure,' and as too practicably voluptuous
when the word 'pleasure' precedes the word 'utility.'" Those who know
anything about the matter are aware that every writer, from Epicurus to
Bentham, who maintained the theory of utility meant by it, not something
to be contradistinguished from pleasure, but pleasure itself, together with
exemption from pain; and instead of opposing the useful to the agreeable
or the ornamental, have always declared that the useful means these,
among other things. Yet the common herd, including the herd of writers,
not only in newspapers and periodicals, but in books of weight and pre-
tension, are perpetually falling into this shallow mistake. Having caught

John Stuart Mill, *Utilitarianism*, George Sher, ed. (Indianapolis, IN: Hackett Publishing Co., 1979), pp. 6–25, 34–40, 46–53.

up the word "utilitarian," while knowing nothing whatever about it but its sound, they habitually express by it the rejection or the neglect of pleasure in some of its forms: of beauty, of ornament, or of amusement. Nor is the term thus ignorantly misapplied solely in disparagement, but occasionally in compliment, as though it implied superiority to frivolity and the mere pleasures of the moment. And this perverted use is the only one in which the word is popularly known, and the one from which the new generation are acquiring their sole notion of its meaning. Those who introduced the word, but who had for many years discontinued it as a distinctive appellation, may well feel themselves called upon to resume it if by doing so they can hope to contribute anything toward rescuing it from this utter degradation.[1]

The creed which accepts as the foundation of morals "utility" or the "greatest happiness principle" holds that actions are right in proportion as they tend to promote happiness; wrong as they tend to produce the reverse of happiness. By happiness is intended pleasure and the absence of pain; by unhappiness, pain and the privation of pleasure. To give a clear view of the moral standard set up by the theory, much more requires to be said; in particular, what things it includes in the ideas of pain and pleasure, and to what extent this is left an open question. But these supplementary explanations do not affect the theory of life on which this theory of morality is grounded – namely, that pleasure and freedom from pain are the only things desirable as ends; and that all desirable things (which are as numerous in the utilitarian as in any other scheme) are desirable either for pleasure inherent in themselves or as means to the promotion of pleasure and the prevention of pain.

Now such a theory of life excites in many minds, and among them in some of the most estimable in feeling and purpose, inveterate dislike. To suppose that life has (as they express it) no higher end than pleasure – no better and nobler object of desire and pursuit – they designate as utterly mean and groveling, as a doctrine worthy only of swine, to whom the followers of Epicurus were, at a very early period, contemptuously likened; and modern holders of the doctrine are occasionally made the subject of equally polite comparisons by its German, French, and English assailants.

When thus attacked, the Epicureans have always answered that it is not they, but their accusers, who represent human nature in a degrading light, since the accusation supposes human beings to be capable of no pleasures except those of which swine are capable. If this supposition were true, the charge could not be gainsaid, but would then be no longer an imputation; for if the sources of pleasure were precisely the same to human beings and to swine, the rule of life which is good enough for the one would be good enough for the other. The comparison of the Epicurean life to that of beasts is felt as degrading, precisely because a beast's pleasures do not satisfy a human being's conceptions of happiness. Human beings have faculties more elevated than the animal appetites and, when once made conscious of them, do not regard anything as happiness which does not include their gratification. I do not indeed, consider the Epicureans to have been by any means faultless in drawing out their scheme of consequences from the utilitarian principle. To do this in any sufficient manner, many Stoic, as well as Christian, elements require to be included. But there is no known Epicurean theory of life which does not assign to the pleasures of the intellect, of the feelings and imagination, and of the moral sentiments a much higher value as pleasures than to those of mere sensation. It must be admitted, however, that utilitarian writers in general have placed the superiority of mental over bodily pleasures chiefly in the greater permanency, safety, uncostliness, etc., of the former – that is, in their circumstantial advantages rather than in their intrinsic nature. And on all these points utilitarians have fully proved their case; but they might have taken the other and, as it may be called, higher ground with entire consistency. It is quite compatible with the principle of utility to recognize the fact that some kinds of pleasure are more desirable and more valuable than others. It would be absurd that, while in estimating all other things quality is considered as well as quantity, the estimation of pleasure should be supposed to depend on quantity alone.

If I am asked what I mean by difference of quality in pleasures, or what makes one pleasure more valuable than another, merely as a pleasure, except its being greater in amount, there is but one possible answer. Of two pleasures, if there be one to which all or almost all who have experience of both give a decided preference, irrespective of any feeling of moral obligation to prefer it, that is the more desirable pleasure. If one of the two is, by those who are competently acquainted with both, placed so far above the other that they prefer it, even though knowing it to be attended with a greater amount of discontent, and would not resign it for any quantity of the other pleasure which their nature is capable of, we are justified in ascribing to the preferred enjoyment a superiority in quality so far outweighing quantity as to render it, in comparison, of small account.

Now it is an unquestionable fact that those who are equally acquainted with and equally capable of appreciating and enjoying both do give a most marked preference to the manner of existence which employs their higher faculties. Few human creatures would consent to be changed into any of the lower animals for a promise of the fullest allowance of a beast's pleasures; no intelligent human being would consent to be a fool, no instructed person would be an ignoramus, no person of feeling and conscience would be selfish and base, even though they should be persuaded that the fool, the dunce, or the rascal is better satisfied with his lot than they are with theirs. They would not resign what they possess more than he for the most complete satisfaction of all the desires which they have in common with him. If they ever fancy they would, it is only in cases of unhappiness so extreme that to escape from it they would exchange their lot for almost any other, however undesirable in their own eyes. A being of higher faculties requires more to make him happy, is capable probably of more acute suffering, and certainly accessible to it at more points, than one of an inferior type; but in spite of these liabilities, he can never really wish to sink into what he feels to be a lower grade of existence. We may give what explanation we please of this unwillingness; we may attribute it to pride, a name which is given indiscriminately to some of the most and to some of the least estimable feelings of which mankind are capable; we may refer it to the love of liberty and personal independence, an appeal to which was with the Stoics one of the most effective means for the inculcation of it; to the love of power or to the love of excitement, both of which do really enter into and contribute to it; but its most appropriate appellation is a sense of dignity, which all human beings possess in one form or other, and in some, though by no means in exact, proportion to their higher faculties, and which is so essential a part of the happiness of those in whom it is strong that nothing which conflicts with it could be otherwise than momentarily an object of desire to them. Whoever supposes that this preference takes place at a sacrifice of happiness – that the superior being, in anything like equal circumstances, is not happier than the inferior – confounds the two very different ideas of happiness and content. It is indisputable that the being whose capacities of enjoyment are low has the greatest chance of having them fully satisfied; and a highly endowed being will always feel that any happiness which he can look for, as the world is constituted, is imperfect. But he can learn to bear its imperfections, if they are at all bearable; and they will not make him envy the being who is indeed unconscious of the imperfections, but only because he feels not at all the good which those imperfections qualify. It is better to be a human being dissatisfied than a pig satisfied; better to be Socrates dissatisfied than a fool satisfied. And if the fool, or the pig, are of a different opinion, it is because they only know their own side of the question. The other party to the comparison knows both sides.

It may be objected that many who are capable of the higher pleasures occasionally, under the influence of temptation, postpone them to the lower. But this is quite compatible with a full appreciation of the intrinsic superiority of the higher. Men often, from infirmity of character, make their election for the nearer good, though they know it to be the less valuable; and this no less when the choice is between two bodily pleasures than when it is between bodily and mental. They pursue sensual indulgences to the injury of health, though perfectly aware that health is the greater good. It may be further objected that many who begin with youthful enthusiasm for everything noble, as they advance in years, sink into indolence and selfishness. But I do not believe that those who undergo this very common change voluntarily choose the lower description of pleasures in preference to the higher. I believe that, before they devote themselves exclusively to the one, they have already become incapable of the other. Capacity for the nobler feelings is in most natures a very tender plant, easily killed, not only by hostile influences, but by mere want of sustenance; and in the majority of young persons it speedily dies away if the occupations to which their position in life has devoted them, and the society into which it has thrown them, are not favorable to keeping that higher capacity in exercise. Men lose their high aspirations as they lose their intellectual tastes, because they have not time or opportunity for indulging them; and they addict themselves to inferior pleasures, not because they deliberately prefer them, but because they are either the only ones to which they have access or the only ones which they are any longer capable of enjoying. It may be questioned whether anyone who has remained equally susceptible to both classes of pleasures ever knowingly and calmly preferred the lower, though many, in all ages, have broken down in an ineffectual attempt to combine both.

From this verdict of the only competent judges, I apprehend there can be no appeal. On a question which is the best worth having of two pleasures, or which of two modes of existence is the most grateful to the feelings, apart from its moral attributes and from its consequences, the judgment of these who are qualified by knowledge of both, or, if they differ, that of the majority among them, must be admitted as final. And there needs be the less hesitation to accept this judgment respecting the quality of pleasures, since there is no other tribunal to be referred to even on the question of quantity. What means are there of determining which is the acutest of two pains, or the intensest of two pleasurable sensations, except the general suffrage of those who are familiar with both? Neither pains nor pleasures are homogeneous, and pain is always heterogeneous with pleasure. What is there to decide whether a particular pleasure is worth purchasing at the cost of a particular pain, except the feelings and judgment of the experienced? When, therefore, those feelings and judgment declare the pleasures derived from the higher faculties to be preferable *in kind*, apart from the question of intensity, to those of which the animal nature, disjoined from the higher faculties, is susceptible, they are entitled on this subject to the same regard.

I have dwelt on this point as being part of a perfectly just conception of utility or happiness considered as the directive rule of human conduct. But it is by no means an indispensable condition to the acceptance of the utilitarian standard; for that standard is not the agent's own greatest happiness, but the greatest amount of happiness altogether; and if it may possibly be doubted whether a noble character is always the happier for its nobleness, there can be no doubt that it makes other people happier, and that the world in general is immensely a gainer by it. Utilitarianism, therefore, could only attain its end by the general cultivation of nobleness of character, even if each individual were only benefited by the nobleness of others, and his own, so far as happiness is concerned, were a sheer deduction from the benefit. But the bare enunciation of such an absurdity as this last renders refutation superfluous.

According to the greatest happiness principle, as above explained, the ultimate end, with reference to and for the sake of which all other things are desirable – whether we are considering our own good or that of other people – is an existence exempt as far as possible from pain, and as rich as possible in enjoyments, both in point of quantity and quality; the test of quality and the rule for measuring it against quantity being the preference felt by those who, in their opportunities of experience, to which must be added their habits of self-consciousness and self-observation, are best furnished with the means of comparison. This, being according to the utilitarian opinion the end of human action, is necessarily also the standard of morality, which may accordingly be defined "the rules and precepts for human conduct," by the observance of which an existence such as has been described might be, to the greatest extent possible, secured to all mankind; and not to them only, but, so far as the nature of things admits, to the whole sentient creation.

Against this doctrine, however, arises another class of objectors who say that happiness, in any form, cannot be the rational purpose of human life and action; because, in the first place, it is unattainable; and they contemptuously ask, What right hast thou to be happy? – a question which Mr. Carlyle clinches by the addition, What right, a short time ago, hadst thou even *to be?* Next they say that men can do *without* happiness; that all noble human beings have felt this, and could not have become noble but by learning the lesson of *Entsagen*, or renunciation; which lesson, thoroughly learned and submitted to, they affirm to be the beginning and necessary condition of all virtue.

The first of these objections would go to the root of the matter were it well founded; for if no happiness is to be had at all by human beings, the attainment of it cannot be the end of morality or of any rational conduct. Though, even in that case, something might still be said for the utilitarian theory, since utility includes not solely the pursuit of happiness, but the prevention or mitigation of unhappiness; and if the former aim be chimerical, there will be all the greater scope and more imperative need for the latter, so long at least as mankind think fit to live and do not take refuge in the simultaneous act of suicide recommended under certain conditions by Novalis. When, however, it is thus positively asserted to be impossible that human life should be happy, the assertion, if not something like a verbal quibble, is at least an exaggeration. If by happiness be meant a continuity of highly pleasurable excitement, it is evident enough that this is impossible. A state of exalted pleasure lasts only moments or in some cases, and with some intermissions, hours or days, and is the occasional brilliant flash of enjoyment, not its permanent and steady flame. Of this the philosophers who have taught that happiness is the end of life were as fully aware as those who taunt them. The happiness which they meant was not a life of rapture, but moments of such, in an existence made up of few and transitory pains, many and various pleasures, with a decided predominance of the active over the passive, and having as the foundation of the whole not to expect more from life than it is capable of bestowing. A life thus composed, to those who have been fortunate enough to obtain it, has always appeared worthy of the name of happiness. And such an existence is even now the lot of many during some considerable portion of their lives. The present wretched education and wretched social arrangements are the only real hindrance to its being attainable by almost all.

The objectors perhaps may doubt whether human beings, if taught to consider happiness as the end of life, would be satisfied with such a moderate share of it. But great numbers of mankind have been satisfied with much less. The main constituents of a satisfied life appear to be two, either of which by itself is often found sufficient for the purpose: tranquillity and excitement. With much tranquillity, many find that they can be content with very little pleasure; with much excitement, many can reconcile themselves to a considerable quantity of pain. There is assuredly no inherent impossibility of enabling even the mass of mankind to unite both, since the two are so far from being incompatible that they are in natural alliance, the prolongation of either being a preparation for, and exciting a wish for, the other. It is only those in whom indolence amounts to a vice that do not desire excitement after an interval of respose; it is only those in whom the need of excitement is a disease that feel the tranquillity which follows excitement dull and insipid, instead of pleasurable in direct proportion to the excitement which preceded it. When people who are tolerably fortunate in their outward lot do not find in life sufficient enjoyment to make it valuable to them, the cause generally is caring for nobody but themselves. To those who have neither public nor private affections, the excitements of life are much curtailed, and in any case dwindle in value as the time approaches when all selfish interests must be terminated by death; while those who leave after them objects of personal affection, and especially those who have also cultivated a fellow-feeling with the collective interests of mankind, retain as lively an interest in life on the eve of death as in the vigor of youth and health. Next to selfishness, the principal cause which makes life unsatisfactory is want of mental cultivation. A cultivated mind – I do not mean that of a philosopher, but any mind to which the fountains of knowledge have been opened, and which has been taught, in any tolerable degree, to exercise its faculties – finds sources of inexhaustible interest in all that surrounds it: in the objects of nature, the achievements of art, the imaginations of poetry, the incidents of history, the ways of mankind, past and present, and their prospects in the future. It is possible, indeed, to become indifferent to all this, and that too without having exhausted a thousandth part of it, but only when one has had from the beginning no moral or human interest in these things and has sought in them only the gratification of curiosity.

Now there is absolutely no reason in the nature of things why an amount of mental culture sufficient to give an intelligent interest in these objects of contemplation should not be the inheritance of everyone born in a civilized country. As little is there an inherent necessity that any human being should be a selfish egotist, devoid of every feeling or care but those which center in his own miserable individuality. Something far superior to this is sufficiently common even now, to give ample earnest of what the human species may be made. Genuine private affections and a sincere interest in the public good are possible, though in unequal degrees, to every rightly brought up human being. In a world in which there is so much to interest, so much to enjoy, and so much also to correct and improve, everyone who has this moderate amount of moral and intellectual requisites is capable of an existence which may be called enviable; and unless such a person, through bad laws or subjection to the will of others, is denied the liberty to use the sources of happiness within his reach, he will not fail to find this enviable existence, if he escapes the positive evils of life, the great sources of physical and mental suffering – such as indigence, disease, and the unkindness, worthlessness, or premature loss of objects of affection. The main stress of the problem lies, therefore, in the contest with these calamities from which it is a rare good fortune entirely to escape; which, as things now are, cannot be obviated, and often cannot be in any material degree mitigated. Yet no one whose opinion deserves a moment's consideration can doubt that most of the great positive evils of the world are in themselves removable, and will, if human affairs continue to improve, be in the end reduced within narrow limits. Poverty, in any sense implying suffering, may be completely extinguished by the wisdom of society combined with the good sense and providence of individuals. Even that most intractable of enemies, disease, may be indefinitely reduced in dimensions by good physical and moral education and proper control of noxious influences, while the progress of science holds out a promise for the future of still more direct conquests over this detestable foe. And every advance in that direction relieves us from some, not only of the chances which cut short our own lives, but, what concerns us still more, which deprive us of those in whom our happiness is wrapt up. As for vicissitudes of fortune and other disappointments connected with worldly circumstances, these are principally the effect either of gross imprudence, of ill-regulated desires, or of bad or imperfect social institutions. All the grand sources, in short, of human suffering are in a great degree, many of them almost entirely, conquerable by human care and effort; and though their removal is grievously slow – though a long succession of generations will perish in the breach before the conquest is completed, and this world becomes all that, if will and knowledge were not wanting, it might easily be made – yet every mind sufficiently intelligent and generous to bear a part, however small and inconspicuous, in the endeavor will draw a noble enjoyment from the contest itself, which he would not for any bribe in the form of selfish indulgence consent to be without.

And this leads to the true estimation of what is said by the objectors concerning the possibility and the obligation of learning to do without happiness. Unquestionably it is possible to do without happiness; it is done involuntarily by nineteen-twentieths of mankind, even in those parts of our present world which are least deep in barbarism; and it often has to be done voluntarily by the hero or the martyr, for the sake of something which he prizes more than his individual happiness. But this something, what is it, unless the happiness of others or some of the requisites of happiness? It is noble to be capable of resigning entirely one's own portion of happiness, or chances of it; but, after all, this self-sacrifice must be for some end; it is not its own end; and if we are told that its end is not happiness but virtue, which is better than happiness, I ask, would the sacrifice be made if the hero or martyr did not believe that it would earn for others immunity from similar sacrifices? Would it be made if he thought that his renunciation of happiness for himself would produce no fruit for any of his fellow creatures, but to make their lot like his and place them also in the condition of persons who have renounced happiness? All honor to those who can abnegate for themselves the personal enjoyment of life when by such renunciation they contribute worthily to increase the amount of happiness in the world; but he who does it or professes to do it for any other purpose is no more deserving of admiration than the ascetic mounted on his pillar. He may be an inspiriting proof of what men *can* do, but assuredly not an example of what they *should*.

Though it is only in a very imperfect state of the world's arrangements that anyone can best serve the happiness of others by the absolute sacrifice of his own, yet, so long as the world is in that imperfect state, I fully acknowledge that the readiness to make such a sacrifice is the highest virtue which can be found in man. I will add that in this condition of the world, paradoxical as the assertion may be, the conscious ability to do without happiness gives the best prospect of realizing such happiness as is attainable. For nothing except that consciousness can raise a person above the chances of life by making him feel that, let fate and fortune do their worst, they have not power to subdue him; which, once felt, frees him from excess of anxiety concerning the evils of life and enables him, like many a Stoic in the worst times of the Roman Empire, to cultivate in tranquillity the sources of satisfaction accessible to him, without concerning himself about the uncertainty of their duration any more than about their inevitable end.

Meanwhile, let utilitarians never cease to claim the morality of self-devotion as a possession which belongs by as good a right to them as either to the Stoic or to the Transcendentalist. The utilitarian morality does recognize in human beings the power of sacrificing their own greatest good for the good of others. It only refuses to admit that the sacrifice is itself a good. A sacrifice which does not increase or tend to increase the sum total of happiness, it considers as wasted. The only self-renunciation which it applauds is devotion to the happiness, or to some of the means of happiness, of others, either of mankind collectively or of individuals within the limits imposed by the collective interests of mankind.

I must again repeat what the assailants of utilitarianism seldom have the justice to acknowledge, that the happiness which forms the utilitarian standard of what is right in conduct is not the agent's own happiness but that of all concerned. As between his own happiness and that of others, utilitarianism requires him to be as strictly impartial as a disinterested and benevolent spectator. In the golden rule of Jesus of Nazareth, we read the complete spirit of the ethics of utility. "To do as you would be done by," and "to love your neighbor as yourself," constitute the ideal perfection of utilitarian morality. As the means of making the nearest approach to this ideal, utility would enjoin, first, that laws and social arrangements should place the happiness or (as, speaking practically, it may be called) the interest of every individual as nearly as possible in harmony with the interest of the whole; and, secondly, that education and opinion, which have so vast a power over human character, should so use that power as to establish in the mind of every individual an indissoluble association between his own happiness and the good of the whole, especially between his own happiness and the practice of such modes of conduct, negative and positive, as regard for the universal happiness prescribes; so that not only he may be unable to conceive the possibility of happiness to himself, consistently with conduct opposed to the general good, but also that a direct impulse to promote the general good may be in every individual one of the habitual motives of action, and the sentiments connected therewith may fill a large and prominent place in every human being's sentient existence. If the impugners of the utilitarian morality represented it to their own minds in this its true character, I know not what recommendation possessed by any other morality they could possibly affirm to be wanting to it; what more beautiful or more exalted developments of human nature any other ethical system can be supposed to foster, or what springs of action, not accessible to the utilitarian, such systems rely on for giving effect to their mandates.

The objectors to utilitarianism cannot always be charged with representing it in a discreditable light. On the contrary, those among them who entertain anything like a just idea of its disinterested character sometimes find fault with its standard as being too high for humanity. They say it is exacting too much to require that people shall always act from the inducement of promoting the general interest of society. But this is to mistake the very meaning of a standard of morals and confound the rule of action with the motive of it. It is the business of ethics to tell us what are our duties, or by what test we may know them; but no system of ethics requires that the sole motive of all we do shall be a feeling of duty; on the contrary, ninety-nine hundredths of all our actions are done from other motives, and rightly so done if the rule of duty does not condemn them. It is the more unjust to utilitarianism that this particular misapprehension should be made a ground of objection to it, inasmuch as utilitarian moralists have gone beyond almost all others in affirming that the motive has nothing to do with the morality of the action, though much with the worth of the agent. He who saves a fellow creature from drowning does what is morally right, whether his motive be duty or the hope of being paid for his trouble; he who betrays the friend that trusts him is guilty of a crime, even if his object be to serve another friend to whom he is under greater obligations.[2] But to speak only of actions done from the motive of duty, and in direct obedience to principle: it is a misapprehension of the utilitarian mode of thought to conceive it as implying that people should fix their minds upon so wide a generality as the world, or society at large. The great majority of good actions are intended not for the benefit of the world, but for that of individuals, of which the good of the world is made up; and the thoughts of the most virtuous man need not on these occasions travel beyond the particular persons concerned, except so far as is necessary to assure himself that in benefiting them he is not violating the rights, that is, the legitimate and authorized expectations, of anyone else. The multiplication of happiness is, according to the utilitarian ethics, the object of virtue: the occasions on which any person (except one in a thousand) has it in his power to do this on an extended scale – in other words, to be a public benefactor – are but exceptional; and on these occasions alone is he called on to consider public utility; in every other case, private utility, the interest or happiness of some few persons, is all he has to attend to. Those alone the influence of whose actions extends to society in general need concern themselves habitually about so large an object. In the case of abstinences indeed – of things which people forbear to do from moral considerations, though the consequences in the particular case might be beneficial – it would be unworthy of an intelligent agent not to be consciously aware that the action is of a class which, if practiced generally, would be generally injurious, and that this is the ground of the obligation to abstain from it. The amount of regard for the public interest implied in this recognition is no greater than is demanded by every system of morals, for they all enjoin to abstain from whatever is manifestly pernicious to society.

The same considerations dispose of another reproach against the doctrine of utility, founded on a still grosser misconception of the purpose of a standard of morality and of the very meaning of the words "right" and "wrong." It is often affirmed that utilitarianism renders men cold and unsympathizing; that it chills their moral feelings toward individuals; that it makes them regard only the dry and hard consideration of the consequences of actions, not taking into their moral estimate the qualities from which those actions emanate. If the assertion means that they do not allow their judgment respecting the rightness or wrongness of an action to be influenced by their opinion of the qualities of the person who does it, this is a complaint not against utilitarianism, but against any standard of morality at all; for certainly no known ethical standard decides an action to be good or bad because it is done by a good or bad man, still less because done by an amiable, a brave, or a benevolent man, or the contrary. These considerations are relevant, not to the estimation of actions, but of persons; and there is nothing in the utilitarian theory inconsistent with the fact that there are other things which interest us in persons besides the rightness and wrongness of their actions. The Stoics, indeed, with the paradoxical misuse of language which was part of their system, and by which they strove to raise themselves above all concern about anything but virtue, were fond of saying that he who has that has everything; that he, and only he, is rich, is beautiful, is a king. But no claim of this description is made for the virtuous man by the utilitarian doctrine. Utilitarians are quite aware that there are other desirable possessions and qualities besides virtue, and are perfectly willing to allow to all of them their full worth. They are also aware that a right action does not necessarily indicate a virtuous character, and that actions which are blamable often proceed from qualities entitled to praise. When this is apparent in any particular case, it modifies their estimation, not certainly of the act, but of the agent. I grant that they are, notwithstanding, of opinion that in the long run the best proof of a good character is good actions; and resolutely refuse to consider any mental disposition as good of which the predominant tendency is to produce bad conduct. This makes them unpopular with many people, but it is an unpopularity which they must share with everyone who regards the distinction between right and wrong in a serious light; and the reproach is not one which a conscientious utilitarian need be anxious to repel.

If no more be meant by the objection than that many utilitarians look on the morality of actions, as measured by the utilitarian standards, with too exclusive a regard, and do not lay sufficient stress upon the other beauties of character which go toward making a human being lovable or admirable, this may be admitted. Utilitarians who have cultivated their moral feelings, but not their sympathies, nor their artistic perceptions, do fall into this mistake; and so do all other moralists under the same conditions. What can be said in excuse for other moralists is equally available for them, namely, that, if there is to be any error, it is better that it should be on that side. As a matter of fact, we may affirm that among utilitarians, as among adherents of other systems, there is every imaginable degree of rigidity and of laxity in the application of their standard; some are even puritanically rigorous, while others are as indulgent as can possibly be desired by sinner or by sentimentalist. But on the whole, a doctrine which brings prominently forward the interest that mankind have in the repression and prevention of conduct which violates the moral law is likely to be inferior to no other in turning the sanctions of opinion against such violations. It is true, the question "What does violate the moral law?" is one on which those who recognize different standards of morality are likely now and then to differ. But difference of opinion on moral questions was not first introduced into the world by utilitarianism, while that doctrine does supply, if not always an easy, at all events a tangible and intelligible, mode of deciding such differences.

It may not be superfluous to notice a few more of the common misapprehensions of utilitarian ethics, even those which are so obvious and gross that it might appear impossible for any person of candor and intelligence to fall into them; since persons, even of considerable mental endowment, often give themselves so little trouble to understand the bearings of any opinion against which they entertain a prejudice, and men are in general so little conscious of this voluntary ignorance as a defect that the vulgarest misunderstandings of ethical doctrines are continually met with in the deliberate writings of persons of the greatest pretensions both to high principle and to philosophy. We not uncommonly hear the doctrine of utility inveighed against a *godless* doctrine. If it be necessary to say anything at all against so mere an assumption, we may say that the question depends upon what idea we have formed of the moral character of the Deity. If it be a true belief that God desires, above all things, the happiness of his creatures, and that this was his purpose in their creation, utility is not only not a godless doctrine, but more profoundly religious than any other. If it be meant that utilitarianism does not recognize the revealed will of God as the supreme law of morals, I answer that a utilitarian who believes in the perfect goodness and wisdom of *God* necessarily believes that whatever God has thought fit to reveal on the subject of morals must fulfill the requirements of utility in a supreme degree. But others besides utilitarians have been of opinion that the Christian revelation was intended, and is fitted, to inform the hearts and minds of mankind with a spirit which should enable them to find for themselves what is right, and incline them to do it when found, rather than to tell them, except in a very general way, what it is; and that we need a doctrine of ethics, carefully followed out, to *interpret* to us the will of God. Whether this opinion is correct or not, it is superfluous here to discuss; since whatever aid religion, either natural or revealed, can afford to ethical investigation is as open to the utilitarian moralist as to any other. He can use it as the testimony of God to the usefulness or hurtfulness of any given course of action by as good a right as others can use it for the indication of a transcendental law having no connection with usefulness or with happiness.

Again, utility is often summarily stigmatized as an immoral doctrine by giving it the name of "expediency," and taking advantage of the popular use of that term to contrast it with principle. But the expedient, in the sense in which it is opposed to the right, generally means that which is expedient for the particular interest of the agent himself; as when a minister sacrifices the interests of his country to keep himself in place. When it means anything better than this, it means that which is expedient for some immediate object, some temporary purpose, but which violates a rule whose observance is expedient in a much higher degree. The expedient, in this sense, instead of being the same thing with the useful, is a branch of the hurtful. Thus it would often be expedient, for the purpose of getting over some momentary embarrassment, or attaining some object immediately useful to ourselves or others, to tell a lie. But inasmuch as the cultivation in ourselves of a sensitive feeling on the subject of veracity is one of the most useful, and the enfeeblement of that feeling one of the most hurtful, things to which our conduct can be instrumental; and inasmuch as any, even unintentional, deviation from truth does that much toward weakening the trustworthiness of human assertion, which is not only the principal support of all present social well-being, but the insufficiency of which does more than any one thing that can be named to keep back civilization, virtue, everything on which human happiness on the largest scale depends – we feel that the violation, for a present advantage, of a rule of such transcendent expediency is not expedient, and that he who, for the sake of convenience to himself or to some other individual, does what depends on him to deprive mankind of the good, and inflict upon them the evil, involved in the greater or less reliance which they can place in each other's words, acts the part of one of their worst enemies. Yet that even this rule, sacred as it is, admits of possible exceptions is acknowledged by all moralists; the chief of which is when the withholding of some fact (as of information from a malefactor, or of bad news from a person dangerously ill) would save an individual (especially an individual other than oneself) from great and unmerited evil, and when the withholding can only be effected by denial. But in order that the exception may not extend itself beyond the need, and may have the least possible effect in weakening reliance on veracity, it ought to be recognized and, if possible, its limits defined; and, if the principle of utility is good for anything, it must be good for weighing these conflicting utilities against one another and marking out the region within which one or the other preponderates.

Again, defenders of utility often find themselves called upon to reply to such objections as this – that there is not time, previous to action, for calculating and weighing the effects of any line of conduct on the general happiness. This is exactly as if anyone were to say that it is impossible to guide our conduct by Christianity because there is not time, on every occasion on which anything has to be done, to read through the Old and New Testaments. The answer to the objection is that there has been ample time, namely, the whole past duration of the human species. During all that time mankind have been learning by experience the tendencies of actions; on which experience all the prudence as well as all the morality of life are dependent. People talk as if the commencement of this course of experience had hitherto been put off, and as if, at the moment when some man feels tempted to meddle with the property or life of another, he had to begin considering for the first time whether murder and theft are injurious to human happiness. Even then I do not think that he would find the question very puzzling; but, at all events, the matter is now done to his hand. It is truly a whimsical supposition that, if mankind were agreed in considering utility to be the test of morality, they would remain without any agreement as to what *is* useful, and would take no measures for having their notions on the subject taught to the young and enforced by law and opinion. There is no difficulty in proving any ethical standard whatever to work ill if we suppose universal idiocy to be conjoined with it; but on any hypothesis short of that, mankind must by this time have acquired positive beliefs as to the effects of some actions on their happiness; and the beliefs which have thus come down are the rules of morality for the multitude, and for the philosopher until he has succeeded in finding better. That philosophers might easily do this, even now, on many subjects; that the received code of ethics is by no means of divine right; and that mankind have still much to learn as to the effects of actions on the general happiness, I admit or rather earnestly maintain. The corollaries from the principle of utility, like the precepts of every practical art, admit of indefinite improvement, and, in a progressive state of the human mind, their improvement is perpetually going on. But to consider the rules of morality as improvable is one thing; to pass over the intermediate generalization entirely and endeavor to test each individual action directly by the first principle is another. It is a strange notion that the acknowledgment of a first principle is inconsistent with the admission of secondary ones. To inform a traveler respecting the place of his ultimate destination is not to forbid the use of landmarks and direction-posts on the way. The proposition that happiness is the end and aim of morality does not mean that no road ought to be laid down to that goal, or that persons going thither should not be advised to take one direction rather than another. Men really ought to leave off talking a kind of nonsense on this subject, which they would neither talk nor listen to on other matters of practical concernment. Nobody argues that the art of navigation is not founded on astronomy because sailors cannot wait to calculate the Nautical Almanac. Being rational creatures, they go to sea with it ready calculated; and all rational creatures go out upon the sea of life with their minds made up on the common questions of right and wrong, as well as on many of the far more difficult questions of wise and foolish. And this, as long as foresight is a human quality, it is to be presumed they will continue to do. Whatever we adopt as the fundamental principle of morality, we require subordinate principles to apply it by; the impossibility of doing without them, being common to all systems, can afford no argument against any one in particular; but gravely to argue as if no such secondary principles could be had, and as if mankind had remained till now, and always must remain, without drawing any general conclusions from the experience of human life is as high a pitch, I think, as absurdity has ever reached in philosophical controversy.

The remainder of the stock arguments against utilitarianism mostly consist in laying to its charge the common infirmities of human nature, and the general difficulties which embarrass conscientious persons in shaping their course through life. We are told that a utilitarian will be apt to make his own particular case an exception to moral rules, and, when under temptation, will see a utility in the breach of a rule, greater than he will see in its observance. But is utility the only creed which is able to furnish us with excuses for evil-doing and means of cheating our own conscience? They are afforded in abundance by all doctrines which recognize as a fact in morals the existence of conflicting considerations, which all doctrines do that have been believed by sane persons. It is not the fault of any creed, but of the complicated nature of human affairs, that rules of conduct cannot be so framed as to require no exceptions, and that hardly any kind of action can safely be laid down as either always obligatory or always condemnable. There is no ethical creed which does not temper the rigidity of its laws by giving a certain latitude, under the moral responsibility of the agent, for accommodation to peculiarities of circumstances; and under every creed, at the opening thus made, self-deception and dishonest casuistry get in. There exists no moral system under which there do not arise unequivocal cases of conflicting obligation. These are the real difficulties, the knotty points both in the theory of ethics and in the conscientious guidance of personal conduct. They are overcome practically, with greater or with less success, according to the intellect and virtue of the individual; but it can hardly be pretended that anyone will be the less qualified for dealing with them, from possessing an ultimate standard to which conflicting rights and duties can be referred. If utility is the ultimate source of moral obligations, utility may be invoked to decide between them when their demands are incompatible. Though the application of the standard may be difficult, it is better than none at all; while in other systems, the moral laws all claiming independent authority, there is no common umpire entitled to interfere between them; their claims to precedence one over another rest on little better than sophistry, and, unless determined, as they generally are, by the unacknowledged influence of consideration of utility, afford a free scope for the action of personal desires and partialities. We must remember that only in these cases of conflict between secondary principles is it requisite that first principles should be appealed to. There is no case of moral obligation in which some secondary principle is not involved; and if only one, there can seldom be any real doubt which one it is, in the mind of any person by whom the principle itself is recognized.

Notes

1   The author of this essay has reason for believing himself to be the first person who brought the word "utilitarian" into use. He did not invent it, but adopted it from a passing expression in Mr. Galt's *Annals of the Parish*. After using it as a designation for several years, he and others abandoned it from a growing dislike to anything resembling a badge or watchword of sectarian distinction. But as a name for one single opinion, not a set of opinions – to denote the recognition of utility as a standard, not any particular way of applying it – the term supplies a want in the language, and offers, in many cases, a convenient mode of avoiding tiresome circumlocutions.

2   An opponent, whose intellectual and moral fairness it is a pleasure to acknowledge (the Rev. J. Llewellyn Davies), has objected to this passage, saying, "Surely the rightness or wrongness of saving a man from drowning does depend very much upon the motive with which it is done. Suppose that a tyrant, when his enemy jumped into the sea to escape from him, saved him from drowning simply in order that he might inflict upon him more exquisite tortures, would it tend to clearness to speak of that rescue as 'a morally right action'? Or suppose again, according to one of the stock illustrations of ethical inquiries, that a man betrayed a trust received from a friend, because the discharge of it would fatally injure that friend himself or someone belonging to him, would utilitarianism compel one to call the betrayal 'a crime' as much as if it had been done from the meanest motive?"

I submit that he who saves another from drowning in order to kill him by torture afterwards does not differ only in motive from him who does the same thing from duty or benevolence; the act itself is different. The rescue of the man is, in the case supposed, only the necessary first step of an act far more atrocious than leaving him to drown would have been. Had Mr. Davies said, "The rightness or wrongness of saving a man from drowning does depend very much" – not upon the motive, but – "upon the *intention*," no utilitarian would have differed from him. Mr. Davies, by an oversight too common not to be quite venial, has in this case confounded the very different ideas of Motive and Intention. There is no point which utilitarian thinkers (and Bentham pre-eminently) have taken more pains to illustrate than this. The morality of the action depends entirely upon the intention – that is, upon what the agent *wills to do*. But the motive, that is, the feeling which makes him will so to do, if it makes no difference in the act, makes none in the morality: though it makes a great difference in our moral estimation of the agent, especially if it indicates a good or a bad habitual *disposition* – a bent of character from which useful, or from which hurtful actions are likely to arise.

CHAPTER IV
Of What Sort of Proof the Principle of Utility is Susceptible

It has already been remarked that questions of ultimate ends do not admit of proof, in the ordinary acceptation of the term. To be incapable of proof by reasoning is common to all first principles, to the first premises of our knowledge, as well as to those of our conduct. But the former, being matters of fact, may be the subject of a direct appeal to the faculties which judge of fact – namely, our senses and our internal consciousness. Can an appeal be made to the same faculties on questions of practical ends? Or by what other faculty is cognizance taken of them?

Questions about ends are, in other words, questions what things are desirable. The utilitarian doctrine is that happiness is desirable, and the only thing desirable, as an end; all other things being only desirable as means to that end. What ought to be required of this doctrine, what conditions is it requisite that the doctrine should fulfill – to make good its claim to be believed?

The only proof capable of being given that an object is visible is that people actually see it. The only proof that a sound is audible is that people hear it; and so of the other sources of our experience. In like manner, I apprehend, the sole evidence it is possible to produce that anything is desirable is that people do actually desire it. If the end which the utilitarian doctrine proposes to itself were not, in theory and in practice, acknowledged to be an end, nothing could ever convince any person that it was so. No reason can be given why the general happiness is desirable, except that each person, so far as he believes it to be attainable, desires his own happiness. This, however, being a fact, we have not only all the proof which the case admits of, but all which it is possible to require, that happiness is a good, that each person's happiness is a good to that person, and the general happiness, therefore, a good to the aggregate of all persons. Happiness has made out its title as *one* of the ends of conduct and, consequently, one of the criteria of morality.

But it has not, by this alone, proved itself to be the sole criterion. To do that, it would seem, by the same rule, necessary to show, not only that people desire happiness, but that they never desire anything else. Now it is palpable that they do desire things which, in common language, are decidedly distinguished from happiness. They desire, for example, virtue and the absence of vice no less really than pleasure and the absence of pain. The desire of virtue is not as universal, but it is as authentic a fact as the desire of happiness. And hence the opponents of the utilitarian standard deem that they have a right to infer that there are other ends of human action besides happiness, and that happiness is not the standard of approbation and disapprobation.

But does the utilitarian doctrine deny that people desire virtue, or maintain that virtue is not a thing to be desired? The very reverse. It maintains not only that virtue is to be desired, but that it is to be desired disinterestedly, for itself. Whatever may be the opinion of utilitarian moralists as to the original conditions by which virtue is made virtue, however they may believe (as they do) that actions and dispositions are only virtuous because they promote another end than virtue, yet this being granted, and it having been decided, from considerations of this description, what *is* virtuous, they not only place virtue at the very head of the things which are good as means to the ultimate end, but they also recognize as a psychological fact the possibility of its being, to the individual, a good in itself, without looking to any end beyond it; and hold that the mind is not in a right state, not in a state conformable to utility, not in the state most conducive to the general happiness, unless it does love virtue in this manner – as a thing desirable in itself, even although, in the individual instance, it should not produce those other desirable consequences which it tends to produce, and on account of which it is held to be virtue. This opinion is not, in the smallest degree, a departure from the happiness principle. The ingredients of happiness are very various, and each of them is desirable in itself, and not merely when considered as swelling an aggregate. The principle of utility does not mean that any given pleasure, as music, for instance, or any given exemption from pain, as for example health, is to be looked upon as means to a collective something termed happiness, and to be desired on that account. They are desired and desirable in and for themselves; besides being means, they are a part of the end. Virtue, according to the utilitarian doctrine, is not naturally and originally part of the end, but it is capable of becoming so; and in those who live it disinterestedly it has become so, and is desired and cherished, not as a means to happiness, but as a part of their happiness.

To illustrate this further, we may remember that virtue is not the only thing originally a means, and which if it were not a means to anything else would be and remain indifferent, but which by association with what it is a means to comes to be desired for itself, and that too with the utmost intensity. What, for example, shall we say of the love of money? There is nothing originally more desirable about money than about any heap of glittering pebbles. Its worth is solely that of the things which it will buy; the desires for other things than itself, which it is a means of gratifying. Yet the love of money is not only one of the strongest moving forces of human life, but money is, in many cases, desired in and for itself; the desire to possess it is often stronger than the desire to use it, and goes on increasing when all the desires which point to ends beyond it, to be compassed by it, are falling off. It may, then, be said truly that money is desired not for the sake of an end, but as part of the end. From being a means to happiness, it has come to be itself a principal ingredient of the individual's conception of happiness. The same may be said of the majority of the great objects of human life: power, for example, or fame, except that to each of these there is a certain amount of immediate pleasure annexed, which has at least the semblance of being naturally inherent in them – a thing which cannot be said of money. Still, however, the strongest natural attraction, both of power and of fame, is the immense aid they give to the attainment of our other wishes; and it is the strong association thus generated between them and all our objects of desire which gives to the direct desire of them the intensity it often assumes, so as in some characters to surpass in strength all other desires. In these cases the means have become a part of the end, and a more important part of it than any of the things which they are means to. What was once desired as an instrument for the attainment of happiness has come to be desired for its own sake. In being desired for its own sake it is, however, desired as *part* of happiness. The person is made, or thinks he would be made, happy by its mere possession; and is made unhappy by failure to obtain it. The desire of it is not a different thing from the desire of happiness any more than the love of music or the desire of health. They are included in happiness. They are some of the elements of which the desire of happiness is made up. Happiness is not an abstract idea but a concrete whole; and these are some of its parts. And the utilitarian standard sanctions and approves their being so. Life would be a poor thing, very ill provided with sources of happiness, if there were not this provision of nature by which things originally indifferent, but conducive to, or otherwise associated with, the satisfaction of our primitive desires, become in themselves sources of pleasure more valuable than the primitive pleasures, both in permanency, in the space of human existence that they are capable of covering, and even in intensity.

Virtue, according to the utilitarian conception, is a good of this description. There was no original desire of it, or motive to it, save its conduciveness to pleasure, and especially to protection from pain. But through the association thus formed it may be felt a good in itself, and desired as such with as great intensity as any other good; and with this difference between it and the love of money, of power, or of fame – that all of these may, and often do, render the individual noxious to the other members of the society to which he belongs, whereas there is nothing which makes him so much a blessing to them as the cultivation of the disinterested love of virtue. And consequently, the utilitarian standard, while it tolerates and approves those other acquired desires, up to the point beyond which they would be more injurious to the general happiness than promotive of it, enjoins and requires the cultivation of the love of virtue up to the greatest strength possible, as being above all things important to the general happiness.

It results from the preceding considerations that there is in reality nothing desired except happiness. Whatever is desired otherwise than as a means to some end beyond itself, and ultimately to happiness, is desired as itself a part of happiness, and is not desired for itself until it has become so. Those who desire virtue for its own sake desire it either because the consciousness of it is a pleasure, or because the consciousness of being without it is a pain, or for both reasons united; as in truth the pleasure and pain seldom exist separately, but almost always together – the same person feeling pleasure in the degree of virtue attained, and pain in not having attained more. If one of these gave him no pleasure, and the other no pain, he would not love or desire virtue, or would desire it only for the other benefits which it might produce to himself or to persons whom he cared for.

We have now, then, an answer to the question, of what sort of proof the principle of utility is susceptible. If the opinion which I have now stated is psychologically true – if human nature is so constituted as to desire nothing which is not either a part of happiness or a means of happiness – we can have no other proof, and we require no other, that these are the only things desirable. If so, happiness is the sole end of human action, and the promotion of it the test by which to judge of all human conduct; from whence it necessarily follows that it must be the criterion of morality, since a part is included in the whole.

And now to decide whether this is really so, whether mankind do desire nothing for itself but that which is a pleasure to them, or of which the absence is a pain, we have evidently arrived at a question of fact and experience, dependent, like all similar questions, upon evidence. It can only be determined by practiced self-consciousness and self-observation, assisted by observation of others. I believe that these sources of evidence, impartially consulted, will declare that desiring a thing and finding it pleasant, aversion to it and thinking of it as painful, are phenomena entirely inseparable or, rather, two parts of the same phenomenon – in strictness of language, two different modes of naming the same psychological fact; that to think of an object as desirable (unless for the sake of its consequences) and to think of it as pleasant are one and the same thing; and that to desire anything except in proportion as the idea of it is pleasant is a physical and metaphysical impossibility.

So obvious does this appear to me that I expect it will hardly be disputed; and the objection made will be, not that desire can possibly be directed to anything ultimately except pleasure and exemption from pain, but that the will is a different thing from desire; that a person of confirmed virtue or any other person whose purposes are fixed carries out his purposes without any thought of the pleasure he has in contemplating them or expects to derive from their fulfillment, and persists in acting on them, even though these pleasures are much diminished by changes in his character or decay of his passive sensibilities, or are outweighed by the pains which the pursuit of the purposes may bring upon him. All this I fully admit and have stated it elsewhere as positively and emphatically as anyone. Will, the active phenomenon, is a different thing from desire, the state of passive sensibility, and, though originally an offshoot from it, may in time take root and detach itself from the parent stock, so much so that in the case of a habitual purpose, instead of willing the thing because we desire it, we often desire it only because we will it. This, however, is but an instance of that familiar fact, the power of habit, and is nowise confined to the case of virtuous actions. Many indifferent things which men originally did from a motive of some sort they continue to do from habit. Sometimes this is done unconsciously, the consciousness coming only after the action; at other times with conscious volition, but volition which has become habitual and is put in operation by the force of habit, in opposition perhaps to the deliberate preference, as often happens with those who have contracted habits of vicious or hurtful indulgence. Third and last comes the case in which the habitual act of will in the individual instance is not in contradiction to the general intention prevailing at other times, but in fulfillment of it, as in the case of the person of confirmed virtue and of all who pursue deliberately and consistently any determinate end. The distinction between will and desire thus understood is an authentic and highly important psychological fact; but the fact consists solely in this – that will, like all other parts of our constitution, is amenable to habit, and that we may will from habit what we no longer desire for itself, or desire only because we will it. It is not the less true that will, in the beginning, is entirely produced by desire, including in that term the repelling influence of pain as well as the attractive one of pleasure. Let us take into consideration no longer the person who has a confirmed will to do right, but him in whom that virtuous will is still feeble, conquerable by temptation, and not to be fully relied on; by what means can it be strengthened? How can the will to be virtuous, where it does not exist in sufficient force, be implanted or awakened? Only by making the person *desire* virtue – by making him think of it in a pleasurable light, or of its absence in a painful one. It is by associating the doing right with pleasure, or the wrong with pain, or by eliciting and impressing and bringing home to the person's experience the pleasure naturally involved in the one or the pain in the other, that it is possible to call forth that will to be virtuous which, when confirmed, acts without any thought of either pleasure or pain. Will is the child of desire, and passes out of the dominion of its parent only to come under that of habit. That which is the result of habit affords no presumption of being intrinsically good; and there would be no reason for wishing that the purpose of virtue should become independent of pleasure and pain were it not that the influence of the pleasurable and painful associations which prompt to virtue is not sufficiently to be depended on for unerring constancy of action until it has acquired the support of habit. Both in feeling and in conduct, habit is the only thing which imparts certainty; and it is because of the importance to others of being able to rely absolutely on one's feelings and conduct, and to oneself of being able to rely on one's own, that the will to do right ought to be cultivated into this habitual independence. In other words, this state of the will is a means to good, not intrinsically a good; and does not contradict the doctrine that nothing is a good to human beings but in so far as it is either itself pleasurable or a means of attaining pleasure or averting pain.

But if this doctrine be true, the principle of utility is proved. Whether it is so or not must now be left to the consideration of the thoughtful reader.

CHAPTER V
On the Connection between Justice and Utility

In most if not in all languages, the etymology of the word which corresponds to "just" points distinctly to an origin connected with the ordinances of law. *Justum* is a form of *jussum*, that which has been ordered. *Dikaion* comes directly from *dike*, a suit at law. *Recht*, from which came *right* and *righteous*, is synonymous with law. The courts of justice, the administration of justice, are the courts and the administration of law. *La justice*, in French, is the established term for judicature. I am not committing the fallacy, imputed with some show of truth to Horne Tooke, of assuming that a word must still continue to mean what it originally meant. Etymology is slight evidence of what the idea now signified is, but the very best evidence of how it sprang up. There can, I think, be no doubt that the *idée mère*, the primitive element, in the formation of the notion of justice was conformity to law. It constituted the entire idea among the Hebrews, up to the birth of Christianity; as might be expected in the case of a people whose laws attempted to embrace all subjects on which precepts were required, and who believed those laws to be a direct emanation from the Supreme Being. But other nations, and in particular the Greeks and Romans, who knew that their laws had been made originally, and still continued to be made, by men, were not afraid to admit that those men might make bad laws; might do, by law, the same things, and from the same motives, which if done by individuals without the sanction of law would be called unjust. And hence the sentiment of injustice came to be attached, not to all violations of law, but only to violations of such laws as *ought* to exist, including such as ought to exist but do not, and to laws themselves if supposed to be contrary to what ought to be law. In this manner the idea of law and of its injunctions was still predominant in the notion of justice, even when the laws actually in force ceased to be accepted as the standard of it.

It is true that mankind consider the idea of justice and its obligations as applicable to many things which neither are, nor is it desired that they should be, regulated by law. Nobody desires that laws should interfere with the whole detail of private life; yet everyone allows that in all daily conduct a person may and does show himself to be either just or unjust. But even here, the idea of the breach of what ought to be law still lingers in a modified shape. It would always give us pleasure, and chime in with our feelings of fitness, that acts which we deem unjust should be punished, though we do not always think it expedient that this should be done by the tribunals. We forgo that gratification on account of incidental inconveniences. We should be glad to see just conduct enforced and injustice repressed, even in the minutest details, if we were not, with reason, afraid of trusting the magistrate with so unlimited an amount of power over individuals. When we think that a person is bound in justice to do a thing, it is an ordinary form of language to say that he ought to be compelled to do it. We should be gratified to see the obligation enforced by anybody who had the power. If we see that its enforcement by law would be inexpedient, we lament the impossibility, we consider the impunity given to injustice as an evil, and strive to make amends for it by bringing a strong expression of our own and the public disapprobation to bear upon the offender. Thus the idea of legal constraint is still the generating idea of the notion of justice, though undergoing several transformations before that notion as it exists in an advanced state of society becomes complete.

The above is, I think, a true account, as far as it goes, of the origin and progressive growth of the idea of justice. But we must observe that it contains as yet nothing to distinguish that obligation from moral obligation in general. For the truth is that the idea of penal sanction, which is the essence of law, enters not only into the conception of injustice, but into that of any kind of wrong. We do not call anything wrong unless we mean to imply that a person ought to be punished in some way or other for doing it – if not by law, by the opinion of his fellow creatures; if not by opinion, by the reproaches of his own conscience. This seems the real turning point of the distinction between morality and simple expediency. It is a part of the notion of duty in every one of its forms that a person may rightfully be compelled to fulfill it. Duty is a thing which may be *exacted* from a person, as one exacts a debt. Unless we think that it may be exacted from him, we do not call it his duty. Reasons of prudence, or the interest of other people, may militate against actually exacting it, but the person himself, it is clearly understood, would not be entitled to complain. There are other things, on the contrary, which we wish that people should do, which we like or admire them for doing, perhaps dislike or despise them for not doing, but yet admit that they are not bound to do;

it is not a case of moral obligation; we do not blame them, that is, we do not think that they are proper objects of punishment. How we come by these ideas of deserving and not deserving punishment will appear, perhaps, in the sequel; but I think there is no doubt that this distinction lies at the bottom of the notions of right and wrong; that we call any conduct wrong, or employ, instead, some other term of dislike or disparagement, according as we think that the person ought, or ought not, to be punished for it; and we say it would be right to do so and so, or merely that it would be desirable or laudable, according as we would wish to see the person whom it concerns compelled, or only persuaded and exhorted, to act in that manner.

This, therefore, being the characteristic difference which marks off, not justice, but morality in general from the remaining provinces of expediency and worthiness, the character is still to be sought which distinguishes justice from other branches of morality. Now it is known that ethical writers divide moral duties into two classes, denoted by the ill-chosen expressions, duties of perfect and of imperfect obligation; the latter being those in which, though the act is obligatory, the particular occasions of performing it are left to our choice, as in the case of charity or beneficence, which we are indeed bound to practice but not toward any definite person, nor at any prescribed time. In the more precise language of philosophic jurists, duties of perfect obligation are those duties in virtue of which a correlative *right* resides in some person or persons; duties of imperfect obligation are those moral obligations which do not give birth to any right. I think it will be found that this distinction exactly coincides with that which exists between justice and the other obligations of morality. In our survey of the various popular acceptations of justice, the term appeared generally to involve the idea of a personal right – a claim on the part of one or more individuals, like that which the law gives when it confers a proprietary or other legal right. Whether the injustice consists in depriving a person of a possession, or in breaking faith with him, or in treating him worse than he deserves, or worse than other people who have no greater claims – in each case the supposition implies two things: a wrong done, and some assignable person who is wronged. Injustice may also be done by treating a person better than others; but the wrong in this case is to his competitors, who are also assignable persons. It seems to me that this feature in the case – a right in some person, correlative to the moral obligation – constitutes the specific difference between justice and generosity or beneficence. Justice implies something which it is not only right to do, and wrong not to do, but which some individual person can claim from us as his moral right. No one has a moral right to our generosity or beneficence because we are not morally bound to practice those virtues toward any given individual. And it will be found with respect to this as to every correct definition that the instances which seem to conflict with it are those which most confirm it. For if a moralist attempts, as some have done, to make out that mankind generally, though not any given individual, have a right to all the good we can do them, he at once, by that thesis, includes generosity and beneficence within the category of justice. He is obliged to say that our utmost exertions are *due* to our fellow creatures, thus assimilating them to a debt; or that nothing less can be a sufficient *return* for what society does for us, thus classing the case as one of gratitude; both of which are acknowledged cases of justice, and not of the virtue of beneficence; and whoever does not place the distinction between justice and morality in general, where we have now placed it, will be found to make no distinction between them at all, but to merge all morality in justice.

Having thus endeavored to determine the distinctive elements which enter into the composition of the idea of justice, we are ready to enter on the inquiry whether the feeling which accompanies the idea is attached to it by a special dispensation of nature, or whether it could have grown up, by any known laws, out of the idea itself; and, in particular, whether it can have originated in considerations of general expediency.

I conceive that the sentiment itself does not arise from anything which would commonly or correctly be termed an idea of expediency, but that, though the sentiment does not, whatever is moral in it does.

We have seen that the two essential ingredients in the sentiment of justice are the desire to punish a person who has done harm and the knowledge or belief that there is some definite individual or individuals to whom harm has been done.

Now it appears to me that the desire to punish a person who has done harm to some individual is a spontaneous outgrowth from two sentiments, both in the highest degree natural and which either are or resemble instincts: the impulse of self-defense and the feeling of sympathy.

It is natural to resent and to repel or retaliate any harm done or attempted against ourselves or against those with whom we sympathize. The origin of this sentiment it is not necessary here to discuss. Whether it be an instinct or a result of intelligence, it is, we know, common to all animal nature; for every animal tries to hurt those who have hurt, or who it thinks are about to hurt, itself or its young. Human beings, on this point, only differ from other animals in two particulars. First, in being capable of sympathizing, not solely with their offspring, or, like some of the more noble animals, with some superior animal who is kind to them, but with all human, and even with all sentient, beings; secondly, in having a more developed intelligence, which gives a wider range to the whole of their sentiments, whether self-regarding or sympathetic. By virtue of his superior intelligence, even apart from his superior range of sympathy, a human being is capable of apprehending a community of interest between himself and the human society of which he forms a part, such that any conduct which threatens the security of the society generally is threatening to his own, and calls forth his instinct (if instinct it be) of self-defense. The same superiority of intelligence, joined to the power of sympathizing with human beings generally, enables him to attach himself to the collective idea of his tribe, his country, or mankind in such a manner that any act hurtful to them raises his instinct of sympathy and urges him to resistance.

The sentiment of justice, in that one of its elements which consists of the desire to punish, is thus, I conceive, the natural feeling of retaliation or vengeance, rendered by intellect and sympathy applicable to those injuries, that is, to those hurts, which wound us through, or in common with, society at large. This sentiment, in itself, has nothing moral in it; what is moral is the exclusive subordination of it to the social sympathies, so as to wait on and obey their call. For the natural feeling would make us resent indiscriminately whatever anyone does that is disagreeable to us; but, when moralized by the social feeling, it only acts in the directions conformable to the general good: just persons resenting a hurt to society, though not otherwise a hurt to themselves, and not resenting a hurt to themselves, however painful, unless it be of the kind which society has a common interest with them in the repression of.

It is no objection against this doctrine to say that, when we feel our sentiment of justice outraged, we are not thinking of society at large or of any collective interest, but only of the individual case. It is common enough, certainly, though the reverse of commendable, to feel resentment merely because we have suffered pain; but a person whose resentment is really a moral feeling, that is, who considers whether an act is blamable before he allows himself to resent it – such a person, though he may not say expressly to himself that he is standing up for the interest of society, certainly does feel that he is asserting a rule which is for the benefit of others as well as for his own. If he is not feeling this, if he is regarding the act solely as it affects him individually, he is not consciously just; he is not concerning himself about the justice of his actions. This is admitted even by anti-utilitarian moralists. When Kant (as before remarked) propounds as the fundamental principle of morals, "So act that thy rule of conduct might be adopted as a law by all rational beings," he virtually acknowledges that the interest of mankind collectively, or at least of mankind indiscriminately, must be in the mind of the agent when conscientiously deciding on the morality of the act. Otherwise he uses words without a meaning; for that a rule even of utter selfishness could not *possibly* be adopted by all rational beings – that there is any insuperable obstacle in the nature of things to its adoption – cannot be even plausibly maintained. To give any meaning to Kant's principle, the sense put upon it must be that we ought to shape our conduct by a rule which all rational beings might adopt *with benefit to their collective interest.*

To recapitulate: the idea of justice supposes two things – a rule of conduct and a sentiment which sanctions the rule. The first must be supposed common to all mankind and intended for their good. The other (the sentiment) is a desire that punishment may be suffered by those who infringe the rule. There is involved, in addition, the conception of some definite person who suffers by the infringement, whose rights (to use the expression appropriated to the case) are violated by it. And the sentiment of justice appears to me to be the animal desire to repel or retaliate a hurt or damage to oneself or to those with whom one sympathizes, widened so as to include all persons, by the human capacity of enlarged sympathy and the human conception of intelligent self-interest. From the latter elements the feeling derives its morality; from the former, its peculiar impressiveness and energy of self-assertion.

I have, throughout, treated the idea of a *right* residing in the injured person and violated by the injury, not as a separate element in the composition of the idea and sentiment, but as one of the forms in which the other two elements clothe themselves. These elements are a hurt to some assignable person or persons, on the one hand, and a demand for punishment, on the other. An examination of our own minds, I think, will show that these two things include all that we mean when we speak of violation of a right. When we call anything a person's right, we mean that he has a valid claim on society to protect him in the possession of it, either by the force of law or by that of education and opinion. If he has what we consider a sufficient claim, on whatever account, to have something guaranteed to him by society, we say that he has a right to it. If we desire to prove that anything does not belong to him by right, we think this done as soon as it is admitted that society ought not to take measure for securing it to him, but should leave him to chance or to his own exertions. Thus a person is said to have a right to what he can earn in fair professional competition, because society ought not to allow any other person to hinder him from endeavoring to earn in that manner as much as he can. But he has not a right to three hundred a year, though he may happen to be earning it; because society is not called on to provide that he shall earn that sum. On the contrary, if he owns ten thousand pounds three-per-cent stock, he *has* a right to three hundred a year because society has come under an obligation to provide him with an income of that amount.

To have a right, then, is, I conceive, to have something which society ought to defend me in the possession of. If the objector goes on to ask why it ought, I can give him no other reason than general utility. If that expression does not seem to convey a sufficient feeling of the strength of the obligation, nor to account for the peculiar energy of the feeling, it is because there goes to the composition of the sentiment, not a rational only but also an animal element – the thirst for retaliation; and this thirst derives its intensity, as well as its moral justification, from the extraordinarily important and impressive kind of utility which is concerned. The interest involved is that of security, to everyone's feelings the most vital of all interests. All other earthly benefits are needed by one person, not needed by another; and many of them can, if necessary, be cheerfully forgone or replaced by something else; but security no human being can possibly do without; on it we depend for all our immunity from evil and for the whole value of all and every good, beyond the passing moment, since nothing but the gratification of the instant could be of any worth to us if we could be deprived of everything the next instant by whoever was momentarily stronger than ourselves. Now this most indispensable of all necessaries, after physical nutriment, cannot be had unless the machinery for providing it is kept unintermittedly in active play. Our notion, therefore, of the claim we have on our fellow creatures to join in making safe for us the very groundwork of our existence gathers feelings around it so much more intense than those concerned in any of the more common cases of utility that the difference in degree (as is often the case in psychology) becomes a real difference in kind. The claim assumes that character of absoluteness, that apparent infinity and incommensurability with all other considerations which constitute the distinction between the feeling of right and wrong and that of ordinary expediency and inexpediency. The feelings concerned are so powerful, and we count so positively on finding a responsive feeling in others (all being alike interested) that *ought* and *should* grow into *must*, and recognized indispensability becomes a moral necessity, analogous to physical, and often not inferior to it in binding force.

If the preceding analysis, or something resembling it, be not the correct account of the notion of justice – if justice be totally independent of utility, and be a standard *per se*, which the mind can recognize by simple intro-spection of itself – it is hard to understand why that internal oracle is so ambiguous, and why so many things appear either just or unjust, accord-ing to the light in which they are regarded.

3

From "Dr Whewell on Moral Philosophy"

John Stuart Mill

Take ordinary cases. I am tempted to utter a flattering falsehood: to gratify some sensual desire contrary to ordinary moral rules. How shall I determine, on the greatest happiness principle, whether the act is virtuous, or the contrary? In the first place, the direct effect of each act is to give pleasure, to another by flattery, to myself by sensual gratification; and pleasure is the material of happiness, in the scheme we are now considering. But by the flattering lie I promote falsehood, which is destructive of confidence, and so, of human comfort. Granted that I do this in some degree – although I may easily say that I shall never allow myself to speak falsely, except when it will give pleasure; and thus I may maintain that I shall not shake confidence in any case in which it is of any value. But granted that I do, in some degree, shake the general fabric of mutual human confidence by my flattering lie, still the question remains, *how much* I do this: whether in such a degree as to overbalance the pleasure, which is the primary and direct consequence of the act. How small must be the effect of my solitary act upon the whole scheme of human action and habit! How clear and decided is the direct affect of increasing the happiness of my hearer! And in the same way we may reason concerning the sensual gratification. Who will know it? Who will be influenced by it of those who do know it? What appreciable amount of pain will it produce in its consequences, to balance the palpable pleasure, which according to our teachers, is the only real good? It appears to me that it is impossible to answer these

John Stuart Mill, "Dr Whewell on Moral Philosophy" was first published as "Whewell on Moral Philosophy" in the *Westminster Review*, October 1852. The text printed here is taken from *Dissertations and Discussions: Political, Philosophical and Historical*, first published by John W. Parker, London, 1859.

questions in any way which will prove on these principles, mendacious flattery, and illegitimate sensuality, to be vicious and immoral. They may possibly produce, take in all their effects, a balance of evil; but if they do, it is by some process which we cannot trace with any clearness, and the result is one which we cannot calculate with any certainty, or even probability; and therefore, on this account, because the resulting evil of such falsehood and sensuality is not calculable or appreciable, we cannot, by calculation of resulting evil, show falsehood and sensuality to be vices. And the like is true of other vices; and, on this ground, the construction of a scheme of morality on Mr Bentham's plan is plainly impossible.

Dr Whewell supposes his self-deceiving utilitarian to be very little master of his own principles. If the effect of a 'solitary act upon the whole scheme of human action and habit' is small, the addition which the accompanying pleasure makes to the general mass of human happiness is small likewise. So small, in the great majority of cases, are both, that we have no scales to weigh them against each other, taken singly. We must look at them multiplied, and in large masses. The portion of the tendencies of an action which belong to it not individually, but as a violation of a general rule, are as certain and as calculable as any other consequences; only they must be examined not in the individual case, but in classes of cases. Take, for example, the case of murder. There are many persons to kill whom would be to remove men who are a cause of no good to any human being, of cruel physical and moral suffering to several, and whose whole influence tends to increase the mass of unhappiness and vice. Were such a man to be assassinated, the balance of traceable consequences would be greatly in favour of the act. The counter-consideration, on the principle of utility, is, that unless persons were punished for killing, and taught not to kill; that if it were thought allowable for any one to put to death at pleasure any human being whom he believes that the world would be well rid of, nobody's life would be safe. To this Dr Whewell answers:

> How does it appear that the evil, that is, the pain, arising from violating a general rule once, is too great to be overbalanced by the pleasurable consequences of that single violation? The actor says, I acknowledge the general rule – I do not deny its value; but I do not intend that this one act should be drawn into consequence.

But it does not depend on him whether or not it shall be drawn into consequence. If one person may break through the rule on his own judgement, the same liberty cannot be refused to others; and since no one could rely on the rule's being observed, the rule would cease to exist. If a hundred infringements would produce all the mischief implied in the abrogation of the rule, a hundredth part of that mischief must be debited to each one of the infringements, though we may not be able to trace it home individually. And this hundredth part will generally far outweigh any good expected to arise from the individual act. We say generally, not universally; for the admission of exceptions to rules is a necessity equally felt in all systems of morality. To take an obvious instance, the rule against homicide, the rule against deceiving, the rule against taking advantage of superior physical strength, and various other important moral rules, are suspended against enemies in the field, and partially against malefactors in private life: in each case suspended as far as is required by the peculiar nature of the case. That the moralities arising from the special circumstances of the action may be so important as to overrule those arising from the class of acts to which it belongs, perhaps to take it out of the category of virtues into that of crimes, or *vice versa*, is a liability common to all ethical systems.

4

From *The Methods of Ethics*

Henry Sidgwick

BOOK IV
CHAPTER XIII
Philosophical Intuitionism

§ 3.   Can we then, between this Scylla and Charybdis of ethical inquiry, avoiding on the one hand doctrines that merely bring us back to common opinion with all its imperfections, and on the other hand doctrines that lead us round in a circle, find any way of obtaining self-evident moral principles of real significance? It would be disheartening to have to regard as altogether illusory the strong instinct of Common Sense that points to the existence of such principles, and the deliberate convictions of the long line of moralists who have enunciated them. At the same time, the more we extend our knowledge of man and his environment, the more we realise the vast variety of human natures and circumstances that have existed in different ages and countries, the less disposed we are to believe that there is any definite code of absolute rules, applicable to all human beings without exception. And we shall find, I think, that the truth lies between these two conclusions. There are certain absolute practical principles, the truth of which, when they are explicitly stated, is manifest; but they are of too abstract a nature, and too universal in their scope, to enable us to ascertain by immediate application of them what we ought to do in any particular case; particular duties have still to be determined by some other method.

Henry Sidgwick, *The Methods of Ethics*, 7th edn. (London: Macmillan, 1967), pp. 379–84, 386–9, 411–26, 453–7.

One such principle was given in [an earlier chapter]; where I pointed out that whatever action any of us judges to be right for himself, he implicitly judges to be right for all similar persons in similar circumstances. Or, as we may otherwise put it, 'if a kind of conduct that is right (or wrong) for me is not right (or wrong) for some one else, it must be on the ground of some difference between the two cases, other than the fact that I and he are different persons.' A corresponding proposition may be stated with equal truth in respect of what ought to be done *to* – not *by* – different individuals. These principles have been most widely recognised, not in their most abstract and universal form, but in their special application to the situation of two (or more) individuals similarly related to each other: as so applied, they appear in what is popularly known as the Golden Rule, 'Do to others as you would have them do to you.' This formula is obviously unprecise in statement; for one might wish for another's co-operation in sin, and be willing to reciprocate it. Nor is it even true to say that we ought to do to others only what we think it right for them to do to us; for no one will deny that there may be differences in the circumstances – and even in the natures – of two individuals, A and B, which would make it wrong for A to treat B in the way in which it is right for B to treat A. In short the self-evident principle strictly stated must take some such negative form as this; 'it cannot be right for A to treat B in a manner in which it would be wrong for B to treat A, merely on the ground that they are two different individuals, and without there being any difference between the natures or circumstances of the two which can be stated as a reasonable ground for difference of treatment.' Such a principle manifestly does not give complete guidance – indeed its effect, strictly speaking, is merely to throw a definite *onus probandi* on the man who applies to another a treatment of which he would complain if applied to himself; but Common Sense has amply recognised the practical importance of the maxim: and its truth, so far as it goes, appears to me self-evident.

A somewhat different application of the same fundamental principle that individuals in similar conditions should be treated similarly finds its sphere in the ordinary administration of Law, or (as we say) of 'Justice.' [Earlier in this Book] I drew attention to 'impartiality in the application of general rules,' as an important element in the common notion of Justice; indeed, there ultimately appeared to be no other element which could be intuitively known with perfect clearness and certainty. Here again it must be plain that this precept of impartiality is insufficient for the complete determination of just conduct, as it does not help us to decide what kind of rules should be thus impartially applied; though all admit the importance of excluding from government, and human conduct generally, all conscious partiality and 'respect of persons.'

The principle just discussed, which seems to be more or less clearly implied in the common notion of 'fairness' or 'equity,' is obtained by considering the similarity of the individuals that make up a Logical Whole or Genus. There are others, no less important, which emerge in the consideration of the similar parts of a Mathematical or Quantitative Whole. Such a Whole is presented in the common notion of the Good – or, as is sometimes said, 'good on the whole' – of any individual human being. The proposition 'that one ought to aim at one's own good' is sometimes given as the maxim of Rational Self-love or Prudence: but as so stated it does not clearly avoid tautology; since we may define 'good' as 'what one ought to aim at.' If, however, we say 'one's good on the whole,' the addition suggests a principle which, when explicitly stated, is, at any rate, not tautological. I have already referred to this principle as that 'of impartial concern for all parts of our conscious life': – we might express it concisely by saying 'that Hereafter *as such* is to be regarded neither less nor more than Now.' It is not, of course, meant that the good of the present may not reasonably be preferred to that of the future on account of its greater certainty: or again, that a week ten years hence may not be more important to us than a week now, through an increase in our means or capacities of happiness. All that the principle affirms is that the mere difference of priority and posteriority in time is not a reasonable ground for having more regard to the consciousness of one moment than to that of another. The form in which it practically presents itself to most men is 'that a smaller present good is not to be preferred to a greater future good' (allowing for difference of certainty): since Prudence is generally exercised in restraining a present desire (the object or satisfaction of which we commonly regard as *pro tanto* 'a good'), on account of the remoter consequences of gratifying it. The commonest view of the principle would no doubt be that the present *pleasure* or *happiness* is reasonably to be forgone with the view of obtaining greater pleasure or happiness hereafter: but the principle need not be restricted to a hedonistic application; it is equally applicable to any other interpretation of 'one's own good,' in which good is conceived as a mathematical whole, of which the integrant parts are realised in different parts or moments of a lifetime. And therefore it is perhaps better to distinguish it here from the principle 'that Pleasure is the sole Ultimate Good,' which does not seem to have any logical connexion with it.

So far we have only been considering the 'Good on the Whole' of a single individual: but just as this notion is constructed by comparison and integration of the different 'goods' that succeed one another in the series of our conscious states, so we have formed the notion of Universal Good by comparison and integration of the goods of all individual human – or sentient – existences. And here again, just as in the former case, by considering the relation of the integrant parts to the whole and to each other, I obtain the self-evident principle that the good of any one individual is of no more importance, from the point of view (if I may say so) of the Universe, than the good of any other; unless, that is, there are special grounds for believing that more good is likely to be realised in the one case than in the other. And it is evident to me that as a rational being I am bound to aim at good generally, – so far as it is attainable by my efforts, – not merely at a particular part of it.

From these two rational intuitions we may deduce, as a necessary inference, the maxim of Benevolence in an abstract form: viz. that each one is morally bound to regard the good of any other individual as much as his own, except in so far as he judges it to be less, when impartially viewed, or less certainly knowable or attainable by him. I before observed that the duty of Benevolence as recognised by common sense seems to fall somewhat short of this. But I think it may be fairly urged in explanation of this that *practically* each man, even with a view to universal Good, ought chiefly to concern himself with promoting the good of a limited number of human beings, and that generally in proportion to the closeness of their connexion with him. I think that a 'plain man,' in a modern civilised society, if his conscience were fairly brought to consider the hypothetical question, whether it would be morally right for him to seek his own happiness on any occasion if it involved a certain sacrifice of the greater happiness of some other human being, – without any counterbalancing gain to any one else, – would answer unhesitatingly in the negative.

I have tried to show how in the principles of Justice, Prudence, and Rational Benevolence as commonly recognised there is at least a self-evident element, immediately cognisable by abstract intuition; depending in each ease on the relation which individuals and their particular ends bear as parts to their wholes, and to other parts of these wholes. I regard the apprehension, with more or less distinctness, of these abstract truths, as the permanent basis of the common conviction that the fundamental precepts of morality are essentially reasonable. No doubt these principles are often placed side by side with other precepts to which custom and general consent have given a merely illusory air of self-evidence: but the distinction between the two kinds of maxims appears to me to become manifest by merely reflecting upon them. I know by direct reflection that the propositions, 'I ought to speak the truth,' 'I ought to keep my promises' – however true they may be – are not self-evident to me; they present themselves as propositions requiring rational justification of some kind. On the other hand, the propositions, 'I ought not to prefer a present lesser good to a future greater good,' and 'I ought not to prefer my own lesser good to the greater good of another,'[1] do present themselves as self-evident; as much (e.g.) as the mathematical axiom that 'if equals be added to equals the wholes are equal.'

It is on account of the fundamental and manifest importance, in my view, of the distinction above drawn between (1) the moral maxims which reflection shows not to possess ultimate validity, and (2) the moral maxims which are or involve genuine ethical axioms, that I refrained at the outset of this investigation from entering at length into the psychogonical question as to the origin of apparent moral intuitions. For no psychogonical theory has ever been put forward professing to discredit the propositions that I regard as really axiomatic, by showing that the causes which produced them were such as had a tendency to make them false: while as regards the former class of maxims, a psychogonical proof that they are untrustworthy when taken as absolutely and without qualification true is in my view, superfluous: since direct reflection shows me they have no claim to be so taken. On the other hand, so far as psychogonical theory represents moral rules as, speaking broadly and generally, means to the ends of individual and social good or well-being, it obviously tends to give a general support to the conclusions to which the preceding discussion has brought us by a different method: since it leads us to regard other moral rules as subordinate to the principles of Prudence and Benevolence. . . .

§ 5.   I must now point out – if it has not long been apparent to the reader – that the self-evident principles laid down in § 3 do not specially belong to Intuitionism in the restricted sense which, for clear distinction of methods, I gave to this term at the outset of our investigation. The axiom of Prudence, as I have given it, is a self-evident principle, implied in Rational Egoism as commonly accepted.[2] Again, the axiom of Justice or Equity as above stated – 'that similar cases ought to be treated similarly' – belongs in all its applications to Utilitarianism as much as to any system commonly called Intuitional: while the axiom of Rational Benevolence is, in my view, required as a rational basis for the Utilitarian system.

Accordingly, I find that I arrive, in my search for really clear and certain ethical intuitions, at the fundamental principle of Utilitarianism. I must, however, admit that the thinkers who in recent times have taught this latter system, have not, for the most part, expressly tried to exhibit the truth of their first principle by means of any such procedure as that above given. Still, when I examine the "proof" of the "principle of Utility" presented by the most persuasive and probably the most influential among

English expositors of Utilitarianism, – J. S. Mill, – I find the need of some such procedure to complete the argument very plain and palpable.

Mill begins by explaining[3] that though "questions of ultimate ends are not amenable" to "proof in the ordinary and popular meaning of the term," there is a "larger meaning of the word proof" in which they are amenable to it. "The subject," he says, is "within the cognisance of the rational faculty. . . . Considerations may be presented capable of determining the intellect to" accept "the Utilitarian formula." He subsequently makes clear that by "acceptance of the Utilitarian formula" he means the acceptance, not of the agent's own greatest happiness, but of "the greatest amount of happiness altogether" as the ultimate "end of human action" and "standard of morality": to promote which is, in the Utilitarian view, the supreme "directive rule of human conduct." Then when he comes to give the "proof" – in the larger sense before explained – of this rule or formula, he offers the following argument. "The sole evidence it is possible to produce that anything is desirable, is that people do actually desire it. . . . No reason can be given why the general happiness is desirable, except that each person, so far as he believes it to be attainable, desires his own happiness. This, however, being a fact, we have not only all the proof which the case admits of, but all which it is possible to require, that happiness is a good: that each person's happiness is a good to that person, and the general happiness, therefore, a good to the aggregate of persons."[4] He then goes on to argue that pleasure, and pleasure alone, is what all men actually do desire.

Now, as we have seen, it is as a "standard of right and wrong," or "directive rule of conduct," that the utilitarian principle is put forward by Mill: hence, in giving as a statement of this principle that "the general happiness is *desirable*," he must be understood to mean (and his whole treatise shows that he does mean) that it is what each individual *ought* to desire, or at least – in the stricter sense of 'ought' – to aim at realising in action.[5] But this proposition is not established by Mill's reasoning, even if we grant that what is actually desired may be legitimately inferred to be in this sense desirable. For an aggregate of actual desires, each directed towards a different part of the general happiness, does not constitute an actual desire for the general happiness, existing in any individual; and Mill would certainly not contend that a desire which does not exist in any individual can possibly exist in an aggregate of individuals. There being therefore no actual desire – so far as this reasoning goes – for the general happiness, the proposition that the general happiness is desirable cannot be in this way established: so that there is a gap in the expressed argument, which can, I think, only be filled by some such proposition as that which I have above tried to exhibit as the intuition of Rational Benevolence.

Utilitarianism is thus presented as the final form into which Intuitionism tends to pass, when the demand for really self-evident first principles is rigorously pressed. In order, however, to make this transition logically complete, we require to interpret 'Universal Good' as 'Universal Happiness.' And this interpretation cannot, in my view, be justified by arguing, as Mill does, from the psychological fact that Happiness is the sole object of men's actual desires, to the ethical conclusion that it alone is desirable or good; because [earlier in] this treatise I attempted to show that Happiness or Pleasure is not the only object that each for himself actually desires. The identification of Ultimate Good with Happiness is properly to be reached, I think, by a more indirect mode of reasoning; which I will endeavour to explain in [a later chapter].

Notes

1 To avoid misapprehension I should state that in these propositions the consideration of the different degrees of *certainty* of Present and Future Good, Own and Others' Good respectively, is supposed to have been fully taken into account *before* the future or alien Good is judged to be greater.
2 On the relation of Rational Egoism to Rational Benevolence – which I regard as the profoundest problem of Ethics – my final view is given in the last chapter of this treatise.
3 *Utilitarianism*, chap. i. pp. 6, 7, and chap. ii. pp. 16, 17.
4 *Utilitarionism*, chap. iv.
5 It has been suggested that I have overlooked a confusion in Mill's mind between two possible meanings of the term 'desirable,' (1) what can be desired and (2) what ought to be desired. I intended to show by the two first sentences of this paragraph that I was aware of this confusion, but thought it unnecessary for my present purpose to discuss it.

BOOK IV
CHAPTER I
The Meaning of Utilitarianism

§ 1.   The term Utilitarianism is, at the present day, in common use, and is supposed to designate a doctrine or method with which we are all familiar. But on closer examination, it appears to be applied to several distinct theories, having no necessary connexion with one another, and not even referring to the same subject-matter. It will be well, therefore, to define, as carefully as possible, the doctrine that is to be denoted by the term in the present Book: at the same time distinguishing this from other doctrines to which usage would allow the name to be applied, and indicating, so far as seems necessary, its relation to these.

By Utilitarianism is here meant the ethical theory, that the conduct which, under any given circumstances, is objectively right, is that which will produce the greatest amount of happiness on the whole; that is, taking into account all whose happiness is affected by the conduct. It would tend to clearness if we might call this principle, and the method based upon it, by some such name as "Universalistic Hedonism": and I have therefore sometimes ventured to use this term, in spite of its cumbrousness.

The first doctrine from which it seems necessary to distinguish this, is the Egoistic Hedonism expounded and discussed [earlier in] this treatise. The difference, however, between the propositions (1) that each ought to seek his own happiness, and (2) that each ought to seek the happiness of all, is so obvious and glaring, that instead of dwelling upon it we seem rather called upon to explain how the two ever came to be confounded, or in any way included under one notion. This question and the general relation between the two doctrines were briefly discussed in a former chapter.[1] Among other points it was there noticed that the confusion between these two ethical theories was partly assisted by the confusion, with both, of the psychological theory that in voluntary actions every agent does, universally or normally, seek his own individual happiness or pleasure. Now there seems to be no *necessary* connexion between this latter proposition and any ethical theory: but in so far as there is a natural tendency to pass from psychological to ethical Hedonism, the transition must be – at least primarily – to the Egoistic phase of the latter. For clearly, from the fact that every one actually does seek his own happiness we cannot conclude, as an immediate and obvious inference, that he ought to seek the happiness of other people.[2]

Nor, again, is Utilitarianism, as an ethical doctrine, necessarily connected with the psychological theory that the moral sentiments are derived, by "association of ideas" or otherwise, from experiences of the non-moral pleasures and pains resulting to the agent or to others from different kinds of conduct. An Intuitionist might accept this theory, so far as it is capable of scientific proof, and still hold that these moral sentiments, being found in our present consciousness as independent impulses, ought to possess the authority that they seem to claim over the more primary desires and aversions from which they have sprung: and an Egoist on the other hand might fully admit the altruistic element of the derivation, and still hold that these and all other impulses (including even Universal Benevolence) are properly under the rule of Rational Self-love: and that it is really only reasonable to gratify them in so far as we may expect to find our private happiness in such gratification. In short, what is often called the "utilitarian" theory of the origin of the moral sentiments cannot by itself provide a proof of the ethical doctrine to which I in this treatise restrict the term Utilitarianism. I shall, however, hereafter try to show that this psychological theory has an important though subordinate place in the establishment of Ethical Utilitarianism.

Finally, the doctrine that Universal Happiness is the ultimate *standard* must not be understood to imply that Universal Benevolence is the only right or always best *motive* of action. For, as we have before observed, it is not necessary that the end which gives the criterion of rightness should always be the end at which we consciously aim: and if experience shows that the general happiness will be more satisfactorily attained if men frequently act from other motives than pure universal philanthropy, it is obvious that these other motives are reasonably to be preferred on Utilitarian principles.

§ 2.   Let us now examine the principle itself somewhat closer. I have already attempted to render the notion of Greatest Happiness as clear and definite as possible; and the results there obtained are of course as applicable to the discussion of Universalistic as to that of Egoistic Hedonism. We shall understand, then, that by Greatest Happiness is meant the greatest possible surplus of pleasure over pain, the pain being conceived as balanced against an equal amount of pleasure, so that the two contrasted amounts annihilate each other for purposes of ethical calculation. And of course, here as before, the assumption is involved that all pleasures included in our calculation are capable of being compared quantitatively with one another and with all pains; that every such feeling has a certain intensive quantity, positive or negative (or, perhaps, zero), in respect of its desirableness, and that this quantity may be to some extent known: so that each may be at least roughly weighed in ideal scales against any other. This assumption is involved in the very notion of Maximum Happiness; as the attempt to make 'as great as possible' a sum of elements not quantitatively commensurable would be a mathematical absurdity. Therefore whatever weight is to be attached to the objections brought against this assumption (which was discussed in [an earlier chapter]) must of course tell against the present method.

We have next to consider who the "all" are, whose happiness is to be taken into account. Are we to extend our concern to all the beings capable of pleasure and pain whose feelings are affected by our conduct? or are we to confine our view to human happiness? The former view is the one adopted by Bentham and Mill, and (I believe) by the Utilitarian school generally: and is obviously most in accordance with the universality that is characteristic of their principle. It is the Good *Universal*, interpreted and defined as 'happiness' or 'pleasure,' at which a Utilitarian considers it his duty to aim: and it seems arbitrary and unreasonable to exclude from the end, as so conceived, any pleasure of any sentient being.

It may be said that by giving this extension to the notion, we considerably increase the scientific difficulties of the hedonistic comparison, which have already been pointed out: for if it be difficult to compare the pleasures and pains of other men accurately with our own, a comparison of either with the pleasures and pains of brutes is obviously still more obscure. Still, the difficulty is at least not greater for Utilitarians than it is for any other moralists who recoil from the paradox of disregarding altogether the pleasures and pains of brutes. But even if we limit our attention to human beings, the extent of the subjects of happiness is not yet quite determinate. In the first place, it may be asked, How far we are to consider the interests of posterity when they seem to conflict with those of existing human beings? It seems, however, clear that the time at which a man exists cannot affect the value of his happiness from a universal point of view; and that the interests of posterity must concern a Utilitarian as much as those of his contemporaries, except in so far as the effect of his actions on posterity – and even the existence of human beings to be affected – must necessarily be more uncertain. But a further question arises when we consider that we can to some extent influence the number of future human (or sentient) beings. We have to ask how, on Utilitarian principles, this influence is to be exercised. Here I shall assume that, for human beings generally, life on the average yields a positive balance of pleasure over pain. This has been denied by thoughtful persons: but the denial seems to me clearly opposed to the common experience of mankind, as expressed in their commonly accepted principles of action. The great majority of men, in the great majority of conditions under which human life is lived, certainly act as if death were one of the worst of evils, for themselves and for those whom they love: and the administration of criminal justice proceeds on a similar assumption.[3]

Assuming, then, that the average happiness of human beings is a positive quantity, it seems clear that, supposing the average happiness enjoyed remains undiminished, Utilitarianism directs us to make the number enjoying it as great as possible. But if we foresee as possible that an increase in numbers will be accompanied by a decrease in average happiness or *vice versa*, a point arises which has not only never been formally noticed, but which seems to have been substantially overlooked by many Utilitarians. For if we take Utilitarianism to prescribe, as the ultimate end of action, happiness on the whole, and not any individual's happiness, unless considered as an element of the whole, it would follow that, if the additional population enjoy on the whole positive happiness, we ought to weigh the amount of happiness gained by the extra number against the amount lost by the remainder. So that, strictly conceived, the point up to which, on Utilitarian principles, population ought to be encouraged to increase, is not that at which average happiness is the greatest possible, – as appears to be often assumed by political economists of the school of Malthus – but that at which the product formed by multiplying the number of persons living into the amount of average happiness reaches its maximum.

It may be well here to make a remark which has a wide application in Utilitarian discussion. The conclusion just given wears a certain air of absurdity to the view of Common Sense; because its show of exactness is grotesquely incongruous with our consciousness of the inevitable inexactness of all such calculations in actual practice. But, that our practical Utilitarian reasonings must necessarily be rough, is no reason for not making them as accurate as the case admits; and we shall be more likely to succeed in this if we keep before our mind as distinctly as possible the strict type of the calculation that we should have to make, if all the relevant considerations could be estimated with mathematical precision.

There is one more point that remains to be noticed. It is evident that there may be many different ways of distributing the same quantum of happiness among the same number of persons; in order, therefore, that the Utilitarian criterion of right conduct may be as complete as possible, we ought to know which of these ways is to be preferred. This question is often ignored in expositions of Utilitarianism. It has perhaps seemed somewhat idle, as suggesting a purely abstract and theoretical perplexity, that could have no practical exemplification; and no doubt, if all the consequences of actions were capable of being estimated and summed up with mathematical precision, we should probably never find the excess of pleasure over pain exactly equal in the case of two competing alternatives of conduct. But the very indefiniteness of all hedonistic calculations, which was sufficiently shown in Book ii., renders it by no means unlikely that there may be no *cognisable* difference between the quantities of happiness involved in two sets of consequences respectively; the more rough our estimates necessarily are, the less likely we shall be to come to any clear decision between two apparently balanced alternatives. In all such cases, therefore, it becomes practically important to ask whether any mode of distributing a given quantum of happiness is better than any other. Now the Utilitarian formula seems to supply no answer to this question: at least we have to supplement the principle of seeking the greatest happiness on the whole by some principle of Just or Right distribution of this happiness. The principle which most Utilitarians have either tacitly or expressly adopted is that of pure equality – as given in Bentham's formula, "everybody to count for one, and nobody for more than one." And this principle seems the only one which does not need a special justification; for, as we saw, it must be reasonable to treat any one man in the same way as any other, if there be no reason apparent for treating him differently.[4]

Notes

1   It may be worth while to notice, that in Mill's well-known treatise on Utilitarianism this confusion, though expressly deprecated, is to some extent encouraged by the author's treatment of the subject.

2   I have already criticised (Book iii. chap. xiii.) the mode in which Mill attempts to exhibit this inference.

3   Those who held the opposite opinion appear generally to assume that the appetites and desires which are the mainspring of ordinary human action are in themselves painful: a view entirely contrary to my own experience, and, I believe, to the common experience of mankind. See chap. iv. § 2 of Book i. So far as their argument is not a development of this psychological error, any plausibility it has seems to me to be obtained by dwelling onesidedly on the annoyances and disappointments undoubtedly incident to normal human life, and on the exceptional sufferings of small minorities of the human race, or perhaps of most men during small portions of their lives.

   The reader who wishes to see the paradoxical results of pessimistic utilitarianism seriously worked out by a thoughtful and suggestive writer, may refer to Professor Macmillan's book on the *Promotion of General Happiness* (Swan Sonnenschein and Co. 1890). The author considers that "the philosophical world is pretty equally divided between optimists and pessimists," and his own judgment on the question at issue between the two schools appears to be held in suspense.

4   It should be observed that the question here is as to the distribution of *Happiness*, not the *means of happiness*. If more happiness on the whole is produced by giving the same means of happiness to B rather than to A, it is an obvious and incontrovertible deduction from the Utilitarian principle that it ought to

be given to B, whatever inequality in the distribution of the *means* of happiness this may involve.

CHAPTER II
The Proof of Utilitarianism

In Book ii., where we discussed the method of Egoistic Hedonism, we did not take occasion to examine any proof of its first principle: and in the case of Universalistic Hedonism also, what primarily concerns us is not how its principle is to be proved to those who do not accept it, but what consequences are logically involved in its acceptance. At the same time it is important to observe that the principle of aiming at universal happiness is more generally felt to require some proof, or at least (as Mill puts it) some "considerations determining the mind to accept it," than the principle of aiming at one's own happiness. From the point of view, indeed, of abstract philosophy, I do not see why the Egoistic principle should pass unchallenged any more than the Universalistic. I do not see why the axiom of Prudence should not be questioned, when it conflicts with present inclination, on a ground similar to that on which Egoists refuse to admit the axiom of Rational Benevolence. If the Utilitarian has to answer the question, 'Why should I sacrifice my own happiness for the greater happiness of another?' it must surely be admissible to ask the Egoist, 'Why should I sacrifice a present pleasure for a greater one in the future? Why should I concern myself about my own future feelings any more than about the feelings of other persons?' It undoubtedly seems to Common Sense paradoxical to ask for a reason why one should seek one's own happiness on the whole; but I do not see how the demand can be repudiated as absurd by those who adopt the views of the extreme empirical school of psychologists, although those views are commonly supposed to have a close affinity with Egoistic Hedonism. Grant that the Ego is merely a system of coherent phenomena, that the permanent identical 'I' is not a fact but a fiction, as Hume and his followers maintain; why, then, should one part of the series of feelings into which the Ego is resolved be concerned with another part of the same series, any more than with any other series?

However, I will not press this question now; since I admit that Common Sense does not think it worth while to supply the individual with reasons for seeking his own interest. Reasons for doing his duty – according to the commonly accepted standard of duty – are not held to be equally superfluous: indeed we find that utilitarian reasons are continually given for one or other of the commonly received rules of morality. Still the fact that certain rules are commonly received as binding, though it does not establish their self-evidence, renders it generally unnecessary to prove their authority to the Common Sense that receives them: while for the same reason a Utilitarian who claims to supersede them by a higher principle is naturally challenged, by Intuitionists no less than by Egoists, to demonstrate the legitimacy of his claim. To this challenge some Utilitarians would reply by saying that it is impossible to "prove" a first principle; and this is of course true, if by proof we mean a process which exhibits the principle in question as an inference from premises upon which it remains dependent for its certainty; for these premises, and not the inference drawn from them, would then be the real first principles. Nay, if Utilitarianism is to be *proved* to a man who already holds some other moral principles, – whether he be an Intuitional moralist, who regards as final the principles of Truth, Justice, Obedience to authority, Purity, etc., or an Egoist who regards his own interest as the ultimately reasonable end of his conduct, – it would seem that the process must be one which establishes a conclusion actually *superior* in validity to the premises from which it starts. For the Utilitarian prescriptions of duty are *prima facie* in conflict, at certain points and under certain circumstances, both with rules which the Intuitionist regards as self-evident, and with the dictates of Rational Egoism; so that Utilitarianism, if accepted at all, must be accepted as overruling Intuitionism and Egoism. At the same time, if the other principles are not throughout taken as valid, the so-called proof does not seem to be addressed to the Intuitionist or Egoist at all. How shall we deal with this dilemma? How is such a process – clearly different from ordinary proof – possible or conceivable? Yet there certainly seems to be a general demand for it. Perhaps we may say that what is needed is a line of argument which on the one hand allows the validity, to a certain extent, of the maxims already accepted, and on the other hand shows them to be not absolutely valid, but needing to be controlled and completed by some more comprehensive principle.

Such a line of argument, addressed to Egoism, was given in chap. xiii. of the foregoing book. It should be observed that the applicability of this argument depends on the manner in which the Egoistic first principle is formulated. If the Egoist strictly confines himself to stating his conviction that he ought to take his own happiness or pleasure as his ultimate end, there seems no opening for any line of reasoning to lead him to Universalistic Hedonism as a first principle;[1] it cannot be proved that the difference between his own happiness and another's happiness is not *for him* all-important. In this case all that the Utilitarian can do is to effect as far as possible a reconciliation between the two principles, by expounding to the Egoist the *sanctions* of rules deduced from the Universalistic principle, – i.e. by pointing out the pleasures and pains that may be expected to accrue to the Egoist himself from the observation and violation respectively of such rules. It is obvious that such an exposition has no tendency to make him accept the greatest happiness of the greatest number as his ultimate end; but only as a means to the end of his own happiness. It is therefore totally different from a *proof* (as above explained) of Universalistic Hedonism. When, however, the Egoist puts forward, implicitly or explicitly, the proposition that his happiness or pleasure is Good, not only *for him* but from the point of view of the Universe, – as (e.g.) by saying that 'nature designed him to seek his own happiness,' – it then becomes relevant to point out to him that *his* happiness cannot be a more important part of Good, taken universally, than the equal happiness of any other person. And thus, starting with his own principle, he may be brought to accept Universal happiness or pleasure as that which is absolutely and without qualification Good or Desirable: as an end, therefore, to which the action of a reasonable agent as such ought to be directed.

This, it will be remembered, is the reasoning[2] that I used in chap. xiii. of the preceding book in exhibiting the principle of Rational Benevolence as one of the few Intuitions which stand the test of rigorous criticism. It should be observed, however, that as addressed to the Intuitionist, this reasoning only shows the Utilitarian first principle to be one moral axiom: it does not prove that it is *sole* or *supreme*. The premises with which the Intuitionist starts commonly include other formulae held as independent and self-evident. Utilitarianism has therefore to exhibit itself in the twofold relation above described, at once negative and positive, to these formulae. The Utilitarian must, in the first place, endeavour to show to the Intuitionist that the principles of Truth, Justice,[3] etc. have only a dependent and subordinate validity: arguing either that the principle is really only affirmed by Common Sense as a general rule admitting of exceptions and qualifications, as in the case of Truth, and that we require some further principle for systematising these exceptions and qualifications; or that the fundamental notion is vague and needs further determination, as in the case of Justice;[3] and further, that the different rules are liable to conflict with each other, and that we require some higher principle to decide the issue thus raised; and again, that the rules are differently formulated by different persons, and that these differences admit of no Intuitional solution, while they show the vagueness and ambiguity of the common moral notions to which the Intuitionist appeals.

This part of the argument I have perhaps sufficiently developed in the preceding book. It remains to supplement this line of reasoning by developing the positive relation that exists between Utilitarianism and the Morality of Common Sense: by showing how Utilitarianism sustains the general validity of the current moral judgments, and thus supplements the defects which reflection finds in the intuitive recognition of their stringency; and at the same time affords a principle of synthesis, and a method for binding the unconnected and occasionally conflicting principles of common moral reasoning into a complete and harmonious system. If systematic reflection upon the morality of Common Sense thus exhibits the Utilitarian principle as that to which Common Sense naturally appeals for that further development of its system which this same reflection shows to be necessary, the proof of Utilitarianism seems as complete as it can be made. And since, further – apart from the question of proof – it is important in considering the method of Utilitarianism to determine exactly its relation to the commonly received rules of morality, it will be proper to examine this relation at some length in the following chapter.

Notes

1   It is to be observed that he may be led to it in other ways than that of argument: i.e. by appeals to his sympathies, or to his moral or quasi-moral sentiments.
2   I ought to remind the reader that the argument in chap. xiii. only leads to the first principle of Utilitarianism, if it be admitted that Happiness is the only thing ultimately and intrinsically Good or Desirable.
3   That is, so far as we mean by Justice anything more than the simple negation of arbitrary inequality.

CHAPTER III
Relation of Utilitarianism to the Morality of Common Sense

§ 1.   It has been before observed that the two sides of the double relation in which Utilitarianism stands to the Morality of Common Sense have been respectively prominent at two different periods in the history of English ethical thought. Since Bentham we have been chiefly familiar with the negative or aggressive aspect of the Utilitarian doctrine. But when

Cumberland, replying to Hobbes, put forward the general tendency of the received moral rules to promote the "common Good[1] of all Rationals" his aim was simply Conservative: it never occurs to him to consider whether these rules as commonly formulated are in any way imperfect, and whether there are any discrepancies between such common moral opinions and the conclusions of Rational Benevolence. So in Shaftesbury's system the "Moral" or "Reflex Sense" is supposed to be always pleased with that "balance" of the affections which tends to the good or happiness of the whole, and displeased with the opposite. In Hume's treatise this coincidence is drawn out more in detail, and with a more definite assertion that the perception of utility[2] (or the reverse) is in each case the source of the moral likings (or aversions) which are excited in us by different qualities of human character and conduct. And we may observe that the most penetrating among Hume's contemporary critics, Adam Smith, admits unreservedly the objective coincidence of Rightness or Approvedness and Utility: though he maintains, in opposition to Hume, that "it is not the view of this utility or hurtfulness, which is either the first or the principal source of our approbation or disapprobation." After stating Hume's theory that "no qualities of the mind are approved of as virtuous, but such as are useful or agreeable either to the person himself or to others, and no qualities are disapproved of as vicious but such as have a contrary tendency"; he remarks that "Nature seems indeed to have so happily adjusted our sentiments of approbation and disapprobation to the conveniency both of the individual and of the society, that after the strictest examination it will be found, I believe, that this is universally the case."

And no one can read Hume's *Inquiry into the First Principles of Morals* without being convinced of this at least, that if a list were drawn up of the qualities of character and conduct that are directly or indirectly productive of pleasure to ourselves or to others, it would include all that are commonly known as virtues. Whatever be the origin of our notion of moral goodness or excellence, there is no doubt that "Utility" is a general characteristic of the dispositions to which we apply it: and that, so far, the Morality of Common Sense may be truly represented as at least unconsciously Utilitarian. But it may still be objected, that this coincidence is merely general and qualitative, and that it breaks down when we attempt to draw it out in detail, with the quantitative precision which Bentham introduced into the discussion. And no doubt there is a great difference between the assertion that virtue is always productive of happiness, and the assertion that the right action is under all circumstances that which will produce the greatest possible happiness on the whole. But it must be borne in mind that Utilitarianism is not concerned to prove the absolute coincidence in results of the Intuitional and Utilitarian methods. Indeed, if it could succeed in proving as much as this, its success would be almost fatal to its practical claims; as the adoption of the Utilitarian principle would then become a matter of complete indifference. Utilitarians are rather called upon to show a natural transition from the Morality of Common Sense to Utilitarianism, somewhat like the transition in special branches of practice from trained instinct and empirical rules to the technical method that embodies and applies the conclusions of science: so that Utilitarianism may be presented as the scientifically complete and systematically reflective form of that regulation of conduct, which through the whole course of human history has always tended substantially in the same direction. For this purpose it is not necessary to prove that existing moral rules are *more* conducive to the general happiness than any others: but only to point out in each case some manifest felicific tendency which they possess.

Hume's dissertation, however, incidentally exhibits much more than a simple and general harmony between the moral sentiments with which we commonly regard actions and their foreseen pleasurable and painful consequences. And, in fact, the Utilitarian argument cannot be fairly judged unless we take fully into account the cumulative force which it derives from the complex character of the coincidence between Utilitarianism and Common Sense.

It may be shown, I think, that the Utilitarian estimate of consequences not only supports broadly the current moral rules, but also sustains their generally received limitations and qualifications: that, again, it explains anomalies in the Morality of Common Sense, which from any other point of view must seem unsatisfactory to the reflective intellect; and moreover, where the current formula is not sufficiently precise for the guidance of conduct, while at the same time difficulties and perplexities arise in the attempt to give it additional precision, the Utilitarian method solves these difficulties and perplexities in general accordance with the vague instincts of Common Sense, and is naturally appealed to for such solution in ordinary moral discussions. It may be shown further, that it not only supports the generally received view of the relative importance of different duties, but is also naturally called in as arbiter, where rules commonly regarded as co-ordinate come into conflict: that, again, when the same rule is interpreted somewhat differently by different persons, each naturally supports his view by urging its Utility, however strongly he may maintain the rule to be self-evident and known *a priori*: that where we meet with marked diversity of moral opinion on any point, in the same age and country, we commonly find manifest and impressive utilitarian reasons on both sides: and that finally the remarkable discrepancies found in comparing the moral codes of different ages and countries are for the most part strikingly correlated to differences in the effects of actions on happiness, or in men's foresight of, or concern for, such effects. Most of these points are noticed by Hume, though in a somewhat casual and fragmentary way: and many of them have been incidentally illustrated in the course of the examination of Common Sense Morality, with which we were occupied in the preceding Book. But considering the importance of the present question, it may be well to exhibit in systematic detail the cumulative argument which has just been summed up, even at the risk of repeating to some extent the results previously given. . . .

§ 7.   The preceding survey has supplied us with several illustrations of the manner in which Utilitarianism is normally introduced as a method for deciding between different conflicting claims, in cases where common sense leaves their relative importance obscure, – as (e.g.) between the different duties of the affections, and the different principles which analysis shows to be involved in our common conception of Justice – : and we have also noticed how, when a dispute is raised as to the precise scope and definition of any current moral rule, the effects of different acceptations of the rule on general happiness or social well-being are commonly regarded as the ultimate grounds on which the dispute is to be decided. In fact these two arguments practically run into one; for it is generally a conflict between maxims that impresses men with the need of giving each a precise definition. It may be urged that the consequences to which reference is commonly made in such cases are rather effects on 'social well-being' than on 'general happiness' as understood by Utilitarians; and that the two notions ought not to be identified. I grant this: but in the last chapter of the preceding Book I have tried to show that Common Sense is unconsciously utilitarian in its practical determination of those very elements in the notion of Ultimate Good or Wellbeing which at first sight least admit of a hedonistic interpretation. We may now observe that this hypothesis of 'Unconscious Utilitarianism' explains the different relative importance attached to particular virtues by different classes of human beings, and the different emphasis with which the same virtue is inculcated on these different classes by mankind generally. For such differences ordinarily correspond to variations – real or apparent – in the Utilitarian importance of the virtues under different circumstances. Thus we have noticed the greater stress laid on chastity in women than in men: courage, on the other hand, is more valued in the latter, as they are more called upon to cope energetically with sudden and severe dangers. And for similar reasons a soldier is expected to show a higher degree of courage than (e.g.) a priest. Again, though we esteem candour and scrupulous sincerity in most persons, we scarcely look for them in a diplomatist who has to conceal secrets, nor do we expect that a tradesman in describing his goods should frankly point out their defects to his customers.

Finally, when we compare the different moral codes of different ages and countries, we see that the discrepancies among them correspond, at least to a great extent, to differences either in the actual effects of actions on happiness, or in the extent to which such effects are generally foreseen – or regarded as important – by the men among whom the codes are maintained. Several instances of this have already been noticed: and the general fact, which has been much dwelt upon by Utilitarian writers, is also admitted and even emphasised by their opponents. Thus Dugald Stewart[3] lays stress on the extent to which the moral judgments of mankind have been modified by "the diversity in their physical circumstances," the "unequal degrees of civilisation which they have attained," and "their unequal measures of knowledge or of capacity." He points out, for instance, that theft is regarded as a very venial offence in the South Sea Islanders, because little or no labour is there required to support life; that the lending of money for interest is commonly reprehended in societies where commerce is imperfectly developed, because the 'usurer' in such communities is commonly in the odious position of wringing a gain out of the hard necessities of his fellows; and that where the legal arrangements for punishing crime are imperfect, private murder is either justified or regarded very leniently. Many other examples might be added to these if it were needful. But I conceive that few persons who have studied the subject will deny that there is a certain degree of correlation between the variations in the moral code from age to age, and the variations in the real or perceived effects on general happiness of actions prescribed or forbidden by the code. And in proportion as the apprehension of consequences becomes more comprehensive and exact, we may trace not only change in the moral code handed down from age to age, but progress in the direction of a closer approximation to a perfectly enlightened Utilitarianism. Only we must distinctly notice another important factor in the progress, which Stewart has not mentioned: the extension, namely, of the capacity for sympathy in an average member of the community. The imperfection of earlier moral codes is at least as much due to defectiveness of sympathy as of intelligence; often, no doubt, the ruder man did not perceive the effects of his conduct on others; but often, again, he perceived them more or less, but felt little or no concern about them. Thus it happens that changes in the conscience of a community often correspond to changes in the extent and degree of the sensitiveness of an average member of it to the feelings of others. Of this the moral development historically worked out under the influence of Christianity affords familiar illustrations.[4]

I am not maintaining that this correlation between the development of current morality and the changes in the consequences of conduct as sympathetically forecast, is perfect and exact. On the contrary, – as I shall have occasion to point cut in [a later] chapter – the history of morality shows us many evidences of what, from the Utilitarian point of view, appear to be partial aberrations of the moral sense. But even in these instances we can often discover a germ of unconscious Utilitarianism; the aberration is often only an exaggeration of an obviously useful sentiment, or the extension of it by mistaken analogy to cases to which it does not properly apply, or perhaps the survival of a sentiment which once was useful but has now ceased to be so.

Further, it must be observed that I have carefully abstained from asserting that the perception of the rightness of any kind of conduct has always – or even ordinarily – been derived by conscious inference from a perception of consequent advantages. This hypothesis is naturally suggested by such a survey as the preceding; but the evidence of history hardly seems to me to support it: since, as we retrace the development of ethical thought, the Utilitarian basis of current morality, which I have endeavoured to exhibit in the present chapter, seems to be rather less than more distinctly apprehended by the common moral consciousness. Thus (e.g.) Aristotle sees that the sphere of the Virtue of Courage (ἀνδρεία), as recognised by the Common Sense of Greece, is restricted to dangers in war: and we can now explain this limitation by a reference to the utilitarian importance of this kind of courage, at a period of history when the individual's happiness was bound up more completely than it now is with the welfare of his state, while the very existence of the latter was more frequently imperilled by hostile invasions: but this explanation lies quite beyond the range of Aristotle's own reflection. The origin of our moral notions and sentiments lies hid in those obscure regions of hypothetical history where conjecture has free scope: but we do not find that, as our retrospect approaches the borders of this realm, the conscious connexion in men's minds between accepted moral rules and foreseen effects on general happiness becomes more clearly traceable. The admiration felt by early man for beauties or excellences of character seems to have been as direct and unreflective as his admiration of any other beauty: and the stringency of law and custom in primitive times presents itself as sanctioned by the evils which divine displeasure will supernaturally inflict on their violators, rather than by even a rude and vague forecast of the natural bad consequences of non-observance. It is therefore not as the mode of regulating conduct with which mankind began, but rather as that to which we can now see that human development has been always tending, as the adult and not the germinal form of Morality, that Utilitarianism may most reasonably claim the acceptance of Common Sense.

Notes

1   It ought to be observed that Cumberland does not adopt a hedonistic interpretation of Good. Still, I have followed Hallam in regarding him as the founder of English Utilitarianism: since it seems to have been by a gradual and half-unconscious process that 'Good' came to have the definitely hedonistic meaning which it has implicitly in Shaftesbury's system, and explicitly in that of Hume.

2   I should point out that Hume uses "utility" in a narrower sense than that which Bentham gave it, and one more in accordance with the usage of ordinary language. He distinguishes the "useful" from the "immediately agreeable": so that while recognising "utility" as the main ground of our moral approbation of the more important virtues, he holds that there are other elements of personal merit which we approve because they are "immediately agreeable," either to the person possessed of them or to others. It appears, however, more convenient to use the word in the wider sense in which it has been current since Bentham.

3   *Active and Moral Powers*, Book ii. chap. iii.

4   Among definite changes in the current morality of the Graeco-Roman civilised world, which are to be attributed mainly if not entirely to the extension and intensification of sympathy due to Christianity, the following may be especially noted: (1) the severe condemnation and final suppression of the practice of exposing infants; (2) effective abhorrence of the barbarism of gladiatorial combats; (3) immediate moral mitigation of slavery, and a strong encouragement of emancipation; (4) great extension of the eleemosynary provision made for the sick and poor.

5

From *Principia Ethica*

G. E. Moore

CHAPTER V
Ethics in Relation to Conduct

88.   I propose, first, to deal with the [*third*] kind of ethical question – the question: What ought we to do?

The answering of this question constitutes the third great division of ethical enquiry; and its nature was briefly explained in [an earlier chapter]. It introduces into Ethics, as was there pointed out, an entirely new question – the question what things are related as *causes* to that which is good in itself; and this question can only be answered by an entirely new method – the method of empirical investigation; by means of which causes are discovered in the other sciences. To ask what kind of actions we ought to perform, or what kind of conduct is right, is to ask what kind of effects such action and conduct will produce. Not a single question in practical Ethics can be answered except by a causal generalisation. All such questions do, indeed, *also* involve an ethical judgment proper – the judgment that certain effects are better, in themselves, than others. But they *do* assert that these better things are effects – are causally connected with the actions in question. Every judgment in practical Ethics may be reduced to the form: This is a cause of that good thing.

89.   That this is the case, that the questions, What is right? what is my duty? what ought I to do? belong exclusively to this third branch of ethical enquiry, is the first point to which I wish to call attention. All moral laws, I wish to shew, are merely statements that certain kinds of actions will

G. E. Moore, *Principia Ethica*, rev. edn. (Cambridge: Cambridge University Press, 1993), pp. 196–200.

have good effects. The very opposite of this view has been generally prevalent in Ethics. 'The right' and 'the useful' have been supposed to be at least *capable* of conflicting with one another, and, at all events, to be essentially distinct. It has been characteristic of a certain school of moralists, as of moral common sense, to declare that the end will never justify the means. What I wish first to point out is that 'right' does and can mean nothing but 'cause of a good result,' and is thus identical with 'useful'; whence it follows that the end always will justify the means, and that no action which is not justified by its results can be right. That there may be a true proposition, meant to be conveyed by the assertion 'The end will not justify the means,' I fully admit: but that, in another sense, and a sense far more fundamental for ethical theory, it is utterly false, must first be shewn.

That the assertion 'I am morally bound to perform this action' is identical with the assertion 'This action will produce the greatest possible amount of good in the Universe' has already been briefly shewn in [an earlier chapter]; but it is important to insist that this fundamental point is demonstrably certain. This may, perhaps, be best made evident in the following way. It is plain that when we assert that a certain action is our absolute duty, we are asserting that the performance of that action at that time is unique in respect of value. But no dutiful action can possibly have unique value in the sense that it is the sole thing of value in the world; since, in that case, *every* such action would be the *sole* good thing, which is a manifest contradiction. And for the same reason its value cannot be unique in the sense that it has more intrinsic value than anything else in the world; since *every* act of duty would then be the *best* thing in the world, which is also a contradiction. It can, therefore, be unique only in the sense that the whole world will be better, if it be performed, than if any possible alternative were taken. And the question whether this is so cannot possibly depend solely on the question of its own intrinsic value. For any action will also have effects different from those of any other action; and if any of these have intrinsic value, their value is exactly as relevant to the total goodness of the Universe as that of their cause. It is, in fact, evident that, however valuable an action may be in itself, yet, owing to its existence, the sum of good in the Universe may conceivably be made less than if some other action, less valuable in itself, had been performed. But to say that this is the case is to say that it would have been better that the action should not have been done; and this again is obviously equivalent to the statement that it ought not to have been done – that it was not what duty required. 'Fiat iustitia, ruat caelum' can only be justified on the ground that by the doing of justice the Universe gains more than it loses by the falling of the heavens. It is, of course, possible that this is the case: but, at all events, to assert that justice *is* a duty, in spite of such consequences, is to assert that it is the case.

Our 'duty,' therefore, can only be defined as that action, which will cause more good to exist in the Universe than any possible alternative. And what is 'right' or 'morally permissible' only differs from this, as what will *not* cause *less* good than any possible alternative. When, therefore, Ethics presumes to assert that certain ways of acting are 'duties' it presumes to assert that to act in those ways will always produce the greatest possible sum of good. If we are told that to 'do no murder' is a duty, we are told that the action, whatever it may be, which is called murder, will under no circumstances cause so much good to exist in the Universe as its avoidance.

90.   But, if this be recognised, several most important consequences follow, with regard to the relation of Ethics to conduct.

(1)   It is plain that no moral law is self-evident, as has commonly been held by the Intuitional school of moralists. The Intuitional view of Ethics consists in the supposition that certain rules, stating that certain actions are always to be done or to be omitted, may be taken as self-evident premisses. I have shewn with regard to judgments of what is *good in itself*, that this is the case; no reason can be given for them. But it is the essence of Intuitionism to suppose that rules of action – statements not of what ought to *be*, but of what we ought to do – are in the same sense intuitively certain. Plausibility has been lent to this view by the fact that we do undoubtedly make immediate judgments that certain actions are obligatory or wrong: we are thus often intuitively certain of our duty, *in a psychological sense*. But, nevertheless, these judgments are not self-evident and cannot be taken as ethical premisses, since, as has now been shewn, they are capable of being confirmed or refuted by an investigation of causes and effects. It is, indeed, possible that some of our immediate intuitions are true; but since *what* we intuit, *what* conscience tells us, is that certain actions will always produce the greatest sum of good possible under the circumstances, it is plain that reasons can be given, which will shew the deliverances of conscience to be true or false.

91.   (2)   In order to shew that any action is a duty, it is necessary to know both what are the other conditions, which will, conjointly with it, determine its effects; to know exactly what will be the effects of these conditions; and to know all the events which will be in any way affected by our action throughout an infinite future. We must have all this causal knowledge, and further we must know accurately the degree of value both of the action itself and of all these effects; and must be able to determine how, in conjunction with the other things in the Universe, they will affect its value as an organic whole. And not only this: we must also possess all this knowledge with regard to the effects of every possible alternative; and must then be able to see by comparison that the total value due to the existence of the action in question will be greater than that which would be produced by any of these alternatives. But it is obvious that our causal knowledge alone is far too incomplete for us ever to assure ourselves of this result. Accordingly it follows that we never have any reason to suppose that an action is our duty: we can never be sure that any action will produce the greatest value possible.

Ethics, therefore, is quite unable to give us a list of duties: but there still remains a humbler task which may be possible for Practical Ethics. Although we cannot hope to discover which, in a given situation, is the best of all possible alternative actions, there may be some possibility of shewing which among the alternatives, *likely to occur to any one*, will produce the greatest sum of good. This second task is certainly all that Ethics can ever have accomplished: and it is certainly all that it has ever collected materials for proving; since no one has ever attempted to exhaust the possible alternative actions in any particular case. Ethical philosophers have in fact confined their attention to a very limited class of actions, which have been selected because they are those which most commonly occur to mankind as possible alternatives. With regard to these they may possibly have shewn that one alternative is better, i.e. produces a greater total of value, than others. But it seems desirable to insist, that though they have represented this result as a determination of *duties*, it can never really have been so. For the term duty is certainly so used that, if we are subsequently persuaded that any possible action would have produced more good than the one we adopted, we admit that we failed to do our duty. It will, however, be a useful task if Ethics can determine which among alternatives *likely to occur* will produce the greatest total value. For, though this alternative cannot be proved to be the best possible, yet it may be better than any course of action which we should otherwise adopt.

Part II
Contemporary Expressions

6

Consequentialism

Philip Pettit

I The Definition of Consequentialism

Moral theories, theories about what individual or institutional agents
ought to do, all involve at least two different components. First, they each
put forward a view about what is good or valuable, though they do not
all make this explicit and may even resist talk of the good: they each put
forward a view about which properties we ought to want realized in our
actions or in the world more generally. A theory like classical utilitarianism holds that the only property that matters is how far sentient beings
enjoy happiness. A natural law theory holds that the property which
matters is compliance with the law of nature. Various other theories
propose that what matters is human freedom, social solidarity, the
autonomous development of nature, or a combination of such features.
The possibilities are endless, since about the only commonly recognized
constraint is that in order to be valuable a property must not involve a
particular individual or setting essentially; it must be a universal feature,
capable of being realized here or there, with this individual or that.

This first component in a moral theory is sometimes described as a
theory of value or a theory of the good. The second component which
every moral theory involves is often described in parallel as a theory of
the right. It is a view, not about which properties are valuable, but about
what individual and institutional agents should do by way of responding to valuable properties. Depending on the view adopted on this question, moral theories are usually divided into two kinds, consequentialist

Philip Pettit, "Consequentialism," *A Companion to Ethics*, Peter Singer, ed. (Oxford:
Blackwell, 1991), pp. 230–40.

and non-consequentialist or, to use an older terminology, teleological and non-teleological: the non-teleological is sometimes identified with, and sometimes taken just to include, the deontological. This essay is concerned with consequentialist theories, as theories of the right, but not with any particular theory of value or of the good.

Suppose I decide, in a moment of intellectualist enthusiasm, that what matters above all in human life is that people understand the history of their species and their universe. How ought I to respond to this perceived value? Is my primary responsibility to honour it in my own life, bearing witness to the importance of such understanding by devoting myself to it? Or is my primary responsibility rather to promote such understanding generally, say by spending most of my time on proselytizing and politics, giving only the hours I cannot better spend to the development of my own understanding? Is the proper response to the value one of promoting its general realization, honouring it in my own actions only when there is nothing better I can do to promote it?

Again, suppose I decide that what is of importance in life is nothing so abstract as intellectual understanding but rather the enjoyment of personal loyalties, whether the loyalties of family or friendship. Here too there is a question about how I should respond to such a value. Should I honour the value in my own life, devoting myself to developing the bonds of kith and kin? Or should I only permit myself such devotion so far as that is part of the more general project of promoting the enjoyment of personal loyalties? Should I be prepared to use my time in the manner most effective for that project even if the cost of doing so – say, the cost of spending so much time on journalism and politics – is that my own personal loyalties are put under severe strain?

These two examples are from the sphere of personal morality but the same question arises in the institutional area. Suppose that a liberal government comes to power, a government which is primarily concerned with people's enjoying liberty. Should such a government honour people's liberty punctiliously in its own conduct, avoiding any interference that offends against liberty? Or should it pursue all measures, including offences against liberty, that make for a greater degree of liberty overall? Imagine that a group forms which begins agitating for a return to authoritarian rule: say, a rule associated with an influential religious tradition. Imagine, to make things harder, that the group has a real chance of success. Should the government permit the group to conduct its activities, on the grounds of honouring people's liberty to form whatever associations they choose? Or should it ban the group, on the grounds that while the ban interferes with people's liberty, it makes for the enjoyment of a greater degree of liberty overall; it means that there will not be a return to an illiberal society.

Consequentialism is the view that whatever values an individual or institutional agent adopts, the proper response to those values is to promote them. The agent should honour the values only so far as honouring them is part of promoting them, or is necessary in order to promote them. Opponents of consequentialism, on the other hand, hold that at least some values call to be honoured whether or not they are thereby promoted. Consequentialists see the relation between values and agents as an instrumental one: agents are required to produce whatever actions have the property of promoting a designated value, even actions that fail intuitively to honour it. Opponents of consequentialism see the relation between values and agents as a non-instrumental one: agents are required or at least allowed to let their actions exemplify a designated value, even if this makes for a lesser realization of the value overall.

This way of introducing the distinction between consequentialism and non-consequentialism, by reference just to agents and values, is unusual but, I hope, intuitively appealing. One drawback it involves is that the notion of promoting a value, and even more so the notion of honouring a value, is not carefully defined. In the next section this fault is remedied in some measure. (The section will be too philosophical for many tastes but it can be read lightly without great loss.)

II Once More, With Some Formality

In order to introduce our more formal approach, it will be useful to define two notions: that of an option and that of a prognosis associated with an option. An option may be a directly behavioural option such as that expressed by a proposition like 'I do A' but equally it may be only indirectly behavioural, as with options such as 'I commit myself to being faithful to this principle of benevolence' or 'I endorse this trait of competitiveness in myself: I shall do nothing to change it'. The defining feature of an option is that it is a possibility which the agent is in a position to realize or not. He can make it the case – or not – that he does A, that he lets the principle of benevolence dictate his actions, or that he remains complacently competitive.

Although an option is a possibility that can be realized, the agent will almost never be able to determine how exactly the possibility works out; that will depend on other agents and on other things in the world. I may do A and it rains or not. I may do A and there is a third world war or not:

the list is open. Given the differences in how such conditions can work out, any option has different prognoses. If an option is a possibility that can be realized, its prognoses are the different possible ways in which the possibility can come to be realised. The notion of a prognosis picks up one version of the familar notion of a consequence.

Returning now to the definition of consequentialism, we can identify two propositions which consequentialists generally defend.

1   Every prognosis for an option, every way the world may be as the result of a choice of option, has a value that is determined, though perhaps not up to uniqueness, by the valuable properties realized there: determined by how far it is a happy world, a world in which liberty is respected, a world where nature thrives, and so on for different valuable properties; the value determined will not be unique, so far as the weightings between such properties are not uniquely fixed.
2   Every option, every possibility which an agent can realize or not, has its value fixed by the values of its prognoses: its value is a function of the values of its different prognoses, a function of the values associated with the different ways it may lead the world to be.

The motivation for going into this level of detail was to give clearer content to the notion of promoting a value. An agent promotes certain values in his or her choices, we can now say, if – and indeed only if – the agent ranks the prognoses of options in terms of these values (proposition 1) and ranks the options – where the ranking determines his choice – in terms of their prognoses (proposition 2). There is an indeterminacy in proposition 2, since it has been left open how exactly the value of an option is fixed by the values of its prognoses. The usual approach among consequentialists, though not the only possible one, is to cast an option as a gamble among the different possible prognoses and borrow a procedure from decision theory to compute its value. On this approach you find the value of the option by adding up the values of the different prognoses – and we assume these are uniquely determined – discounting each such value by the probability the prognosis has – say, a quarter or a half – of being the correct one; I leave open the question of whether the appropriate probability to use is objective chance, subjective credence, 'rational' credence, or whatever. Suppose that the agent's concern is to save life and that in some dire circumstances two options present themselves: one gives a fifty per cent probability of saving one hundred lives, the other a certainty of saving forty. Other things being equal – which they will rarely be – the approach would favour the first option.

We now have a better grasp of what it is the consequentialist says. The consequentialist holds that the proper way for an agent to respond to any values recognized is to promote them: that is, in every choice to select the option with prognoses that mean it is the best gamble with those values. But we can now also be somewhat more specific about what the non-consequentialist says. There are two varieties of non-consequentialism, two ways of holding that certain values should be honoured, not promoted. One variety insists that while there are respectful or loyal options, there is no sense to the notion of promoting the abstract value of loyalty or respect. This is to deny the consequentialist's first proposition, holding that values like loyalty and respect do not determine abstract scores for the different prognoses of an option; the values are irrelevant to prognoses, failing even to determine non-unique scores. The other position which the non-consequentialist may take is to admit the first proposition, acknowledging that the notion of an agent promoting values at least makes sense, but to deny the second: that is, deny that the best option is necessarily determined by the values of its prognoses. The important thing is not to produce the goods but to keep your hands clean.

One last thought, while we are being more formal, on non-consequentialism. This is that non-consequentialists assume with the properties they think should be honoured rather than promoted, that the agent will always be in a position to know for certain whether an option will or will not have one of those properties. Faced with a value like that of respect or loyalty, the idea is that I will never be uncertain whether or not a given option will be respectful or loyal. The assumption of certainty may be reasonable with such examples but it will not generally be so. And that means that with some valuable properties, the non-consequentialist strategy will often be undefined. Take a property like that of happiness. This value can lend itself to being honoured as well as being promoted: honouring it might require concern for the happiness of those you deal with directly, regardless of indirect effects. But it will not always be clear in practice what a non-consequentialist attachment to happiness requires. Non-consequentialists do not tell us how to choose when none of the available options is going to display the relevant value for sure. And there will often be cases of this kind with a value like that of happiness. There will often be cases where none of the options offers a certainty of doing well by the happiness of those you are dealing with directly: cases where one option offers a certain chance of that result and a second option offers the best prospect for happiness overall. The non-consequentialist response in such cases is simply not defined.

III   The Main Argument Against Consequentialism

It is usually said against consequentialism that it would lead an agent to do horrendous deeds, so long as they promised the best consequences. It would forbid nothing absolutely: not rape, not torture, not even murder. This charge is on target but it is only relevant of course in horrendous circumstances. Thus if someone of ordinary values condoned torture, that would only be in circumstances where there was a great potential gain – the saving of innocent lives, the prevention of a catastrophe – and where there were not the bad consequences involved, say, in state authorities claiming the right to torture. Once it is clear that the charge is relevant only in horrendous circumstances, it ceases to be clearly damaging. After all the non-consequentialist will often have to defend an equally unattractive response in such circumstances. It may be awful to think of torturing someone but it must be equally awful to think of not doing so and consequently allowing, say, a massive bomb to go off in some public place.

Probably in view of this stand-off, the charge against consequentialism usually reduces to the associated claim that not only would it allow horrendous deeds in exceptional circumstances, it would allow and indeed encourage the general habit of contemplating such deeds: or if not of actively contemplating the deeds, at least of countenancing the possibility that they may be necessary. Consequentialism, it is said, would make nothing unthinkable. It would not allow agents to admit any constraints on what they can do, whether constraints associated with the rights of other people as independent agents or constraints associated with the claims of those who relate to them as intimates or dependants.

The idea behind this charge is that any consequentialist moral theory requires agents to change their deliberative habits in an objectionable fashion. They will have to calculate about every choice, it is said, identifying the different prognoses for every option, the value associated with each prognosis and the upshot of those various values for the value of the option. Doing this, they will be unable to recognize the rights of others as considerations that ought to constrain them without further thought to consequences; they will be unable to acknowledge the special claims of those near and dear to them, claims that ought normally to brook no calculation; and they will be unable to mark distinctions between permissible options, obligatory options and options of supererogatory virtue. They will become moralistic computers, insensitive to all such nuances. F. H. Bradley made the point nicely in the last century, in *Ethical Studies* (p. 107). 'So far as my lights go, this is to make possible, to justify, and even to encourage, an incessant practical casuistry; and that, it need scarcely be added, is the death of morality.'

But if this sort of charge was made in the last century, so it was also rebutted then, particularly by writers like John Austin and Henry Sidgwick. Such writers defended classical utilitarianism, the consequentialist moral theory according to which the only value is the happiness of human, or at least sentient beings. Austin picked a nice example when arguing in *The Province of Jurisprudence* (p. 108) that the utilitarian does not require agents to be incessant casuists. 'Though he approves of love because it accords with his principle, he is far from maintaining that the general good ought to be the motive of the lover. It was never contended or conceived by a sound, orthodox utilitarian, that the lover should kiss his mistress with an eye to a common weal.'

The point which Austin is making in this passage is that a consequentialist theory like utilitarianism is an account of what justifies an option over alternatives – the fact that it promotes the relevant value – not an account of how agents ought to deliberate in selecting the option. The lover's act may be justified by its promotion of human happiness, in which case the utilitarian will applaud. But that does not mean that the utilitarian expects lovers to select and monitor their overtures by reference to that abstract goal.

The line which non-consequentialists generally run against this response is to deny that it is available to their opponents. They say that if a consequentialist thinks that an agent's choices are justified or not by whether they promote certain values, then the consequentialist is committed to saying that the moral agent – the agent who seeks to be justified – should deliberate over how far in any setting the different options promote those values. In saying this, they assume that such deliberation is the best way for an agent to guarantee that the choice made promotes the values espoused.

This non-consequentialist rejoinder is unpersuasive, however, because that assumption is clearly false. Consider again the lover and his mistress. If the lover calculates his every embrace, fine-tuning it to the demands of the general happiness, there will probably be little pleasure in it for either party. A condition of the embrace's producing pleasure, and therefore of its contributing to the general happiness, is that it is relatively spontaneous, coming of natural and unreflective affections. The point hardly needs labouring.

But though the point is clear, and though it clearly applies in a variety of cases, it raises a question which consequentialists have been too slow to tackle, at least until recently. The question is this. Granted that consequentialism is a theory of justification, not a theory of deliberation, what practical difference – what difference in deliberative policy – is made by being a consequentialist? Suppose the lover in Austin's example were to become himself a utilitarian. What sort of policy could he then adopt, granted he would not tie himself to considering the utilitarian pros and cons of his every action?

The answer usually offered by consequentialists nowadays is motivated by the observation in the last section that the options that call for assessment in consequentialist terms – the possibilities over which an agent is decisive – include options which are only indirectly behavioural as well as alternative actions he may take in any context. They include options such as whether or not to endorse a certain motive or trait of character, letting it have its untrammelled way in some settings, and options such as whether or not to make a commitment to a certain principle – say, the principle of respecting a particular right in others – giving it the status of an automatic behavioural pilot in suitable circumstances.

The fact that the option-sets faced by agents include many of this kind means that if they become consequentialists, their conversion to that doctrine can have a practical effect on how they behave without having the clearly undesirable effect of turning them into incessant calculators. It may have the effect of leading an agent to endorse certain traits or principles, traits or principles that lead him or her in suitable contexts to act in a spontaneous, uncalculating way. It will have this effect, in particular, if choosing to go in thrall to such pre-emptors of calculation is the best way to promote the values that the agent cherishes.

But won't it always be best if agents keep their calculative wits sharpened, having an eye in every case as to whether following the automatic pilot of trait or principle really does best promote their values? And in that case shouldn't the consequentialist agent still remain, in a sense, an incessant calculator?

This is a question at the forefront of contemporary consequentialist discussions. The answers canvassed among consequentialists are various. One answer is that agents are so fallible, at least in the heat of decision-making, that the calculative monitoring envisaged here would probably do more harm than good. Another is that some of the relevant pre-emptors of calculation, for example certain traits that the agent may nurture – say, the trait of being obsessional about completing tasks – are such that once in play they are incapable of being controlled via monitoring. Yet another answer, one particularly favoured by the present writer, is that many values are such that their promotion is undermined if habits of deliberation – pre-emptors of calculation – which are designed to promote them are subjected to calculative monitoring. Suppose I commit myself to the principle of saying what first comes to mind in conversation in order to promote my spontaneity. I will undermine the promotion of that value if I attempt to monitor and control my remarks. Or suppose I commit myself to the principle of letting my teenage daughter have her way in a certain sphere – say, in her choice of clothes – in order to promote her sense of independence and self. Again I will subvert the promotion of that value, at least assuming that I am relatively scrutable, if I try to monitor and moderate the tolerance I offer. In each case, within suitable contexts, I must put myself more or less blindly on automatic pilot if I am to promote the value in question.

The brand of consequentialism which is explicit about the possibility that being a consequentialist may motivate an agent to restrict calculation over consequences is sometimes described as indirect, sometimes as strategic, sometimes as restrictive. Such restrictive consequentialism promises to be capable of answering the various challenges associated with the main argument against consequentialism, but that claim can hardly be documented here. In concluding our discussion of that argument the only point that calls to be made is that restrictive consequentialism in this sense should not be confused with what is called restricted or rule-consequentialism, as distinct from extreme or act-consequentialism. That doctrine, no longer much in vogue, claims that rules of behaviour are justified by whether compliance or attempted compliance best promotes the relevant values, but that behavioural options are justified in other terms: specifically, by whether they comply or attempt to comply with the optimal rules. The restrictive consequentialism to which we have been introduced is not half-hearted in this way; it is a form of extreme or act-consequentialism. It holds that the test for whether any option is justified is consequentialist, whether the option be directly or indirectly behavioural: the best option is that which best promotes the agent's values. What makes it restrictive is simply the recognition that agents may best promote their values in behavioural choices, if they restrict the tendency to calculate, abjuring the right to consider all relevant consequences.

IV The Main Argument for Consequentialism

The key to the main argument for consequentialism is a proposition which we have so far taken for granted, that every moral theory invokes values such that it can make sense to recommend in consequentialist fashion that they be promoted or in non-consequentialist that they be honoured. The proposition is fairly compelling. Every moral theory designates certain choices as the right ones for an agent to make. In any such case, however, what the theory is committed to recommending is not just this or that choice by this or that agent but the choice of this type of option by that sort of agent in these kinds of circumstances; this is a commitment, as it is sometimes said, of universalizability. The commitment means that every moral theory invokes values, for the fact that such and such choices are made is now seen as a desirable property to have realized.

The other aspect of our key proposition is that with any value at all, with any property that is hailed as desirable, we can identify a consequentialist and a non-consequentialist response. We can make sense of the notion of promoting or honouring the value. I hope that this claim can be supported by the sorts of examples introduced at the beginning. We saw there that an agent might think of honouring or promoting values to do with intellectual understanding, personal loyalty and political liberty. It should be clear by analogy that the same possibilities arise with all desirable properties. As we also saw, I can think of honouring a value traditionally associated with consequentialism such as that of people's enjoying happiness, though uncertainty about options may sometimes leave the strategy undefined; to honour this will be to try not to cause anyone unhappiness directly, even if doing so would increase happiness overall. And I can think of promoting a value as intimately linked with non-consequentialist theories as that of respect for persons; to promote this will be to try to ensure that people respect one another as much as possible, even if this requires disrespecting some.

Our key proposition motivates an argument for consequentialism, because it shows that the non-consequentialist is committed to a theory which is seriously defective in regard to the methodological virtue of simplicity. It is common practice in the sciences and in intellectual disciplines generally to prefer the more simple hypothesis to the less, when otherwise they are equally satisfactory. Consequentialism, it turns out, is indisputably a simpler hypothesis than any form of non-consequentialism and that means that, failing objections such as those rejected in the last section, it ought to be preferred to it. If non-consequentialists have not seen how much their view loses on the side of simplicity, that may be because they do not generally assent to our key proposition. They imagine that there are certain values which are susceptible only to being promoted, others that are susceptible only to being honoured.

There are at least three respects in which consequentialism scores on simplicity. The first is that whereas consequentialists endorse only one way of responding to values, non-consequentialists endorse two. Non-consequentialists all commit themselves to the view that certain values should be honoured rather than promoted: say, values like those associated with loyalty and respect. But they all agree, whether or not in their role as moral theorists, that certain other values should be promoted: values as various as economic prosperity, personal hygiene, and the safety of nuclear installations. Thus where consequentialists introduce a single axiom on how values justify choices, non-consequentialists must introduce two.

But not only is non-consequentialism less simple for losing the numbers game. It is also less simple for playing the game in an *ad hoc* way. Non-consequentialists all identify certain values as suitable for honouring rather than promoting. But they do not generally explain what it is about the values identified which means that justification comes from their being honoured rather than promoted. And indeed it is not clear what satisfactory explanation can be provided. It is one thing to make a list of the values which allegedly require honouring: values, say, like personal loyalty, respect for others, and punishment for wrongdoing. It is another to say why these values are so very different from the ordinary run of desirable properties. There may be features that mark them off from other values, but why do those features matter so much? That question typically goes unconsidered by non-consequentialists. Not only do they have a duality then where consequentialists have a unity; they also have an unexplained duality.

The third respect in which consequentialism scores on the simplicity count is that it fits nicely with our standard views of what rationality requires, whereas non-consequentialism is in tension with such views. The agent concerned with a value is in a parallel position to that of an agent concerned with some personal good: say, health or income or status. In thinking about how an agent should act on the concern for a personal good, we unhesitatingly say that of course the rational thing to do, the rationally justified action, is to act so that the good is promoted. That means then that whereas the consequentialist line on how values justify choices is continuous with the standard line on rationality in the pursuit of personal goods, the non-consequentialist line is not. The non-consequentialist has the embarrassment of having to defend a position on what certain values require which is without analogue in the non-moral area of practical rationality.

If these considerations of simplicity are not sufficient to motivate a consequentialist outlook, the only recourse for a consequentialist is probably to draw attention to the detail of what the non-consequentialist says, inviting reflection on whether this really is plausible. In the second section above we saw that non-consequentialists have to deny either that the values they espouse determine values for the prognoses of an option or that the value of an option is a function of the values associated with those different prognoses. The consequentialist can reasonably argue that either claim is implausible. If one prognosis realizes my values more than another then that surely fixes its value. And if one option has prognoses such that it represents a better gamble than another with those values, then that surely suggests that it is the best option for me to take. So how can the non-consequentialist think otherwise?

Of course, the consequentialist should ideally have an answer to that question. The consequentialist should be able to offer some explanation of how non-consequentialists come mistakenly to think the things they believe. It may be useful to say a word on this in conclusion.

There are at least two observations which ought to figure in a consequentialist explanation of how non-consequentialists come to hold their views. The first has already been suggested in this essay. It is that non-consequentialists probably focus on deliberation rather than justification and, noticing that it will often be counter-productive to deliberate about the promotion of a value involved in action – a value like loyalty or respect – conclude that in such cases choices are justified by honouring the values, not by promoting them. Here there is a mistake but at least it is an intelligible mistake. Thus it may help the consequentialist to make sense of the commitments of opponents.

The second observation is one that we have not made explicitly before and it offers a good ending note. This is that many deontological theories come from acknowledging the force of the consequentialist point about justification but then containing it in some way. One example is the rule-consequentialist who restricts his consequentialism to choices between rules, arguing that behavioural choices are justified by reference to the rules so chosen. Another example, more significantly, is the non-consequentialist who holds that each agent ought to choose in such a way that were everyone to make that sort of choice then the value or values in question would be promoted. Here the thought is that consequentialism is suitable for assessing the choices of the collectivity but not of its members. The collectivity ought to choose so that the values are promoted, the individual ought to choose, not necessarily in the way that actually promotes the values, but in the way that would promote them if everybody else made a similar choice. Here as in the other case the non-consequentialist position is motivated by the consequentialist thought. That will not make it congenial to the consequentialist, who will think

that the thought is not systematically enough applied: the consequentialist will say that it is as relevant to the individual agent as to the collectivity.
But the observation may help consequentialists to make sense of their
opponents and thereby reinforce their own position. They can argue that
they are not overlooking any consideration that non-consequentialists
find persuasive. What non-consequentialists find persuasive is something
which consequentialists are able to understand, and to undermine.

References

Austin, J.: *The Province of Jurisprudence Determined* (1832); ed. H. L. A. Hart
(London: Weidenfeld, 1954).
Bradley, F. H.: *Ethical Studies* (1876); (Oxford: Clarendon Press, 1962).
Sidgwick, H.: *The Methods of Ethics* (New York: Don Press, 1966).

Further Reading

Adams, R. M.: 'Motive utilitarianism', *Journal of Philosophy*, 73 (1976).
Hare, R. M.: *Moral Thinking* (Oxford: Clarendon Press, 1981).
Lyons, D.: *Forms and Limits of Utilitarianism* (Oxford: Clarendon Press, 1965).
Parfit, D.: *Reasons and Persons* (Oxford: Clarendon Press, 1984).
Pettit, P.: 'The consequentialist can recognise rights', *Philosophical Quarterly*, 35
(1988).
Pettit, P. and Brennan, G.: 'Restrictive consequentialism', *Australasian Journal of
Philosophy*, 64 (1984).
Railton, P.: 'Alienation, consequentialism and morality', *Philosophy and Public
Affairs*, 13 (1984).
Regan, D. H.: *Utilitarianism and Cooperation* (Oxford: Clarendon Press, 1980).
Scheffler, S.: *The Rejection of Consequentialism* (Oxford: Clarendon Press, 1982).
—— ed.: *Consequentialism and its Critics* (Oxford: Clarendon Press, 1988).
Slote, M.: *Common-Sense Morality and Consequentialism* (London: Routledge and
Kegan Paul, 1985).
Smart, J. J. C. and Williams, B.: *Utilitarianism: For and Against* (Cambridge:
Cambridge University Press, 1973).
Stocker, M.: 'The schizophrenia of modern ethical theories', *Journal of Philosophy*,
73 (1976).

7

From *The Rejection of Consequentialism*

Samuel Scheffler

1
The Project and its Motivation

As John Rawls has written, 'The two main concepts of ethics are those of the right and the good . . . The structure of an ethical theory is . . . largely determined by how it defines and connects these two basic notions.'[1] Among ethical theories, those that I call 'act-consequentialist' may be characterized roughly as follows. Such theories first specify some principle for ranking overall states of affairs from best to worst from an impersonal point of view. In other words, the rankings generated by the designated principle are not agent-relative; they do not vary from person to person, depending on what one's particular situation is. For they do not embody judgements about which overall states of affairs are best for particular individuals, but rather judgements about which states of affairs are best, all things considered, from an impartial standpoint. After giving some principle for generating such rankings, act-consequentialists then require that each agent in all cases act in such a way as to produce the highest-ranked state of affairs that he is in a position to produce.[2] Different act-consequentialist theories incorporate different conceptions of the overall good: that is, different principles for ranking overall states of affairs from best to worst. But all such theories share the same conception of the right which requires each agent in all cases to produce the best available outcome overall.

Act-consequentialism is not the only kind of consequentialism; other variants include rule-consequentialism and motive-consequentialism.

Samuel Scheffler, *The Rejection of Consequentialism*, rev. edn. (Oxford: Clarendon Press, 1994), pp. 1–6, 80–101.

These views typically differ somewhat from act-consequentialism in what they require of agents,[3] though they share with act-consequentialism the feature of ranking overall states of affairs impersonally, and the general idea that the best states of affairs are *somehow* to be promoted. I will not be discussing these other variants of consequentialism in this book. Although I believe that my main lines of argument could be modified to cover them, the only kind of consequentialism that I will actually consider in the book is act-consequentialism. Since this is so, and since the term 'act-consequentialism' is cumbersome, I will, beginning with the next paragraph and throughout the rest of the book, use the terms 'consequentialism' and 'consequentialist' to mean 'act-consequentialism' and 'act-consequentialist', except where I explicitly state otherwise. This is purely an abbreviatory device, adopted for the sake of simplicity and ease of exposition; it is not intended to suggest either that my discussion encompasses all of the various forms of consequentialism, or that act-consequentialism is the only legitimate form of consequentialism.

In contrast to consequentialist conceptions, standard deontological views maintain that it is sometimes wrong to do what will produce the best available outcome overall. In other words, these views incorporate what I shall call 'agent-centred restrictions': restrictions on action which have the effect of denying that there is any non-agent-relative principle for ranking overall states of affairs from best to worst such that it is always permissible to produce the best available state of affairs so characterized.

Classical utilitarianism, which ranks states of affairs according to the amount of total satisfaction they contain, is the most familiar consequentialist view.[4] But classical utilitarianism is widely thought to be too crude a theory. Although its defenders point with approval to its simplicity, critics charge that this simplicity is achieved at too high a cost. They argue that utilitarianism relies on implausible assumptions about human motivation, incorporates a strained and superficial view of the human good, and ignores a host of important considerations about justice, fairness, and the character of human agency. More generally, they accuse utilitarianism of relentless insensitivity to the nature of a person, and suggest that it has forfeited any serious claim to account for the complex and varied considerations that intrude on the moral life, and which give rise to the severest tests of our decency. Indeed, utilitarianism has gained a reputation for moral clumsiness that is unparalleled among ethical theories. Bernard Williams, writing that 'the simple-mindedness of utilitarianism disqualifies it totally', suggests that '[t]he day cannot be too far off in which we hear no more of it'.[5]

And yet that day refuses to come; we continue to hear a great deal about utilitarianism. Cynics may suppose that the explanation for this lies in the philosopher's penchant for keeping half-dead horses just barely alive so that he can continue to beat them with a moderately clear conscience. My diagnosis is different: I believe that utilitarianism refuses to fade from the scene in large part because, as the most familiar consequentialist theory, it is the major recognized normative theory incorporating the deeply plausible-sounding feature that one may always do what would lead to the best available outcome overall. Despite all of utilitarianism's faults (including, no doubt, its misidentification of the best outcomes), its incorporation of this one plausible feature is in my opinion responsible for its persistence. Moral conceptions that include agent-centred restrictions, of course, reject this feature. Although a full characterization and discussion of these restrictions will not be presented until Chapter Four, they have already been identified as restrictions on action which have the effect of denying that there is *any* non-agent-relative principle for ranking overall states of affairs such that it is always permissible to produce the best available state of affairs so construed. If an adequate theoretical rationale for such restrictions could be identified, it would provide a reason for rejecting utilitarianism's deeply plausible-sounding feature. But although, as I will indicate in Chapter Four, it is easy to think of cases in which agent-centred restrictions seem intuitively appropriate, and although such restrictions constitute the heart of most familiar deontological moral conceptions, it is, as I will also indicate in Chapter Four, surprisingly difficult to find persuasive hypotheses in the literature as to what their underlying theoretical rationale might be.

Faced with what I take to be serious difficulties in the attempt to provide an adequate rationale for agent-centred restrictions, and faced with the plausibility of the idea that it is always permissible to do what would have the best outcome overall, I wish in this book to reconsider the rejection of consequentialism. What I will do, more specifically, is to undertake a comparative examination of two different kinds of non-consequentialist moral conceptions. The standard deontological theories I call 'fully agent-centred' conceptions constitute the more familiar of these two kinds. By virtue of including agent-centred restrictions, these conceptions deny that there is any non-agent-relative principle for ranking overall states of affairs from best to worst such that it is always permissible to produce the best available state of affairs so characterized. And in addition to including such restrictions, these conceptions also deny that one must do what would have the best outcome overall on all of those occasions when the restrictions do *not* forbid it. In other words, fully agent-centred conceptions maintain that, given any impersonal principle for ranking overall states of affairs from best to worst, there will be some circumstances in which one is not permitted to produce the best available state of affairs, and still other circumstances in which one is permitted but not required to do so.

Non-consequentialist conceptions of the second kind I will consider are much less familiar. Indeed, I am unaware of any previous discussion of them in the literature. These 'hybrid' conceptions, as I refer to them, depart from consequentialism through their incorporation of something I call an 'agent-centred prerogative', which has the effect of denying that one is always required to produce the best overall states of affairs, and which is thus in some form a feature of fully agent-centred conceptions as well.[6] At the same time, however, hybrid conceptions are akin to consequentialist conceptions in their rejection of agent-centred restrictions: that is, in their acceptance of the idea that it is always permissible to do what would produce the best overall state of affairs. In other words, hybrid conceptions are like fully agent-centred conceptions and unlike consequentialist conceptions in maintaining that one need not always do what would produce the best outcome; but they are like consequentialist conceptions and unlike fully agent-centred conceptions in accepting the plausible-sounding idea that one *may* always do what would produce the best outcome.

The agent-centred prerogative, as I will argue, is responsive to certain important anti-consequentialist intuitions. To this extent it is on a par with agent-centred restrictions. But, as I will also argue, there is a significant asymmetry between the two agent-centred features; that is, it is much easier to identify a plausible theoretical foundation for the former than it is for the latter. Thus an agent-centred prerogative can be motivated and defended not merely by showing that it has intuitive appeal in certain cases, but also by demonstrating that there is a plausible principled rationale which underlies it. To the extent that this rationale is compelling, hybrid conceptions may, by virtue of incorporating such a prerogative, seem more attractive than consequentialist conceptions. And at the same time, the fact that it is indeed possible to provide a persuasive theoretical rationale for one departure from consequentialism will make the difficulties in providing such a rationale for agent-centred restrictions seem all the more striking, whatever the intuitive appeal of such restrictions. The upshot is that hybrid theories, intermediate between consequentialist and fully agent-centred conceptions and less familiar than either, may in the end seem preferable to both. At the very least, they will emerge as a serious alternative. Or so I hope to show.

112   *Samuel Scheffler*

Notes

1   *A Theory of Justice* (Harvard University Press, 1971), p. 24.
2   Obviously, this formulation is oversimplified. Most such theories do not require the agent to act in such a way as to produce the best actual state of affairs that is available. Rather they require that the agent perform the available act that has the highest expected value, where the expected value of an act is a function of each of its various possible outcomes and of their probabilities of occurrence. I will, however, continue to use the oversimplified formulation because it highlights the features of consequentialism that are relevant to this discussion. For my purposes, nothing is lost by avoiding the more complicated and more accurate formulation.

It should also be emphasized that when I speak of the act-consequentialist as requiring agents to produce the best overall outcomes or states of affairs, I do not mean that the act-consequentialist divides what happens into the act and the outcome, and evaluates only the latter with his overall ranking principle. Rather, the act itself is initially evaluated as part of the overall outcome or state of affairs. The act-consequentialist first ranks overall outcomes, which are understood, in this broad way, to include the acts necessary to produce them, and then directs the agent to produce the best available outcome so construed.

3   For some complications, see David Lyons, *Forms and Limits of Utilitarianism* (Oxford University Press, 1965).
4   To avoid confusion, there are a number of points about this characterization of the view that I call 'classical utilitarianism' which should be noted at the outset. First, I intend it to be understood that whenever I speak of this view as ranking states of affairs according to the amount of total or aggregate satisfaction they contain, I mean, of course, total *net* satisfaction (that is, total satisfaction minus dissatisfaction). Second, classical utilitarianism as I understand it is a view that has hedonistic and non-hedonistic variants. Thus in characterizing the view I have deliberately used the term 'satisfaction', which can be understood either hedonistically, as referring to a kind of feeling, or non-hedonistically, as referring to the satisfaction of people's preferences, whatever the preferences may be for. [In the course of this book,] I will distinguish between the hedonistic and non-hedonistic variants of classical utilitarianism only when the distinction is relevant to the topic under discussion. Whenever I do not make the distinction explicitly, the reader is to understand what I say as applying to both the hedonistic and non-hedonistic variants. Finally, the term 'utilitarianism' is used in the philosophical literature in connection with a wide range of moral views, from rule-utilitarianism to the principle that the right act maximizes average utility to the so-called 'ideal utilitarianism' associated with G. E. Moore. But I will use the term exclusively to refer to the classical act-utilitarianism described in the text.
5   J. J. C. Smart and Bernard Williams, *Utilitarianism For and Against* (Cambridge University Press, 1973), p. 150.

6   That is, since fully agent-centred conceptions do, as I have said, deny that one
     is required to do what would have the best overall outcome on all of those
     occasions when the agent-centred restrictions do not forbid it, they in effect
     include an agent-centred prerogative of some form, although not necessarily
     of the very same form as I describe in [a later chapter], and although the term
     'agent-centred prerogative' is of course my own.

4
The Defence of Agent-centred Restrictions: Intuitions in Search of a Foundation

Agent-centred restrictions, I have said, are restrictions on action which
have the effect of denying that there is any non-agent-relative principle
for ranking overall states of affairs such that it is always permissible to
produce the best available state of affairs so construed. I want now to characterize these restrictions more fully, and to explain why they have this
effect. An agent-centred restriction is a restriction which it is at least sometimes impermissible to violate in circumstances where a violation would
prevent either more numerous violations, of no less weight from an
impersonal point of view, of the very same restriction, or other events at
least as objectionable, and would have no other morally relevant consequences. Imagine a theory according to which there is some restriction S,
such that it is at least sometimes impermissible to violate S in circumstances where doing so would prevent a still greater number of equally
weighty violations of S, and would have no other morally relevant consequences. Now S is an agent-centred restriction; due to the inclusion of
S in the theory, there exists no non-agent-relative principle for ranking
overall states of affairs from best to worst such that it will always be permissible to produce the best state of affairs so characterized. If the best
overall state of affairs is construed as the one containing fewest violations
of S, for example, it will at least sometimes be impermissible for an agent
to produce that state of affairs if he can only do so by actually committing one of the (minimized) violations of S. Thus agent-centred restrictions
are limitations on the conduct of the individual agent which take priority
over calculations of overall impersonal value.

An agent-centred prerogative, as we have seen, serves to deny that
agents are always *required* to produce the best overall states of affairs.
Agent-centred restrictions, on the other hand, serve to deny that there is
any non-agent-relative principle for ranking states of affairs such that
agents are always *permitted* to produce the best state of affairs. Both

devices thus represent departures from consequentialism, which takes the impersonal standpoint to be the only moral standpoint. Intuitively, it may therefore seem plausible that the rejection of agent-centred restrictions should be ultimately incompatible with acceptance of an agent-centred prerogative. For it may seem that if there is a motivation for introducing any agent-centredness into a moral theory at all, then there is a motivation for introducing *both* agent-centred components. And if the introduction of one agent-centred component is poorly motivated, then the introduction of the other component must be poorly motivated as well. Hence it may appear that there are only two positions one can consistently hold: one can either reject agent-centredness altogether and retreat to some kind of consequentialism, or accept a fully agent-centred view incorporating both an agent-centred prerogative and agent-centred restrictions. Hybrid conceptions, it may seem, represent an attempt to stake out a middle ground that does not exist; there is no room for a view intermediate between consequentialist and fully agent-centred conceptions. There is no room for a conception that incorporates an agent-centred prerogative but not agent-centred restrictions.

I believe that this intuitive line of reasoning is mistaken, and that hybrid views constitute a bona fide alternative to consequentialist and fully agent-centred conceptions. I believe that there is an underlying principled motivation for an agent-centred prerogative, and that this motivation has been identified in [an earlier] chapter. And I believe that this motivation is independent of any rationale there may be for agent-centred restrictions, in the sense that someone who is motivated in this way to accept a prerogative can at the same time consistently refuse to accept such restrictions. I will call this *the independence thesis*. The truth of the independence thesis is of course compatible with the existence of some separate principled motivation for agent-centred restrictions. Not only do I believe that the independence thesis is true, however, I also believe, as I have indicated, that it is surprisingly difficult to find plausible suggestions in the literature as to what an underlying motivation for such restrictions might be. There is thus another thesis that in my opinion merits our close attention. *The asymmetry thesis* asserts that although it is possible to identify an underlying principled rationale for an agent-centred prerogative, it is not possible to identify any comparable rationale for agent-centred restrictions. If the independence thesis alone were true, then hybrid theories would still represent a bona fide alternative to consequentialist and fully agent-centred conceptions. But if the asymmetry thesis were also true, then fully agent-centred conceptions might begin to look particularly problematic. In this chapter, I want to examine possible rationales for agent-centred restrictions. In the course of the discussion, I will defend the independence thesis, and try to explain why the asymmetry thesis must also be taken seriously.

As I suggested in Chapter One, there are some prima-facie difficulties with agent-centred restrictions. The main problem is the apparent air of irrationality surrounding the claim that some acts are so objectionable that one ought not to perform them even if this means that more equally weighty acts of the very same kind or other comparably objectionable events will ensue, and even if there are no other morally relevant consequences to be considered. An adequate principled motivation for agent-centred restrictions must dispel this air of irrationality. It must provide answers to a series of questions posed by Robert Nozick:

> Isn't it *irrational* to accept a side constraint C, rather than a view that directs minimizing the violations of C? . . . If nonviolation of C is so important, shouldn't that be the goal? How can a concern for the nonviolation of C lead to the refusal to violate C even when this would prevent other more extensive violations of C? What is the rationale for placing the nonviolation of rights as a side constraint upon action instead of including it solely as a goal of one's actions?[1]

As I begin to explore possible answers to these questions, I want to re-emphasize at the outset that, despite the apparent air of irrationality to which I have called attention, the intuitive appeal of agent-centred restrictions is not in question. Such restrictions are certainly responsive to widely shared anti-consequentialist sentiments. There are many imaginable cases, for example, in which many people would intuitively feel it wrong to kill an innocent person even if doing so would prevent two or three other equally objectionable killings, and would have no other morally relevant consequences. It is to feelings of this sort that agent-centred restrictions respond, or appear to respond. Thus the intuitive appeal of such restrictions is not in question, just as the intuitive appeal of an agent-centred prerogative was never in question.

However, while the fact that a structural feature has intuitive appeal constitutes a reason for trying to identify a plausible rationale for that feature, it does not constitute a rationale of the sort I am looking for, nor guarantee that there is one. In now familiar fashion, a consequentialist might respond in either of two ways to the charge that his theory regularly generates results which violate the intuitions to which agent-centred restrictions answer. He could respond either by denying that such cases arise often in real life and claiming that occasionally counter-intuitive positions may nevertheless be acceptable, or by conceding that such cases arise regularly but denying the importance of the counter-intuitive character of the consequentialist position, especially in light of the prima-facie irrationality of the more intuitive fully agent-centred conceptions. So what we wish to know is whether it is possible to establish that whether or not consequentialism regularly yields counter-intuitive consequences in real-life cases, there is in any event a principled rationale for agent-centred restrictions. If this could be established, then if the consequentialist took his second option, conceding that his theory yields systematically counter-intuitive results but denying the importance of that point, the defender of agent-centred restrictions could respond by insisting that there *is* a serious underlying motivation for the restrictions which respond to those anti-consequentialist intuitions. And even if the consequentialist took his first option and succeeded in showing that his theory does not regularly yield counter-intuitive results in real cases, the defender of the restrictions could respond that there is nevertheless a plausible rationale for preferring a fully agent-centred conception. With the restrictions as with the agent-centred prerogative, then, the existence of supporting intuitions marks the beginning and not the end of the search for an underlying principled rationale.

To focus the discussion of possible rationales for agent-centred restrictions, let us consider a schematic example of a disagreement between those who accept such restrictions and those who reject them. Suppose that if agent A_1 fails to violate a restriction R by harming some undeserving person P_1, then five other agents, $A_2 \ldots A_6$, will each violate restriction R by identically harming five other persons, $P_2 \ldots P_6$, who are just as undeserving as P_1, and whom it would be just as undesirable from an impersonal standpoint to have harmed. We may make the following simplifying assumptions: (1) A_1 has no way out of this dilemma, and (2) there are no morally relevant consequences of A_1's action or non-action beyond those already mentioned. Neither these simplifying assumptions nor the case as I have described it manifests any bias against agent-centred restrictions. Consider the simplifying assumptions first. Obviously, in real-life cases there are likely to be more options available to the agent, some important long-term consequences to take into account, and greater uncertainty about the outcomes of the various actions. But the assumptions that exclude these complications serve only to guarantee that we have a clear example of the kind of case that gives rise to disagreement between those who accept agent-centred restrictions and those who reject them; the simplifications in themselves count neither for nor against such restrictions.

Consider now the description of the case itself. Different fully agent-centred conceptions differ with regard to what exactly they take the agent-centred restrictions on action to be, and so they would differ about which specific restriction should play the role of restriction R. Just for this reason, the content of R was left deliberately vague in describing the case; no unusual or prejudicial assumptions were made about the character of the restriction.[2] Similarly, there is wide variation among fully agent-centred conceptions with regard to the circumstances, if any, under which the restrictions are thought to be overridable. At one end of the spectrum, 'absolutist' conceptions hold that some restrictions cannot be overridden and must not be violated, whatever the consequences. Some non-absolutists occupy an intermediate position, conceding only that agent-centred restrictions *sometimes* give way: when we are threatened by an evil that is so great as to seem immeasurable, and honouring *them* means losing everything. Toward the other end or the spectrum, finally, there are those non-absolutists who go much further, holding that it is often (though not always) permissible to violate the restrictions in circumstances where doing so is the only way to prevent a still greater number of equally weighty violations of the very same restrictions, or other events at least as objectionable. One might caricature these differing positions by saying that the absolutist would prohibit the violation of a restriction even if a violation were the only way to prevent a genocidal catastrophe,[3] the more restrictive non-absolutist would permit a violation in circumstances such as these but not in situations any less catastrophic, and the less restrictive non-absolutist would permit one violation if that would prevent twenty comparable violations but not if it would prevent only three. Although the absolutist variant may place the greatest strain on the credibility of fully agent-centred conceptions, the case I have described does not respond to distinctive features of absolutist conceptions, and hence in using this example I am not attempting to exploit specially problematic aspects of such conceptions. In other words, the example does not prejudice the issue by depicting catastrophic consequences if A_1 fails to violate R and then assuming that defenders of agent-centred restrictions as a class are committed to forbidding violation. The outcome of non-violation is not extreme, relatively speaking, and the case could easily be redescribed in such a way as to make the outcome still less extreme, without changing the basic issues. For if the non-absolutist is committed to agent-centred restrictions at all, then there must be some restriction R, such that in some situation, he will say that an agent is required not to violate R even though a still greater number of equally weighty violations of R, or other comparably objectionable events, will ensue if the agent does not violate R, and even if there are no other morally relevant consequences to be considered. And it is claims of this type about cases of this sort, made by absolutists and non-absolutists alike, which I wish to explore. The example sketched is intended as a schematic idealization of one such case: no more and no less.

Let me then adapt Nozick's question to my example: why isn't the view that it is wrong for A_1 to violate R irrational?[4] There is one way of trying to answer the question which may seem tempting initially, but which is also clearly unacceptable. That is, it is tempting to suggest that acts that violate R have some feature that is very bad or has high disvalue, and that it is for this reason that A_1 may not violate R. But this suggestion is clearly inadequate, for, *ex hypothesi*, however high the disvalue of a violation of R, a greater number of equally weighty violations – and hence at least as much disvalue – will ensue if A_1 does *not* violate R. Appeals to the disvalue of violations of R are powerless to explain why it is wrong to violate R when doing so will prevent five identical violations of R.[5]

Nevertheless, defences of agent-centred restrictions in the literature often seem to take the form of an appeal to the disvalue of violation. Thus, for example, Nozick, answering his own question about the apparent irrationality of 'side constraints', says: 'Side constraints upon action reflect the underlying Kantian principle that individuals are ends and not merely means; they may not be sacrificed or used for the achieving of other ends without their consent. Individuals are inviolable.'[6] It is natural to interpret this passage as a suggestion that violations of agent-centred restrictions involve violating the victimized individuals themselves, treating them as means instead of ends, and that since being violated or treated as a means is a bad thing, violations of such restrictions are impermissible. It is natural, in other words, to interpret Nozick's defence of side constraints as an appeal to the disvalue of certain features of violations of the constraints. But if this is the proper interpretation of his defence, then clearly that defence is inadequate for the reasons just mentioned.

The general point, which applies to agent-centred restrictions of all kinds, may be illuminated by looking at this particular defence, as applied to our schematic example, more closely. Presumably, persons $P_1 \ldots P_6$ in our example are all equally 'inviolable', in the sense that Nozick intends. Yet, *ex hypothesi*, *someone* in that example is going to be violated. Either A_1 will harm P_1 or five other agents will identically harm $P_2 \ldots P_6$. Either way, someone loses: *some* inviolable person is violated. Why isn't it at least permissible to prevent the violation of five people by violating one? An appeal to the value of an unviolated life or the disvalue of the violation of a life cannot possibly provide a satisfactory answer to this question. For the question is not whether to choose an unviolated life over a violated one; the relative value of violated and unviolated lives is not at issue. Instead, the choice is between one person inflicting a relatively smaller number of violations, and five other persons inflicting a relatively larger number of violations of equal weight from an impersonal standpoint. And the question is what possible ground there is for holding that the one person must not inflict the smaller number of violations in order to prevent their more numerous occurrence. The badness of a violation cannot provide such a ground, for surely five violations are at least as bad as one.

Similarly, the badness of being treated as a means to some end cannot account for the impermissibility of A_1's violating R by harming P_1 in order to prevent five other agents from identically harming $P_2 \ldots P_6$. For once again, *ex hypothesi*, *someone* will be treated as a means to an end whatever A_1 does. If it is indeed a bad thing to be treated as a means to an end, why isn't it at least permissible for A_1 to treat one person as a means to some end if that will prevent five other equally undeserving people from being so treated? At least the person A_1 uses will be treated as a means to the end of minimizing the treatment of people as means. Even if we leave this last point aside, however, the badness of being treated as a means to an end cannot provide a ground for the impermissibility of A_1's treating P_1 as a means to an end in this case. For surely five such treatments of no less weight from an impersonal standpoint are at least as bad as one.

As we have seen, the problem is with the general strategy for the defence of agent-centred restrictions that is employed here. So long as the strategy is to single out some feature of violations of the restrictions as having high disvalue, no adequate defence of such restrictions will emerge. It makes no difference, in particular, *which* feature of violation is singled out as having a high disvalue: no difference, for example, whether the focus is on the victim of violation, the agent, or the relationship between them. One might address the defender of agent-centred restrictions as follows. If, in our example, you are concerned about the badness of what will happen to P_1 if A_1 violates R (P_1 will be used, treated as a means, or whatever), why isn't it permissible to be at least as concerned about the fivefold badness of what will happen to $P_2 \ldots P_6$ if A_1 does *not* violate R (then they will be used, treated as means, etc.)? If instead you are concerned about the badness of a human agent *doing* something harmful to another human being, why isn't it permissible to be at least as concerned about the badness of *five* human beings doing equally harmful things to five other human beings. And if you are worried that a violation of R corrupts the *relationship* between the agent and the victim, and that the corruption of a human relationship is a bad thing, then why isn't it at least permissible to corrupt one valuable relationship if that is the only way to prevent the corruption of five equally valuable human relationships?

An attempt to motivate agent-centred restrictions by appealing to the disvalue of violations of such restrictions is directly analogous to an attempt to motivate an agent-centred prerogative by appealing to the value or goodness of an agent's carrying out his projects and plans. Both attempts fail, for parallel reasons. An appeal to the disvalue of violations of a restriction is powerless to explain why one may not violate that restriction in order to prevent still more numerous violations, of no less weight from an impersonal standpoint, of the very same restriction. Thus such an appeal cannot motivate agent-centred restrictions. It can only motivate a consequentialist presumption against performing the kinds of acts that such restrictions forbid, a presumption that is overridable whenever the disvalue of a violation would be exceeded by the disvalue of the consequences of non-violation. Similarly, an appeal to the value of an individual's carrying out his plans is powerless to explain why one is not required to abandon one's *own* plans if doing so would enable still more people to carry out *their* plans. Such an appeal cannot therefore motivate an agent-centred prerogative. All it can do is to motivate a provisional consequentialist dispensation to devote more attention to one's own happiness and well-being than to the happiness and well-being of other people so long as doing so will have the best results overall. In sum, appeals to value cannot succeed in motivating either of the agent-centred structural components we are examining. They cannot provide a rationale either for agent-centred restrictions or for an agent-centred prerogative. They can only serve to motivate consequentialist presumptions and consequentialist dispensations: those strategic manoeuvres internal to consequentialism which constitute that conception's alternative to, and substitute for, the radical departures of agent-centred morality.[7]

Clearly, the failure of attempts to motivate agent-centred restrictions by appealing to the disvalue of violations of such restrictions does not indicate that no plausible rationale whatsoever can be found for such restrictions, any more than the failure of attempts to motivate the agent-centred prerogative by appealing to the value of individual plans indicates that there is no plausible rationale for that device. The lesson to be learned from the failure of the parallel appeals to value is rather that any successful attempt to motivate either agent-centred component will have to take a different form. Although an agent-centred prerogative cannot be motivated through an appeal to value, I have of course already argued that it is possible to motivate such a prerogative by showing how it embodies a rational strategy for taking account of the independence of the personal point of view, given one construal of the importance of that aspect of persons. The question now to be faced is the question of whether, similarly, it is possible to identify a plausible underlying rationale for agent-centred restrictions, even though *they* cannot be motivated through an appeal to value.

The first possibility to consider, along these lines, is the possibility that someone who embraces the motivation for an agent-centred prerogative is thereby committed, on pain of inconsistency, to accepting agent-centred restrictions as well. The suggestion here, in other words, is that the independence thesis is false. This suggestion has a certain amount of initial implausibility. For, as we have seen, the prerogative and the restrictions respond to different sorts of anti-consequentialist intuitions. This is not conclusive, however, for intuitions with differing content may nevertheless have sources which are closely linked, or even a single source in common. So despite its initial implausibility, the suggestion that the independence thesis is false needs to be taken seriously. As I have characterized it, the motivation for an agent-centred prerogative is that it embodies a rational strategy for responding to the natural independence of the personal point of view, given a certain legitimate construal of the importance of independence. Now this implies that one is not rationally required to go beyond that strategy and accept agent-centred restrictions additionally in response to the fact of independence so conceived. Thus, assuming that my characterization of the motivation for an agent-centred prerogative is accurate, it seems quite likely that the independence thesis is true, and the suggestion we are considering false. It is not yet certain, however. For even if someone who accepts the prerogative as embodying a rational response to the independence of the personal point of view, given a certain construal of the importance of independence, is not thereby committed to accepting agent-centred restrictions additionally in response to the fact of independence so construed, there remains the possibility that such a person *is* also thereby committed to some separate strategy for responding to something *other* than the fact of independence so construed, and that this second strategy *does* constitute a motivation for agent-centred restrictions. But although this is an abstract possibility, I cannot think of any way to make it concretely plausible. There is nothing that emerged in the course of the discussion of the liberation strategy that provides any reason for thinking that the employment of this strategy commits one to using other sorts of strategies in other sorts of circumstances. I conclude that this abstract possibility may be discounted, and that therefore the independence thesis is true, and the suggestion we have been considering is false. It is not the case that someone who embraces the motivation for an agent-centred prerogative is thereby committed, on pain of inconsistency, to accepting agent-centred restrictions as well. It is not the case that one must either reject agent-centredness altogether and retreat to consequentialism, or accept a fully agent-centred view which incorporates both an agent-centred prerogative and agent-centred restrictions. Hybrid theories constitute a bona fide, stable alternative to consequentialist and fully agent-centred conceptions.

It is important to note that the independence thesis is nevertheless compatible with the possibility that fully agent-centred conceptions embody *some* rational strategy for responding to the independence of the personal point of view. For all that has been said so far, it may be that fully agent-centred conceptions and hybrid conceptions employ two equally rational strategies for responding to the fact of personal independence, given two equally legitimate construals of the importance of that fact, or even given the very same construal of its importance. It may be that the choice between these strategies depends on one's ultimate moral attitudes. All that has been ruled out is the possibility that everyone who accepts an agent-centred prerogative as part of a response to personal independence must also accept agent-centred restrictions. The possibility that hybrid conceptions and fully agent-centred conceptions represent *alternative* responses to the fact of independence remains open, and it is natural to examine this possibility next.

Do agent-centred restrictions embody all or part of a rational strategy for responding to the natural independence of the personal point of view, given some legitimate construal of the importance of that aspect of persons? There is an initial implausibility about the suggestion that they do, just as there was an initial implausibility about the suggestion that the independence thesis is false. The implausibility of both proposals derives from the fact that they both take the underlying motivations for the two agent-centred devices to be closely connected, even though those devices respond on the surface to very different kinds of anti-consequentialist intuitions. As I noted in connection with the previous proposal, however, surface differences can conceal underlying connections. So the current proposal, like the previous one, must be taken seriously.

It seems to me that the most plausible way of developing the proposal is by trying to understand agent-centred restrictions as representing all or part of a rational response to the independence of the personal point of view, given an interpretation of the importance of that aspect of persons which is just the same as the interpretation relied on by the liberation strategy. For the current proposal is like the liberation strategy in seeking to construe an agent-centred feature of moral theories as a rational response to the independence of the personal point of view. It is thus most plausible to suppose that, if agent-centred restrictions do represent a rational response to personal independence, they, like the agent-centred prerogative, do so given a conception of the importance of independence which emphasizes its significance for human agency. Since this is the most plausible way of developing the current proposal, I will make it the focus for my consideration of the proposal as a whole. If the proposal in its strongest form is ultimately defective, it is reasonable to pass over alternative construals that had less promise from the start.

Thus the question is whether it is in fact appropriate to conceive of agent-centred restrictions as constituting all or part of a rational response to the natural independence of the personal point of view, given that the importance of independence is conceived as stemming primarily from its impact on the character of human agency and motivation. I believe that the answer to this question is 'no'. Someone who disagreed might reason thus. Agent-centred restrictions, which have the effect of denying that there is any non-agent-relative principle for ranking overall states of affairs from best to worst such that it is always permissible to produce the best available state of affairs so characterized, serve to protect individuals from the demand that they organize their conduct in accordance with some canon of impersonal optimality. They prevent individuals from becoming slaves of the impersonal standpoint, and in so doing they serve to insulate the personal point of view against external demands. For this reason they represent a rational response to the fact that individuals are naturally independent of the impersonal perspective.

As it stands, this line of argument is inadequate. The *permission* not to produce the best states of affairs suffices to free individual agents from the demands of impersonal optimality, and thus to prevent them from becoming slaves of the impersonal standpoint. That is the whole point of the liberation strategy, which underlies the agent-centred prerogative. What must be provided is a rationale for going beyond such permissions and *prohibiting* the production of the best states of affairs. Of course, since prohibitions against producing the best states of affairs entail permissions not to produce those states of affairs, it is true that agent-centred restrictions do free agents from the requirement always to do what would have the best outcome overall.[8] But this does not show that such restrictions are, after all, a rational response to the natural independence of the personal point of view, for the fact that a prohibition entails a motivated permission does not constitute a motivation for the prohibition.

Someone might try in the following way to improve on the argument I have just rejected. It is true, it might be conceded, that an agent-centred prerogative suffices to free individuals from the requirement always to do what would have the best outcome overall. But it is not true that prohibitions against doing what would have the best outcome accomplish nothing further, in this regard. By always permitting actions that would have the best outcome overall, hybrid conceptions leave open the possibility of morally acceptable conduct which is guided exclusively by the standard of impersonal optimality. Fully agent-centred conceptions, by contrast, eliminate this option. They insist that the acceptability of an individual's conduct must be determined by the intrinsic characteristics of his personal projects, actions, and intentions, and not by an extrinsic, impersonal appraisal of those overall states of affairs which his actions may produce. In this way, fully agent-centred conceptions grant more extensive moral independence to the personal point of view than hybrid conceptions do. For while hybrid conceptions regard it as morally tolerable if an individual always does what will have the best overall outcome impersonally judged, fully agent-centred conceptions insist that the standards of individual conduct must be specially tailored to fit the *personal* perspective of the individual agent. Thus, the argument might be summed up, fully agent-centred conceptions do embody a rational response to the natural independence of the personal point of view, given one legitimate construal of the importance of independence. Like hybrid conceptions, they regard independence as important primarily for its impact on the character of human agency. Unlike hybrid conceptions, however, they respond by insisting that human agents must be held to a standard of accountability which gives the intrinsic qualities of an individual's acts moral priority over their impersonal optimality.

This revised argument seems to me to represent the strongest kind of case that can be made for construing agent-centred restrictions as part of a rational response to the independence of the personal point of view, but I believe that it is flawed none the less. The intuitive idea behind the argument is that a moral conception gives priority to the personal point of view over the impersonal point of view, and thus emphasizes the independence of the former from the latter, by insisting that individuals be judged on the basis of the intrinsic qualities of their personal actions, projects, and intentions, and not on the basis of an impersonal appraisal of the tendency of their conduct to promote the overall good. However, in so far as the argument does suggest a principled motivation for departing from consequentialism, the motivation suggested is for an agent-centred prerogative only. And in so far as the argument purports to provide a motivation for agent-centred restrictions, it fails to do so.

The basic problem is that the argument misconceives the nature of the individual point of view. It implicitly assumes that an individual cannot, from his own point of view, form and act on intentions to do things that will have the best overall outcome, either because they will have the best outcome, or for other reasons. Individuals cannot identify with acts and intentions of this kind. Activities that promote the best overall states of affairs cannot be among a person's projects. If the argument were not relying on these assumptions, there would be no plausibility whatsoever to its claim that fully agent-centred conceptions give the personal point of view priority over the impersonal point of view by holding the individual to a standard of accountability which gives the intrinsic personal qualities of his actions and projects priority over their impersonal optimality. For if actions which will have the best overall outcome *can* be undertaken from within the individual's own point of view, then the agent-centred restrictions which limit such actions, far from representing a way of giving the personal point of view priority over the impersonal point of view, will appear instead as arbitrary and unexplained constraints on the projects and activities of the individual.

The assumptions that the argument thus relies on are evidently false. A person may want to do what will have the best overall outcome, either because it will have the best outcome or for some other reason. Thus A_1, in our schematic example, might decide to violate R because he genuinely wanted to do what would have the best overall outcome, and believed that violating R would, or because he had compassion for all six potential victims and wanted to prevent as many of them as possible from suffering. One can also intend to do and *actually* do that which will have the best outcome, either because it will have that outcome or for other reasons. Moreover, one can identify with these wants, intentions, and actions in just the same way that one identifies with others of one's wants, intentions and actions. They are just as compatible with the personal point of view as, for example, desires, intentions, and actions to promote the good of particular people one cares about. The promotion of the general good, like the promotion of the good of one's intimates, can be undertaken from *within* one's personal standpoint. This is unproblematic. Since the assumptions relied on by the argument are thus false, the argument fails to support agent-centred restrictions. For, as I have already noted, once it is recognized that actions and projects that promote optimal outcomes can be undertaken from within one's personal point of view, then the agent-centred restrictions which limit such actions no longer appear to be a way of giving the personal point of view priority over the impersonal point of view, but look instead like arbitrary and unmotivated constraints on the projects and activities of the individual. Hybrid conceptions, by contrast, do not impose restrictions of this kind on personal projects. And, of course, they give the agent permission to devote energy and attention to his projects, plans, and personal relationships out of proportion to the weight in the impersonal calculus of his doing so. Thus they, more than fully agent-centred conceptions, may be thought of as specially tailoring the standards of individual conduct to fit the personal perspective of the individual agent, and in this way of giving moral priority to the personal point of view. That is what I meant when I said earlier that, in so far as the argument I have been considering does suggest a principled motivation for departing from consequentialism, the motivation suggested is for an agent-centred prerogative only, and in so far as the argument purports to provide a motivation for agent-centred restrictions, it fails to do so. It seems fair to conclude that, even in its most plausible form, the idea of construing agent-centred restrictions as part of a rational response to the independence of the personal point of view is unacceptable.[9] Let us thus turn our attention to other suggestions for motivating such restrictions.

If agent-centred restrictions cannot be construed as part of a rational response to the natural independence of the personal point of view, can they instead be seen as part of a rational strategy for responding to some other feature of the person? We may consider, in this connection, another suggestion of Nozick's, which is reminiscent of the proposals of his that we have already considered, though somewhat different:

... why may not one violate persons for the greater social good? Individually, we each sometimes choose to undergo some pain or sacrifice for a greater benefit or to avoid a greater harm: we go to the dentist to avoid worse suffering later; we do some unpleasant work for its results; some persons diet to improve their health or looks; some save money to support themselves when they are older. In each case, some cost is borne for the sake of the greater overall good. Why not, *similarly*, hold that some persons have to bear some costs that benefit other persons more, for the sake of the overall social good? But there is no *social entity* with a good that undergoes some sacrifice for its own good. There are only individual people, different individual people, with their own individual lives. Using one of these people for the benefit of others, uses him and benefits the others. Nothing more. What happens is that something is done to him for the sake of others. Talk of an overall social good covers this up. (Intentionally?) To use a person in this way does not sufficiently respect and take account of the fact that he is a separate person, that his is the only life he has. He does not get some overbalancing good from his sacrifice, and no one is entitled to force this upon him ... .[10]

If this passage is interpreted as appealing, in defence of agent-centred restrictions like R, to the disvalue of some features of violations of such restrictions – the feature of disrupting the only life the victim has, for example – then it will of course fail to provide an adequate defence, for the now familiar reasons. But suppose the passage is interpreted instead as suggesting that such restrictions constitute a rational response to the separateness of persons, even if they cannot be defended by appealing to the disvalue of violations. Is this suggestion more adequate? I think not. Though it avoids the fruitless appeal to the disvalue of violations, the proposal is defective for other reasons. The passage suggests that the rationality of agent-centred restrictions like R as a response to the separateness of persons derives from the fact that the violation of such a restriction harms some victim without compensating him for this harm. But the relevance of this fact is unclear. Why does this consideration make rational the view that it is wrong to violate such a restriction even in order to prevent a still greater number of equally weighty violations of the very same restriction? Whether A_1 harms P_1, in our schematic example, or $A_2 \ldots A_6$ harm $P_2 \ldots P_6$, *someone's* separate and distinct life will be violated without compensation. There is no question here of avoiding uncompensated violations altogether. The question instead is: why isn't it at least permissible to disrupt one distinct individual life, without compensation, in order to prevent the uncompensated disruption of five equally distinct lives? It is obviously no answer to this question to simply reiterate that people are distinct, that each has only one life to lead, and that P_1 will not be compensated for the harm he suffers if A_1 violates R. This restatement provides no explanation whatsoever of the impermissibility of A_1's inflicting one uncompensated violation in order to prevent $A_2 \ldots A_6$ from inflicting five similarly uncompensated violations.

The problem with this particular attempt to motivate agent-centred restrictions like R is that it focuses on the possession of some allegedly significant property by the *victims* of violations. But agent-centred restrictions are restrictions which prohibit the victimizing of one person even to prevent the multiple victimization of other people, or comparably objectionable events. As noted in [an earlier chapter], the conceptual distinction to which such restrictions respond is the distinction between what would have the best overall outcome impersonally judged and what a person may permissibly do. And nothing one can say about the features of persons which make it undesirable for them to be victims will be capable of explaining a moral rule whose function is to deny that it is permissible to minimize equally undesirable victimizations. The question is not: what is it about people that makes it objectionable for them to be victimized? But rather: what is it about a person that makes it imper-missible for him to victimize someone else even in order to minimize victimizations which are equally objectionable from an impersonal standpoint?

There is thus a general lesson to be learned from the failure of this particular attempt to motivate agent-centred restrictions like R. The lesson is that proposals to motivate agent-centred restrictions by constru-ing them as a rational response to the possession of some allegedly sig-nificant property by the victims of violations, like proposals to motivate them by appealing to the *disvalue* of violations, are doomed to failure. Indeed, there is strong pressure for proposals of the first sort to collapse into proposals of the second sort. For if one tries to think of agent-centred restrictions as a rational response to the possession of some feature by the victims of violations, then it is natural to suppose, as I did in the last para-graph, that the feature in question must be one in virtue of which it is undesirable for persons to be victimized. And it is then only a short step to the thought that the feature must be one in virtue of which violations are very bad things to have happen: one in virtue of which they have very high disvalue. But whether or not proposals of the first sort do in this way collapse into proposals of the second sort, both types of proposals for motivating agent-centred restrictions fail, and for just the same sorts of reasons. An appeal to the disvalue of violations of such restrictions is powerless to explain why one may not commit one violation in order to prevent more numerous violations, of no less weight from an impersonal standpoint, of the very same restriction, and hence to avert an outcome with higher disvalue. An appeal to the victims' possession of some prop-erty is powerless to explain why one may not victimize one person with the feature in order to prevent the victimization of still more people with the very same feature. In each case, the appeal is to a consideration that simply makes all violations of the restrictions seem equally objectionable, and which thus appears to militate in favour of permitting, rather than prohibiting, the minimization of total overall violations. So, if there is to be an adequate rationale for agent-centred restrictions, it cannot take the form of an appeal to the victims' possession of some property, any more than it can take the form of an appeal to the disvalue of violations.

Notes

1   *Anarchy, State, and Utopia* (New York: Basic Books, 1974), p. 30. 'Side con-straint' is Nozick's term for the kind of agent-centred restriction he favours.

2   There is, however, an important qualification that must be made at this point. It is true that I am taking R to be a restriction against nothing more specific than 'harming some undeserving person'. And it is true that every fully agent-centred view which has any degree of plausibility does include restrictions which answer to that description. But it is also true that most such conceptions also take there to be other sorts of agent-centred restrictions as well. Thus, according to most such conceptions, we are at least sometimes obligated to keep our promises even if we could produce a better overall outcome by not doing so. And it is also typically held that we have special obligations to protect and promote the interests of people to whom we stand in certain special relations, to our parents, children, spouses, patients, students, and so on, and that these obligations may not be violated whenever a violation would lead to a better overall outcome. Agent-centred restrictions of these two kinds are not most accurately described simply as restrictions against harming.

As I have argued, a hybrid conception, unlike a consequentialist conception, would ordinarily *permit* agents to keep their promises, or to promote the interests of people to whom they stand in special relations, even if by not doing so they could produce better overall outcomes. For a hybrid conception permits people to devote energy and attention to their projects, commitments, and personal relationships out of proportion to the weight from an impersonal standpoint of their doing so. And, as I have also argued, a hybrid conception might additionally require agents to keep their promises and fulfil their voluntarily incurred special obligations *unless* their not doing so would result in a better overall outcome. But fully agent-centred conceptions obviously go further, maintaining that there are times when promises must be kept and obligations fulfilled *even if* failure to do so would result in a better overall outcome.

Now in my discussion of possible rationales for agent-centred restrictions, I will, as I have said, be treating a restriction R against harming some undeserving person as my paradigm case of such restrictions. But although some of the arguments I will offer will be in criticism of supposed rationales for agent-centred restrictions like R in particular, I will also offer a number of arguments in criticism of supposed rationales for agent-centred restrictions in general, and, as a result, a number of perfectly general arguments about the form that a rationale for *any* kind of agent-centred restriction must take. It is true, however, that I will not directly discuss any specific proposals that might be made for motivating *only* those agent-centred restrictions which prohibit the breaking of one's promises or the neglect of one's special obligations. And, strictly speaking, this leaves it open to a defender of a fully agent-centred outlook to maintain that those restrictions have a rationale of the appropriate form which is independent of any putative rationale for restrictions like R, and which remains compelling even if doubt is cast on the strength of supposed general rationales for agent-centred restrictions, and on the strength of specific rationales for agent-centred restrictions against harming in particular.

3   Consider Ivan Karamazov's challenge to his brother Alyosha in Dostoevsky's novel:

> Tell me yourself, I challenge you – answer. Imagine that you are creating a fabric of human destiny with the object of making men happy in the end, giving them peace and rest at last. Imagine that you arc doing this but that it is essential and inevitable to torture to death only one tiny creature – that child beating its breast with its fist, for instance – in order to found that edifice on its unavenged tears. Would you consent to be the architect on those conditions? Tell me. Tell the truth.
>
> (*The Brothers Karamazov* [New York: New American Library, 1957], p. 226)

Ivan's question does not constitute a sufficient test for absolutism. In order to be an absolutist, it is not enough to hold that it would be impermissible to torture one child to death even if that would produce universal happiness. One must also hold that it would be impermissible to torture one child to death even if that were the only way to prevent, say, everyone else in the world's being tortured to death.

4   There is one kind of possible answer to this question that I will not even consider: the kind of answer that might be given by defenders of rule-consequentialism, act-and-motive consequentialism, or other such views. For an elaboration of this point, see note 7 of this chapter.

5   Compare T. Nagel:

> . . . the constraints on action represented by rights cannot be equivalent to an assignment of large disvalue to their violation, for that would make it permissible to violate such a right if by doing so one could prevent more numerous or more serious violations of the same right by others. This is not in general true. It is not permissible . . . to kill an innocent person even to prevent the deliberate killing of three other innocent persons. A general feature of anything worthy of being called a right is that it is not translatable into a mere assignment of disvalue to its violation. ('Libertarianism Without Foundations', *Yale Law Review* 85 [1975], at p. 144)

6   *Anarchy, State, and Utopia*, pp. 30–1.

7   Remember that, in speaking of consequentialist presumptions and dispensations, I am referring to the strategic manoeuvres available to the standard act-consequentialist. As I noted in [an earlier chapter], defenders of other forms of consequentialism might argue in favour of some other kind of dispensation which represented a departure from strict act-consequentialism. Now it is also true that some rule-consequentialists, or act-and-motive consequentialists, might try to defend something stronger than an act-consequentialist presumption against performing the acts which agent-centred restrictions forbid. Some might go so far as to say that, depending on how our schematic example was filled out, with regard to such things as the motives of A_2 . . .

A_6, it might indeed be wrong for A_1 to violate R. Others who insisted that it would be right for A_1 to violate R might nevertheless add that there are good, broadly consequentialist reasons for agents not to be disposed to do the right thing in such cases. As I have repeatedly emphasized, I am limiting my discussion of consequentialism in this book to act-consequentialism, so I will not attempt to assess the merits of any broadly consequentialist arguments for the view that A_1 ought not to violate R, or that A_1 ought to be disposed not to violate R even if violating R is what he really ought to do. What I am trying to determine is whether or not traditional deontological views are correct to maintain, as I believe they do maintain, that just as there is a rationale for an agent-centred prerogative which is independent of even broadly consequentialist considerations, so too there is a rationale for agent-centred restrictions which is independent of even broadly consequentialist considerations.

8   This passage calls to mind a kind of moral conception of which I have not yet taken note. The non-consequentialist conceptions I have been discussing depart from consequentialism either by incorporating an agent-centred prerogative alone, or an agent-centred prerogative *and* agent-centred restrictions. Non-consequentialist conceptions of the second type, which I have been calling 'fully-agent centred' conceptions, include two kinds of permissions not to produce the best states of affairs: those conferred by the prerogative and those entailed by the restrictions. As this passage suggests, however, one can imagine moral conceptions that did include agent-centred restrictions but that did not include any permissions not to produce the best states of affairs *except* those entailed by the restrictions.

9   The argument of the last three paragraphs has been intended in a very general way as a response to the account given by Thomas Nagel, in his Tanner Lectures, of the foundations of deontological moral conceptions. Those lectures have been published, with the overall title 'The Limits of Objectivity', in *The Tanner Lectures on Human Values I*, Sterling McMurrin, ed. (University of Utah Press and Cambridge University Press, 1980): 77–139. See especially pp. 126–39.

10   *Anarchy, State, and Utopia*, pp. 32–3.

8

From *Reasons and Persons*

Derek Parfit

10. How Consequentialism is Indirectly Self-defeating

Most of my claims could, with little change, cover one group of moral theories. These are the different versions of *Consequentialism*, or *C*. C's *central claim* is

> (C1)   There is one ultimate moral aim: that outcomes be as good as possible.

C applies to everything. Applied to acts, C claims both

> (C2)   What each of us ought to do is whatever would make the outcome best, and
>
> (C3)   If someone does what he believes will make the outcome worse, he is acting wrongly.

I distinguished between what we have most reason to do, and what it would be rational for us to do, given what we believe, or ought to believe. We must now distinguish between what is *objectively* and *subjectively* right or wrong. This distinction has nothing to do with whether moral theories can be objectively true. The distinction is between what some theory implies, given (i) what are or would have been the effects of what some person does or could have done, and (ii) what this person believes, or ought to believe, about these effects.

Derek Parfit, *Reasons and Persons* (Oxford: Oxford University Press, 1984), pp. 24–43.

It may help to mention a similar distinction. The medical treatment that is objectively right is the one that would in fact be best for the patient. The treatment that is subjectively right is the one that, given the medical evidence, it would be most rational for the doctor to prescribe. As this example shows, what it would be best to know is what is objectively right. The central part of a moral theory answers this question. We need an account of subjective rightness for two reasons. We often do not know what the effects of our acts would be. And we ought to be blamed for doing what is subjectively wrong. We ought to be blamed for such acts even if they are objectively right. A doctor should be blamed for doing what was very likely to kill his patient, even if his act in fact saves this patient's life.

In most of what follows, I shall use *right, ought, good,* and *bad* in the objective sense. But *wrong* will usually mean *subjectively* wrong, or *blameworthy*. Which sense I mean will often be obvious given the context. Thus it is clear that, of the claims given above, (C2) is about what we ought objectively to do, and (C3) is about what is subjectively wrong.

To cover risky cases, C claims

(C4)   What we ought subjectively to do is the act whose outcome has the greatest *expected* goodness.

In calculating the expected goodness of an act's outcome, the value of each possible good effect is multiplied by the chance that the act will produce it. The same is done with the disvalue of each possible bad effect. The expected goodness of the outcome is the sum of these values minus these disvalues. Suppose, for example, that if I go West I have a chance of 1 in 4 of saving 100 lives, and a chance of 3 in 4 of saving 20 lives. The expected goodness of my going West, valued in terms of the number of lives saved, is $100 \times 1/4 + 20 \times 3/4$, or $25 + 15$, or 40. Suppose next that, if I go East, I shall certainly save 30 lives. The expected goodness of my going East is 30×1, or 30. According to (C4), I ought to go West, since the expected number of lives saved would be greater.

Consequentialism covers, not just acts and outcomes, but also desires, dispositions, beliefs, emotions, the colour of our eyes, the climate, and everything else. More exactly, C covers anything that could make outcomes better or worse. According to C, the best possible climate is the one that would make outcomes best. I shall again use 'motives' to cover both desires and dispositions. C claims

(C5)   The best possible motives are those of which it is true that, if we have them, the outcome will be best.

As before, 'possible' means 'causally possible'. And there would be many different sets of motives that would be in this sense best: there would be no other possible set of motives of which it would be true that, if we had this set, the outcome would be better. I have described some of the ways in which we can change our motives. (C2) implies that we ought to try to cause ourselves to have, or to keep, any of the best possible sets of motives. More generally, we ought to change both ourselves, and anything else, in any way that would make the outcome better. If we believe that we could make such a change, (C3) implies that failing to do so would be wrong.[1]

To apply C, we must ask what makes outcomes better or worse. The simplest answer is given by *Utilitarianism*. This theory combines C with the following claim: the best outcome is the one that gives to people the greatest net sum of benefits minus burdens, or, on the Hedonistic version of this claim, the greatest net sum of happiness minus misery.

There are many other versions of C. These can be *pluralist* theories, appealing to several different principles about what makes outcomes better or worse. Thus, one version of C appeals both to the Utilitarian claim and to the Principle of Equality. This principle claims that it is bad if, through no fault of theirs, some people are worse off than others. On this version of C, the goodness of an outcome depends both on how great the net sum of benefits would be, and on how equally the benefits and burdens would be distributed between different people. One of two outcomes might be better, though it involved a smaller sum of benefits, because these benefits would be shared more equally.

A Consequentialist could appeal to many other principles. According to three such principles, it is bad if people are deceived, coerced, and betrayed. And some of these principles may essentially refer to past events. Two such principles appeal to past entitlements, and to just deserts. The Principle of Equality may claim that people should receive equal shares, not at particular times, but in the whole of their lives. If it makes this claim, this principle essentially refers to past events. If our moral theory contains such principles, we are not concerned only with *consequences* in the narrow sense: with what happens *after* we act. But we can still be, in a wider sense, Consequentialists. In this wider sense our ultimate moral aim is, not that outcomes be as good as possible, but that history go as well as possible. What I say below could be restated in these terms.

With the word 'Consequentialism', and the letter 'C', I shall refer to all these different theories. As with the different theories about self-interest, it would take at least a book to decide between these different versions of C. This book [*Reasons and Persons*] does not discuss this decision. I discuss only what these different versions have in common. My arguments and conclusions would apply to all, or nearly all, the plausible theories of this kind. It is worth emphasizing that, if a Consequentialist appeals to all of the principles I have mentioned, his moral theory is *very* different from Utilitarianism. Since such theories have seldom been discussed, this is easy to forget.

Some have thought that, if Consequentialism appeals to many different principles, it ceases to be a distinctive theory, since it can be made to cover all moral theories. This is a mistake. C appeals only to principles about what makes outcomes better or worse. Thus C might claim that it would be worse if there was more deception or coercion. C would then give to all of us two common aims. We should try to cause it to be true that there is less deception or coercion. Since C gives to all agents common moral aims, I shall call C *agent-neutral.*

Many moral theories do not take this form. These theories are *agent-relative,* giving to different agents different aims. It can be claimed, for example, that each of us should have the aim that *he* does not coerce other people. On this view, it would be wrong for me to coerce other people, even if by doing so I could cause it to be true that there would be less coercion. Similar claims might be made about deceiving or betraying others. On these claims, each person's aim should be, not that there be less deception or betrayal, but that he himself does not deceive or betray others. These claims are not Consequentialist. And these are the kinds of claim that most of us accept. C can appeal to principles about deception and betrayal, but it does not appeal to these principles in their familiar form.

I shall now describe a different way in which some theory T might be self-defeating. Call T

indirectly collectively self-defeating when it is true that, if several people try to achieve their T-given aims, these aims would be worse achieved.

On all or most of its different versions, this may be true of C. C implies that, whenever we can, we should try to do what would make the outcome as good as possible. If we are disposed to act in this way, we are *pure do-gooders.* If we were all pure do-gooders, this might make the outcome worse. This might be true even if we always did what, of the acts that are possible for us, would make the outcome best. The bad effects would come, not from our acts, but from our disposition.

There are many ways in which, if we were all pure do-gooders, this might have bad effects. One is the effect on the sum of happiness. On any plausible version of C, happiness is a large part of what makes outcomes better. Most of our happiness comes from acting on certain strong desires. These include the desires that are involved in loving certain other people, the desire to work well, and most of the strong desires on which we act when we are not working. If we become pure do-gooders, most of our acts would be attempts to make outcomes better, not just in our own community, but in the world as a whole. We would therefore seldom act on these strong desires. It is likely that this would enormously reduce the sum of happiness. This might make the outcome worse, even if we always did what, of the acts that are possible for us, made the outcome best. It might not make the outcome worse than it *actually* is, given what people are actually like. But it would make the outcome worse than it would be, if we were not pure do-gooders, but had certain other causally possible desires and dispositions.

There are several other ways in which, if we were all pure do-gooders, this might make the outcome worse. One rests on the fact that, when we want to act in certain ways, we shall be likely to deceive ourselves about the effects of our acts. We shall be likely to believe, falsely, that these acts will produce the best outcome. Consider, for example, killing other people. If we want someone to be dead, it is easy to believe, falsely, that this would make the outcome better. It would therefore make the outcome better if we were strongly disposed not to kill, even when we believe that this would make the outcome better. Our disposition not to kill should give way only when we believe that, by killing, we would make the outcome *very much* better. Similar though weaker claims apply to deception, coercion, and several other kinds of act.[2]

11.   Why C Does Not Fail in its Own Terms

I shall assume that, in these and other ways, C is indirectly collectively self-defeating. If we were all pure do-gooders, the outcome would be worse than it would be if we had certain other sets of motives. If we know this, C tells us that it would be wrong to cause ourselves to be, or to remain, pure do-gooders. Because C makes this claim, it is not failing in its own terms. C does not condemn itself.

This defence of C is like my defence of S ['For each person, there is one supremely rational aim: that his life go, for him, as well as possible']. It is worth pointing out one difference. S is indirectly individually self-defeating when it is true of some person that, if he was never self-denying, this would be worse for him than if he had some other set of desires and dispositions. This would be a bad effect in S's terms. And this bad effect often occurs. There are many people whose lives are going worse because they are never, or very seldom, self-denying. C is indirectly collectively self-defeating when it is true that, if some or all of us were pure do-gooders, this would make the outcome worse than it would be if we had certain other motives. This would be a bad effect in C's terms. But this bad effect may *not* occur. There are few people who are pure do-gooders. Because there are few such people, the fact that they have this disposition may not, on the whole, make the outcome worse.

The bad effect in S's terms often occurs. The bad effect in C's terms may not occur. But this difference does not affect my defence of S and C. Both theories tell us not to have the dispositions that would have these bad effects. This is why S is not, and C would not be, failing in their own terms. It is irrelevant whether these bad effects actually occur.

My defence of C assumes that we can change our dispositions. It may be objected: 'Suppose that we were all pure do-gooders, because we believe C. And suppose that we could not change our dispositions. Our dispositions would have bad effects, in C's terms, and these bad effects would be the result of belief in C. C would here be failing in its own terms.' There was a similar objection to my defence of S. I discuss these objections in [a later Section].

12.   The Ethics of Fantasy

I have assumed that C is indirectly collectively self-defeating. I have assumed that, if we were all pure do-gooders, the outcome would be worse than it would be if we had certain other sets of motives. If this claim is true, C tells us that we should try to have one of these other sets of motives.

Whether this claim is true is in part a factual question. And I would need to say much more if, rather than assuming this claim, I wished to *show* that this claim is true. I shall not try to show this, for three reasons. I believe that this claim is probably true. Rather than arguing about the facts, I believe that it is more worthwhile to discuss what this claim implies. My third reason is that I assume that most of us would not *in fact* become pure do-gooders, even if we became convinced that Consequentialism is the best moral theory.

Because he makes a similar assumption, Mackie calls Act Utilitarianism 'the ethics of fantasy'.[3] Like several other writers, he assumes that we should reject a moral theory if it is in this sense *unrealistically demanding*:

if it is true that, even if we all accepted this theory, most of us would in fact seldom do what this theory claims that we ought to do. Mackie believes that a moral theory is something that we *invent*. If this is so, it is plausible to claim that an acceptable theory cannot be unrealistically demanding. But, on several other views about the nature of morality, this claim is not plausible. We may *hope* that the best theory is not unrealistically demanding. But, on these views, this can only be a hope. We cannot assume that this must be true.

Suppose that I am wrong to assume that C is indirectly collectively self-defeating. Even if this is false, we can plausibly assume that C is unrealistically demanding. Even if it would not make the outcome worse if we were all pure do-gooders, it is probably causally impossible that all or most of us become pure do-gooders.

Though these are quite different assumptions, they have the *same* implication. If it is causally impossible that we become pure do-gooders, C again implies that we ought to try to have one of the best possible sets of motives, in Consequentialist terms. This implication is therefore worth discussing if (1) C is either indirectly self-defeating or unrealistically demanding, or both, and (2) neither of these facts would show that C cannot be the best theory. Though I am not yet convinced that C is the best theory, I believe both (1) and (2).

13.   Collective Consequentialism

It is worth distinguishing C from another form of Consequentialism. As stated so far, C is *individualistic* and concerned with *actual* effects. According to C, *each* of us should try to do what would make the outcome best, *given what others will actually do*. And each of us should try to have one of the possible sets of motives whose effects would be best, given the actual sets of motives that will be had by others. Each of us should ask: Is there some other set of motives that is both possible for *me* and is such that, if *I* had this set, the outcome would be better?' Our answers would depend on what we know, or can predict, about the sets of motives that will be had by others.

What can I predict as I type these words, in January 1983? I know that most of us will continue to have motives much like those that we have now. Most of us will love certain other people, and will have the other strong desires on which most happiness depends. Since I know this, C may tell *me* to try to be a pure do-gooder. This may make the outcome better even though, if we were *all* pure do-gooders, this would make the outcome worse. If most people are *not* pure do-gooders, it may make the outcome better if a few people are. If most people remain as they are now, there will be much suffering, much inequality, and much of most of the other things that make outcomes bad. Much of this suffering I could fairly easily prevent, and I could in other ways do much to make the outcome better. It may therefore make the outcome better if I avoid close personal ties, and cause my other strong desires to become comparatively weaker, so that I can be a pure do-gooder.

If I am lucky, it may not be bad for me to become like this. My life will be stripped of most of the sources of happiness. But one source of happiness is the belief that one is doing good. This belief may give me happiness, making my austere life, not only morally good, but also a good life for me.

I may be less lucky. It may be true that, though I could come close to being a pure do-gooder, this would not be a good life for me. And there may be many other possible lives that would be much better for me. This could be true on most of the plausible theories about self-interest. The demands made on me by C may then seem unfair. Why should *I* be the one who strips his life of most of the sources of happiness? More exactly, why should I be among the few who, according to C, ought to try to do this? Would it not be fairer if we all did more to make outcomes better?

This suggests a form of Consequentialism that is both *collective* and concerned with *ideal* effects. On this theory, each of us should try to have one of the sets of desires and dispositions which is such that, if *everyone* had one of these sets, this would make the outcome better than if everyone had other sets. This statement can be interpreted in several ways, and there are well-known difficulties in removing the ambiguities. Moreover, some versions of this theory are open to strong objections. They tell us to ignore what would in fact happen, in ways that may be disastrous. But Collective Consequentialism, or CC, has much appeal. I shall suggest later how a more complicated theory might keep what is appealing in CC, while avoiding the objections.

CC does not differ from C only in its claims about our desires and dispositions. The two theories disagree about what we ought to do. Consider the question of how much the rich should give to the poor. For most Consequentialists, this question ignores national boundaries. Since I know that most other rich people will give very little, it would be hard for me to deny that it would be better if I gave away almost all my income. Even if I gave nine-tenths, some of my remaining tenth would do more good if spent by the very poor. Consequentialism thus tells me that I ought to give away almost all my income.

Collective Consequentialism is much less demanding. It does not tell me to give the amount that would in fact make the outcome best. It tells me to give the amount which is such that if we *all* gave this amount, the outcome would be best. More exactly, it tells me to give what would be demanded by the particular International Income Tax that would make the outcome best. This tax would be progressive, requiring larger proportions from those who are richer. But the demands made on each person would be much smaller than the demands made by C, on any plausible prediction about the amounts that others will in fact give. It might be best if those as rich as me all give only half their income, or only a quarter. It might be true that, if we all gave more, this would so disrupt our own economies that in the future we would have much less to give. And it might be true that, if we all gave more, our gift would be too large to be absorbed by the economies of the poorer countries.

The difference that I have been discussing arises only within what is called *partial compliance theory*. This is the part of a moral theory that covers cases where we know that some other people will not do what they ought to do. C might require that a few people give away almost all their money, and try to make themselves pure do-gooders. But this would only be because most other people are *not* doing what C claims that they ought to do. They are not giving to the poor the amounts that they ought to give.

In its partial compliance theory, C has been claimed to be excessively demanding. This is not the claim that C is *unrealistically* demanding. As I have said, I believe that this would be no objection. What is claimed is that, in its partial compliance theory, C makes *unfair* or *unreasonable* demands. This objection may not apply to C's *full compliance theory*. C would be much less demanding if we *all* had one of the possible sets of motives that, according to C, we ought to try to cause ourselves to have.[4]

14.   Blameless Wrongdoing

Though C is indirectly self-defeating, it is not failing in its own terms. But it may seem open to other objections. These are like those I raised when discussing S. Suppose that we all believe C, and all have sets of motives that are among the best possible sets in Consequentialist terms. I have claimed that, at least for most of us, these sets would not include being a pure do-gooder. If we are not pure do-gooders, we shall sometimes do what we believe will make the outcome worse. According to C, we shall then be acting wrongly.

Here is one example. Most of the best possible sets of motives would include strong love for our children. Suppose that *Clare* has one of these sets of motives. Consider

Clare's Decision. Clare could either give her child some benefit, or give much greater benefits to some unfortunate stranger. Because she loves her child, she benefits him rather than the stranger.

As a Consequentialist, Clare may give moral weight, not just to how much children are benefited, but also to whether they are benefited *by their own parents*. She may believe that parental care and love are intrinsically, or in themselves, part of what makes outcomes better. Even so, Clare may believe that she is doing what makes the outcome worse. She may therefore believe that she is acting wrongly. And this act is quite voluntary. She could avoid doing what she believes to be wrong, if she wanted to. She fails to do so simply because her desire to benefit her child is stronger than her desire to avoid doing what she believes to be wrong.

If someone freely does what she believes to be wrong, she is usually open to serious moral criticism. Ought Clare to regard herself as open to such criticism? As a Consequentialist, she could deny this. Her reply would be like Kate's [in an earlier section] when Kate claimed that she was not irrational. Clare could say: 'I act wrongly because I love my child. But it would be wrong for me to cause myself to lose this love. This bad effect is part of a set of effects that are, on the whole, one of the best possible sets of effects. It would be wrong for me to change my motives so that I would not in future act wrongly in this kind of way. Since this is so, when I do act wrongly in this way, I need not regard *myself* as morally bad. We have seen that there can be rational irrationality. In the same way, there can be *moral immorality*, or *blameless wrongdoing*. In such a case, it is the act and not the agent that is immoral.'

It may again be objected: 'The bad effect that you produced could have been avoided. It is not like the pain that some surgeon cannot help causing when he gives the best possible treatment. The bad effect was the result of a separate and voluntary act. Since it could have been avoided, it cannot be claimed to be part of one of the best possible sets of effects.'

Clare could reply: 'I could have acted differently. But this only means that I *would* have done so if my motives had been different. Given my actual motives, it is causally impossible that I act differently. And, if my motives had been different, this would have made the outcome, on the whole, worse. Since my actual motives are one of the best possible sets, in Consequentialist terms, the bad effects *are*, in the relevant sense, part of one of the best possible sets of effects.'

It may be objected: 'If it is not causally possible that you act differently, given your actual motives, you cannot make claims about what you ought to do. *Ought* implies *can*.'

Kate answered this objection in [an earlier Section]. It cannot be claimed that Clare ought to have acted differently if she could not have done so. This last clause does not mean 'if this would have been causally impossible, given her actual motives'. It means 'if this would have been causally impossible, whatever her motives might have been'.

Like Kate, Clare may be wrong to assume Psychological Determinism. If this is so, her claims can be revised. She should cease to claim that, if she has one of the best possible sets of motives, this will inevitably cause her to do what she believes to be wrong. She could claim instead: 'If I was a pure do-gooder, it would be easy not to do what I believe to be wrong. Since I have another set of motives, it is very hard not to act in this way. And it would be wrong for me to change my motives so that it would be easier not to act in this way. Since this is so, when I act in this way, I am morally bad only in a very weak sense.'

Consider next

The Imagined Case. It might have been true that Clare could either save her child's life, or save the lives of several strangers. Because she loves her child, she would have saved him, and the strangers would have died.

If this had happened, could Clare have made the same claims? The deaths of several strangers would have been a very bad effect. Could Clare have claimed that it was part of one of the best possible sets of effects? The answer may be No. It might have made the outcome better if Clare had not loved her child. This would have been worse for her, and much worse for her child. But she would then have saved the lives of these several strangers. This good effect might have outweighed the bad effects, making the outcome, on the whole, better.

If this is so, Clare could have said: 'I had no reason to believe that my love for my child would have this very bad effect. It was subjectively right for me to allow myself to love my child. And causing myself to lose this love would have been blameworthy, or subjectively wrong. When I save my child rather than the strangers, I am acting on a set of motives that it would have been wrong for me to cause myself to lose. This is enough to justify my claim that, when I act in this way, this is a case of blameless wrongdoing.'

A Consequentialist might have claimed: 'When Clare learns that she could save the strangers, it would *not* be subjectively wrong for her to cause herself not to love her child. This would be right, since she would then save the strangers.' Clare could have answered: 'I could not possibly have lost this love with the speed that would have been required. There are ways in which we can change our motives. But, in the case of our deepest motives, this takes a long time. It *would* have been wrong for me to try to lose my love for my child. If I had tried, I would have succeeded only after the strangers had died. After they had died, this change in my motives would have made the outcome worse.'

As this answer shows, Clare's claims essentially appeal to certain factual assumptions. It might have been true that, if she had the disposition of a pure do-gooder, this would on the whole have made the outcome better. But we are assuming that this is false. We are assuming that the outcome would be better if Clare has some set of motives that will sometimes cause her to choose to do what she believes will make the outcome worse. And we are assuming that her actual set of motives is one of the best possible sets.

We could imagine other motives that would have made the outcome even better. But such motives are not causally possible, given the facts about human nature. Since Clare loves her child, she would have saved him rather than several strangers. We could imagine that our love for our children would 'switch off' whenever other people's lives are at stake. It might be true that, if we all had this kind of love, this would make the outcome better. If we all gave such priority to saving more lives, there would be few cases when our love for our children would have to switch off. This love could therefore be much as it is now. But it is in fact impossible that our love could be like this. We could not bring about such 'fine-tuning'. If there is a threat to the life of Clare's child, her love for him could not switch off merely because several strangers are also threatened.[5]

Clare claims that, when she does what she believes will make the outcome worse, she is acting wrongly. But she also claims: 'Because I am acting on a set of motives that it would be wrong for me to lose, these acts are blameless. When I act in this way, I need not regard myself as bad. If Psychological Determinism was not true, I would be bad only in a very weak sense. When I act in this way, I should not feel remorse. Nor should I intend to try not to act in this way again.'

It may now be objected that, since she makes these claims, Clare cannot really *believe* that she is acting wrongly. But there are sufficient grounds for thinking that she does have this belief. Consider the imagined case in which Clare saves her child rather than several strangers. Though she loves her child, Clare would not have believed that his death would be a worse outcome than the deaths of the several strangers. His death would have been worse for him and her. But she would have believed that the deaths of several strangers would, on the whole, be much worse. In saving her child rather than the strangers, she would have done what she be-lieves will make the outcome much worse. She would therefore have believed that she is acting wrongly. Her moral theory directly implies this belief. She would also have believed that she should not feel remorse. But her reason for believing this would not have casted doubt on her belief that she is acting wrongly. Her reason would have been that she is acting on a motive – love for her child – that it would have been wrong for her to cause herself to lose. This supports the claim that she deserves no blame, but it does not support the claim that her act is not wrong.

It might be said

(G4)   If someone acts on a motive that he ought to cause himself to have, and that it would be wrong for him to cause himself to lose, he cannot be acting wrongly.

If (G4) was justified, it would support the claim that Clare's act would not have been wrong. And this would support the claim that she cannot really believe that her act would have been wrong. But in Section 16 I describe a case where (G4) is not plausible.

Clare could add that, in many other possible cases, if she believed that her act was wrong, she *would* believe herself to be bad, and she would feel remorse. This would often be so if she did what she believed would make the outcome worse, and she was *not* acting on a set of motives that it would be wrong for her to cause herself to lose. Consequentialism does not in general break the link between the belief that an act is wrong, and blame and remorse. This link is broken only in special cases. We have been discussing one of these kinds of case: those in which someone acts on a motive that it would be wrong for him to cause himself to lose.

There is another kind of case where the link is broken. C applies to everything, including blame and remorse. According to C we ought to blame others, and feel remorse, when this would make the outcome better. This would be so when blame or remorse would cause our motives to change in a way that would make the outcome better. This would not be true when, like Clare, we have one of the best possible sets of motives. And it might not be true even when we do not have such motives. If we are blamed too often, blame may be less effective. C may thus imply that, even if we do not have one of the best sets of motives, we should be blamed only for acts that we believe will make the outcome *much* worse.

15. Could it be Impossible to Avoid Acting Wrongly?

Clare's claims imply that she cannot avoid doing what she believes to be wrong. She might say: 'It is not causally possible *both* that I have one of the best possible sets of motives, *and* that I never do what I believe to be wrong. If I was a pure do-gooder, my ordinary acts would never be wrong. But I would be acting wrongly in allowing myself to remain a pure do-gooder. If instead I cause myself to have one of the best possible sets of motives, as I ought to do, I would then sometimes do what I believe to be wrong. If I do not have the disposition of a pure do-gooder, it is not causally possible that I *always* act like a pure do-gooder, never doing what I believe to be wrong. Since this is not causally possible, and it would be wrong for me to cause myself to be a pure do-gooder, I cannot be morally criticised for failing always to act like a pure do-gooder.'

It may now be said that, as described by Clare, C lacks one of the essential features of any moral theory. It may be objected: 'No theory can demand what is impossible. Since we cannot avoid doing what C claims to be wrong, we cannot always do what C claims that we ought to do. We should therefore reject C. As before, *ought* implies *can*.'

This objection applies even if we deny Psychological Determinism. Suppose that Clare had saved her child rather than several strangers. She would have acted in this way because she does not have the disposition of a pure do-gooder. Her love for her child would have been stronger than her desire to avoid doing what she believes to be wrong. If we deny Determinism, we shall deny that, in this case, it would have been causally impossible for Clare to avoid doing what she believes to be wrong. By an effort of will, she could have acted against her strongest desire. Even if we claim this, we cannot claim that Clare could *always* act like a pure do-gooder *without* having a pure do-gooder's disposition. Even those who deny Determinism cannot completely break the link between our acts and our dispositions.

If we cannot always act like pure do-gooders, without having a pure do-gooder's disposition, the objection given above still applies. Even if we deny Determinism, we must admit the following. We are assuming that we believe truly that the outcome would be worse if we were all pure do-gooders. If we have this belief, it is not possible that we never do what we believe will make the outcome worse. If we cause ourselves to be, or allow ourselves to remain, pure do-gooders, we are thereby doing what we believe will make the outcome worse. If instead we have other desires and dispositions, it is not possible that we always act like pure do-gooders, never doing what we believe will make the outcome worse. The objector can therefore say: 'Even if Determinism is not true, it is not possible that we never do what we believe will make the outcome worse. In claiming that we ought never to act in this way, C is demanding what is impossible. Since ought implies can, C's claim is indefensible.'

Clare could answer: 'In most cases, when someone acts wrongly, he deserves to be blamed, and should feel remorse. This is what is most plausible in the doctrine that ought implies can. It is hard to believe that there could be cases where, *whatever* someone does, or might have earlier done, he deserves to be blamed, and should feel remorse. It is hard to believe that it could be impossible for someone to avoid acting in a way that deserves to be blamed. C does *not* imply this belief. If I saved my child rather than several strangers, I would believe that I am doing what will make the outcome much worse. I would therefore believe that I am acting wrongly. But this would be a case of *blameless* wrongdoing. According to C, we *can* always avoid doing *what deserves to be blamed*. This is enough to satisfy the doctrine that ought implies can.'

We may believe that these claims do not sufficiently meet this objection. There was a similar objection to S. It is impossible that we never do what S claims to be irrational. I began to meet that objection by appealing to the case in [an earlier Section]: Schelling's Answer to Armed Robbery. In this case, on any plausible theory about rationality, I could not avoid acting irrationally. To meet the objection to C, Clare might appeal to other cases where we cannot avoid acting wrongly. That there are such cases has been claimed by some of the writers who are most opposed to C.[6]

16.   Could it be Right to Cause Oneself to Act Wrongly?

Since C is indirectly self-defeating, it tells us to cause ourselves to do, or to be more likely to do, what it claims to be morally wrong. This is not a defect in C's terms. We can ask a question like the one I asked about the Self-interest Theory. C gives us one substantive moral aim: that history go as well as possible. Does it also give us a second substantive aim: that we never act wrongly? On the best known form of C, Utilitarianism, the answer is No. For Utilitarians, avoiding wrong-doing is a mere means to the achievement of the one substantive moral aim. It is not itself a substantive aim. And this could also be claimed on the versions of C that judge the goodness of outcomes in terms not of one but of several moral principles. It might be claimed, for instance, by the theory that appeals both to the Utilitarian claim and to the Principle of Equality. All these theories give us the *formal* aim of acting morally, and avoiding wrong-doing. But these theories could all claim that this formal aim is not part of our substantive moral aim.

Though this claim might be made by any Consequentialist, it would not be made on several other moral theories. On these theories, the avoidance of wrong-doing is itself a substantive moral aim. If we accept one of these theories, we may object to C in at least two ways. We may say, 'An acceptable theory cannot treat acting morally as a mere means.' We may also say, 'An acceptable theory cannot tell us to cause ourselves to do what this theory itself claims to be wrong.'

We should ask whether, if we raise this objection, we ourselves believe that the acts in question would be wrong. We are considering cases where a Consequentialist believes that, though he is acting wrongly, he is not morally bad, because he is acting on motives that it would be wrong for him to cause himself to lose. In such cases, do we ourselves believe that this Consequentialist is acting wrongly?

This is unlikely in the imagined case where Clare saves her child rather than several strangers. If we are not Consequentialists, we shall be likely to believe that Clare's act would not have been wrong. We may think the same about some of the other cases of this kind. Suppose that Clare refrains from killing me, though she has the true belief that killing me would make the outcome better. Clare would think that, in refraining from killing me, she would be acting wrongly. But she would regard this as a case of blameless wrongdoing. She acts wrongly because she is strongly disposed not to kill, and, for the reason given at the end of Section 10, she believes that this is a disposition that it would be wrong for her to cause herself to lose. We may again believe that, in refraining from killing me, Clare is *not* acting wrongly.

If this is what we believe about these cases, it is less clear that we should object to this part of C. We accept C's claim that, in these cases, Clare would not show herself to be morally bad, or deserve to be blamed. Over this there is no disagreement. We may object to C's claim that, though Clare is blameless, her acts would be wrong. But perhaps we should not object to this claim, if it does not have its usual implications.

We may still object that an acceptable moral theory cannot tell us to cause ourselves to do what this theory claims to be wrong. But consider

My Moral Corruption. Suppose that I have some public career that would be wrecked if I was involved in a scandal. I have an enemy, a criminal whom I exposed. This enemy, now released, wants revenge. Rather than simply injuring me, he decides to force me to corrupt myself, knowing that I shall think this worse than most injuries. He threatens that either he or some member of his gang will kill all my children, unless I act in some obscene way, that he will film. If he later sent this film to some journalist, my career would be wrecked. He will thus be able later, by threatening to wreck my career, to cause me to choose to act wrongly. He will cause me to choose to help him commit various minor crimes. Though I am morally as good as most people, I am not a saint. I would not act very wrongly merely to save my career; but I would help my enemy to commit minor crimes. I would here be acting wrongly even given the fact that, if I refuse to help my enemy, my career would be wrecked. We can next suppose that, since I know my enemy well, I have good reason to believe both that, if I refuse to let him make his film, my children will be killed, and to believe that, if I do not refuse, they will not be killed.

I ought to let this man make his film. We can plausibly claim that *governments* should not give in to such threats, because this would merely expose them to later threats. But such a claim would not cover this threat made to me by my enemy. It would be wrong for me to refuse his demand, with the foreseen result that my children are killed. I ought to let him make his film, even though I know that the effect will be that I shall later often act wrongly. After my children are freed, I shall often, to save my career, help my enemy commit minor crimes. These later acts will be quite voluntary. I cannot claim that my enemy's later threats force me to act in these ways. I could refuse to act wrongly, even though this would wreck my career.

I have claimed that I ought to let this man make his film. This would be agreed even by most of those who reject Consequentialism. These people would agree that, since it is the only way to save my children's lives, I ought to cause it to be true that I shall later often act wrongly. These people thus believe that an acceptable moral theory *can* tell someone to cause himself to do what this theory claims to be wrong. Since they believe this, they cannot object to Consequentialism that it can have this implication.

If I let my enemy make his film, I would become disposed to help him commit minor crimes. Let us now add some features to this case. I could cause myself to lose this disposition, by abandoning my career. But my enemy has threatened that, if I abandon my career, his gang will kill my children. It would therefore be wrong for me to cause myself to lose this disposition. In contrast, if I refuse to help my enemy commit his crimes, he will merely wreck my career, by sending to some journalist the film in which I act obscenely. My enemy assures me that, if he wrecks my career, my children will not be killed. He gets perverse pleasure from causing me to do what I believe to be wrong, by threatening to wreck my career. This pleasure would be lost if his threat was to kill my children. If I help him to commit his crimes because this is the only way to save my children's lives, I would not believe that I was acting wrongly. Since my enemy wants me to believe that I am acting wrongly, he does not make *this* threat.

Knowing my enemy, I have good reason to believe what he says. Since it is the only way to save my children's lives, I ought to let him make his film. I ought to make myself disposed to help him commit his minor crimes. And it would be wrong for me to cause myself to lose this disposition, since, if I do, my children will be killed. But, when I act on this disposition, I am acting wrongly. I ought not to help this man to commit his crimes, merely in order to save my career.

This case shows that we should reject what I called (G4). This is the claim that, if I ought to cause myself to have some disposition, and it would be wrong for me to cause myself to lose this disposition, I cannot be acting wrongly when I act upon this disposition. In the case just described, when I act on such a disposition, I *am* acting wrongly.

I shall now state together four similar mistakes. Some people claim that, if it is rational for me to cause myself to have some disposition, it cannot be irrational to act upon this disposition. This was shown to be false by the case I called *Schelling's Answer to Armed Robbery*. A second claim is that, if it is rational for me to cause myself to believe that some act is rational, this act *is* rational. This was shown to be false by the case that I called *My Slavery*. A third claim is that, if there is some disposition that I ought to cause myself to have, and that it would be wrong for me to cause myself to lose, it cannot be wrong for me to act upon this disposition. The case just given shows this to be false. A fourth claim is that, if I ought to cause myself to believe that some act would not be wrong, this act cannot be wrong. In Section 18 I show that this is false. These four claims assume that rationality and rightness can be *inherited*, or *transferred*.

If it is rational or right for me either to cause myself to be disposed to act in some way, or to make myself believe that this act is rational or right, this act *is* rational or right. My examples show that this is not so. Rationality and rightness cannot be inherited in this way. In this respect the truth is simpler than these claims imply. These claims cannot show that, if we believe some act to be irrational or wrong, we are making a mistake.

17.   How C Might be Self-effacing

It might be claimed that, if Consequentialism sometimes breaks the link between the belief that our act is wrong and the belief that we are bad, we would not in fact continue to regard morality with sufficient seriousness. Our desire to avoid wrongdoing may be undermined if we have other desires which are often stronger. This desire may survive only if we believe that it should *always* be overriding, and feel remorse when it is not. It might be claimed, on these or other grounds, that it would make the outcome better if we always keep the link between our moral beliefs and our intentions and emotions. If this is so, it would make the outcome better if we did not believe C.

I doubt these claims. But it is worth considering what they would imply. According to C, each of us should try to have one of the best possible sets of desires and dispositions, in Consequentialist terms. It might make the outcome better if we did not merely have these desires and dispositions, but had corresponding moral emotions and beliefs.

Consider, for example, theft. On some versions of C, it is intrinsically bad if property is stolen. On other versions of C, this is not so. On these versions, theft is bad only when it makes the outcome worse. Avoiding theft is not part of the ultimate moral aim given to us by C. It might be true that it would make the outcome better if we are strongly disposed not to steal. And it might make the outcome better if we believed stealing to be intrinsically wrong, and would feel remorse when we do steal. Similar claims might be made about many other kinds of act.

If these claims are true, C would be self-effacing. It would tell us that we should try to believe, not itself, but some other theory. We should try to believe the theory which is such that, if we believe it, the outcome would be best. On the claims made above, this theory might not be C. It might be some version of what Sidgwick called *Common-Sense Morality*.

If C told us to believe some version of this morality, this would not be Common-Sense Morality as it is now, but an improved version. Common-

Sense Morality is *not* the moral theory belief in which would make the outcome best. Such a theory would, for example, demand much more from the rich. It might make the outcome best if those in the richer nations gave to the poor at least a quarter or even half of their incomes every year. The rich now give, and seem to believe that they are justified in giving, less than one per cent.

Suppose that C told us to believe some other theory. As I have said, it would be hard to change our beliefs, if our reason for doing so is not a reason which casts doubt on our old beliefs, but is merely that it would have good effects if we had different beliefs. But there are various ways in which we might bring about this change. Perhaps we could all be hypnotized, and the next generation brought up differently. We would have to be made to forget how and why we acquired our new beliefs, and the process would have to be hidden from future historians.

It would make a difference here if we accept, not C, but Collective Consequentialism. If we accept C, we might conclude that C ought to be rejected by most people, but should still be believed by a few. Our theory would then be partly self-effacing, and partly *esoteric*, telling those who believe it not to enlighten the ignorant majority. On Collective Consequentialism, we ought to believe the moral theory which is such that, if we *all* believe it, the outcome would be best. This theory cannot be esoteric.

Some find it especially objectionable that a moral theory might be esoteric. If we believe that deception is morally wrong, deception about morality may seem especially wrong. Sidgwick wrote: 'it seems expedient that the doctrine that esoteric morality is expedient should itself be kept esoteric. Or, if this concealment be difficult to maintain, it may be desirable that Common Sense should repudiate the doctrines which it is expedient to confine to an enlightened few.'[7] This is what Williams calls 'Government House' Consequentialism, since it treats the majority like the natives in a colony.[8] As Williams claims, we cannot welcome such a conclusion. Sidgwick regretted his conclusions, but he did not think regret a ground for doubt.[9]

I have claimed that it is unlikely that C is wholly self-effacing. It would at most be partly self-effacing and partly esoteric. It might make the outcome better if some people do not believe C; but it is unlikely that it would make the outcome better if C was believed by no one.

Here is another ground for doubting this. Suppose that we all come to believe C. (This will seem less implausible when we remember that C can be a pluralist theory, appealing to many different moral principles.) We then decide that C is wholly self-effacing. We decide that it would make the outcome best if we caused ourselves to believe some improved version of Common-Sense Morality. We might succeed in bringing about this change in our beliefs. Given changes in the world, and in our technology, it might later come to be true that the outcome would be better if we revised our moral beliefs. But if we no longer believe C, and now believe some version of Common-Sense Morality, we would not be led to make these needed revisions in our morality. Our reason for believing this morality would not be that we *now* believe it to be the morality belief in which would make the outcome best. This would be why we caused ourselves to believe this morality. But, in order to believe this morality, we must have forgotten that this is what we did. We would now simply believe this morality. We would therefore not be led to revise our morality even if it came to be true that our belief in this morality would increase the chances of some disaster, such as a nuclear war.

These claims should affect our answer to the question whether it would make the outcome better if we all ceased to believe C. We might believe correctly that there is some other moral theory belief in which would, in the short run, make the outcome better. But once Consequentialism has effaced itself, and the cord is cut, the long-term consequences might be much worse.

This suggests that the most that could be true is that C is partly self-effacing. It might be better if most people cause themselves to believe some other theory, by some process of self-deception that, to succeed, must also be forgotten. But, as a precaution, a few people should continue to believe C, and should keep convincing evidence about this self-deception. These people need not live in Government House, or have any other special status. If things went well, the few would do nothing. But if the moral theory believed by most did become disastrous, the few could then produce their evidence. When most people learn that their moral beliefs are the result of self-deception, this would undermine these beliefs, and prevent the disaster.

Though I have claimed that this is unlikely, suppose that C *was* wholly self-effacing. Suppose that it told all of us to make ourselves believe, not itself, but some other theory. Williams claims that, if this is so, the theory ceases to deserve its name, since it 'determines nothing of how thought in the world is conducted'.[10] This claim is puzzling since, as Williams also claims, C would be demanding that the way in which we think about morality, and our set of desires and dispositions, 'must be for the best'.[11] This is demanding something fairly specific, and wholly Consequentialist.

Williams makes the third claim that, if C was wholly self-effacing, it would cease to be effective.[12] This need not be so. Suppose that things happen as described above. We all come to believe in some form of C. We then believe truly that, if we all believed some other theory, this would produce the best possible outcome. C tells us all to believe this other theory. In some indirect way, we cause ourselves to believe this other theory. No one now believes C. This does not justify the claim that C has ceased to be effective. It has had the effect that we all now believe some other particular theory. Because we believe this other theory, this will affect what we do. And our belief in this other theory will produce the best possible outcome. Though no one believes C, C is still effective. There are two continuing facts that are the effects of our earlier belief in C: our new moral beliefs, and the fact that, because we have these beliefs, the outcome is as good as it can possibly be.

Williams rightly claims that, if C was wholly self-effacing, it would not be clear what this shows. We would have to decide whether it showed that this theory 'is unacceptable, or merely that no one ought to accept it.'[13] It is clear that, on our last assumptions, no one ought morally to accept this theory. If anyone does accept this theory, the theory would itself tell him that he ought morally to try to reject the theory, and instead believe some other theory. But, as Williams suggests, there are two questions. It is one question whether some theory is the one that we *ought morally* to try to believe. It is another question whether this is the theory that we *ought intellectually* or *in truth-seeking terms* to believe – whether this theory is the true, or best, or best justified theory. I claimed earlier that, if a theory about rationality was self-effacing, this would not show that this theory cannot be the true or the best justified theory. Can we make a similar claim about moral theories?

Our answer to this question will depend in part on our beliefs about the nature of moral reasoning. If a moral theory can be quite straightforwardly *true*, it is clear that, if it is self-effacing, this does not show that it cannot be true. But we may instead regard morality as a social product, either actually or in some 'ideal constructivist' way. We may then claim that, to be acceptable, a moral theory must fulfil what Rawls calls 'the publicity condition': it must be a theory that everyone ought to accept, and publicly acknowledge to each other.[14] On these meta-ethical views, a moral theory cannot be self-effacing. On other views, it can be. It would take at least a book to decide between these different views. I must therefore, in this book, leave this question open. This does not matter if, as I believe, C would *not* be self-effacing.

Notes

1   Cf. Adams.
2   This is argued in Sidgwick, pp. 431–9, and Adams, throughout. Adams discusses what he calls *Act and Motive Utilitarianism*, claiming that Motive Utilitarianism is not just a special case of Act Utilitarianism. A Motive Utilitarian claims that everyone should have the dispositions having which will make the outcome best, even if there is nothing that this person could have done to cause himself to have these dispositions. Adams is right to claim that Motive Utilitarianism is different from Act Utilitarianism, just as Rule Utilitarianism, at least in some versions, is not a special case of Act Utilitarianism. I shall not discuss these distinctions here.
3   Mackie, Ch. 4, Section 2.
4   Collective Consequentialism is not the Cooperative Consequentialism advanced in Regan.
5   Cf. Hare, p. 36.
6   We should first note the sense of 'can' in the doctrine that ought implies can. Suppose it is claimed that, in some case, I ought to have acted in some other way. On the doctrine, I ought to have acted in this other way only if I could have done so. If I could not have acted in this other way, it cannot be claimed that this is what I ought to have done. As I argued in [an earlier section], the claim (1) that I could not have acted in this other way is not the claim (2) that acting in this way would have been impossible, given my actual desires and dispositions. The claim is rather (3) that acting in this way would have been impossible, even if my desires and dispositions had been different. Acting in this way would have been impossible, *whatever* my desires and dispositions might have been.

   We are sometimes right to claim that ought implies can. Suppose that someone believes:

   (A)   It is always wrong to fail to save someone's life.

   Assume that I can either save one life, or save another life, but that I cannot save both. Whichever life I save, I am failing to save someone's life. According to (A), I cannot avoid acting wrongly. I would avoid acting wrongly only if I save both lives, and this is impossible. We can plausibly reject (A) by claiming that ought implies can. I could not save both these lives. This is not the claim that this is not possible, given my actual desires and dispositions. I could not save both these lives, whatever my desires and dispositions were. Since it is in this sense impossible for me to save both lives, it cannot defensibly be claimed that this is what I ought to do, and that in failing to save both lives I am acting wrongly.

   Return now to Consequentialism. C claims that it is wrong for anyone to do what he believes will make the outcome worse. We are assuming that, if we were all pure do-gooders, the outcome would be worse than it would be if we had certain other desires and dispositions. If we believe this, it is impossible that we never do what we believe will make the outcome worse. We shall believe that, if we are pure do-gooders, we have made the outcome worse by causing ourselves to be, or allowing ourselves to remain, pure do-gooders. If we are not pure do-gooders, but have the desires and dispositions that we believe would make the outcome better, it is not possible that we always act like pure do-gooders. It is not possible that we never do what we believe will make the outcome worse. On either of these alternatives, it is impossible that we never act in this way.

Is this impossible in the sense that justifies an appeal to the doctrine that ought implies can? Is it impossible that we never act in this way, whatever our desires and dispositions are, or might have been? This is true, but misleading. It suggests that this impossibility has nothing to do with what our desires and dispositions are. This is not so. This impossibility essentially involves claims about our desires and dispositions. Why is it impossible that we never do what we believe will make the outcome worse? This is impossible because there is only one disposition given which it would be causally possible *never* to do what we believe will make the outcome worse, and causing ourselves to have or to keep this disposition would *itself* be a case of doing what we believe will make the outcome worse. Because this impossibility essentially involves these claims about our desires and dispositions, it is not clear that this is the kind of impossibility that justifies an appeal to the doctrine that ought implies can. It can at least be said that this case is very different from the case where it is impossible for me to save both of a pair of lives. That impossibility had nothing to do with my desires and dispositions. In that case we could plausibly appeal to the doctrine that ought implies can. This does not show that we can plausibly appeal to this doctrine in this very different case. Perhaps we can. But I believe that we cannot support an appeal to this doctrine here by claiming that this appeal is plausible in the case where I cannot save both of a pair of lives. Because they are so different, I believe that case to be irrelevant.

The irrelevance may be denied. If we believe that the outcome would be worse if we were all pure do-gooders, it is impossible that we never do what we believe will make the outcome worse. I have called it misleading to claim that this is impossible whatever our desires and dispositions are, or might have been. This claim suggests, falsely, that this impossibility has nothing to do with our desires and dispositions. But, even if this claim is misleading, it is still true. And this might be claimed to make this case sufficiently similar to that in which I cannot save both of a pair of lives.

Are there any cases where we can deny that ought implies can, even when the impossibility has nothing to do with our desires and dispositions? Some writers claim that there are. Nagel claims that there can be moral tragedies, cases where, whatever someone does, he will be acting wrongly. Nagel admits that, in making his claims, he is denying that *ought* implies *can*. In the cases he describes, someone ought to avoid acting wrongly, though he could not have avoided acting wrongly, whatever his desires and dispositions might have been. It is natural to hope that there cannot be such cases. But Nagel writes, 'it is naive to suppose that there is a solution to every moral problem with which the world can face us'. The world may give us problems to which there is no solution which avoids wrong-doing. (Nagel, p. 79.)

Nagel suggests that there can be such cases because the best moral theory contains *conflicting* principles. He might claim: 'A single moral principle cannot have such implications. If such a principle implies that we cannot avoid wrong-doing, this principle is indefensible.' This claim is plausible when applied to cases like that where I cannot save both of a pair of lives. Principle (A) implies that, in failing to save both lives, I am acting wrongly. The fault here lies in this principle, not in the world.

If it is true that the outcome would be worse if we were all pure do-gooders, Consequentialism implies that we cannot avoid acting wrongly. Though a Consequentialist may appeal to many different moral principles, this particular conclusion is implied by a single principle. It is implied by the claim that it is wrong to do what we believe will make the outcome worse. But, if there can be cases where we cannot avoid acting wrongly, as Nagel claims, the explanation may not have to be that there is a conflict between two different principles. The explanation cannot simply appeal to the fact that it is causally impossible to act in both of two different ways. The explanation must appeal to something deeper – something like the conflict between two different principles. And, in the case we are considering, the explanation may be claimed to be of this kind. There is a conflict, not between two different principles, but between what would be the best set of acts, and what would be the best set of desires and dispositions. We are assuming that it is causally impossible, given the facts about human nature, *both* that we perform the set of acts that would make the outcome best, *and* that we have the desires and dispositions having which would make the outcome best. This kind of conflict may be held to be sufficiently similar to that produced by the conflict between two different principles. And the fault here may be claimed to lie, not in the principle that it is wrong to do what we believe will make the outcome worse, but in the world. A Consequentialist could repeat part of Nagel's claim. He might say: 'It may be true that, if we have the disposition that will enable us never to do what we believe will make the outcome worse, we have made the outcome worse by causing ourselves to have or to keep this very disposition. If this is true, the world has given us a problem to which there is no solution. More exactly there is a solution, but it does not enable us to avoid wrong-doing. There is something that we ought to do, all things considered. We ought to cause ourselves to have, or to keep, one of the sets of desires and dispositions having which will make the outcome better. But, if we do have one of these sets, it is impossible that we never do what we believe will make the outcome worse. If we do what, all things considered, we ought to do, it is impossible that we never act wrongly.'

There is another difference between this case and those discussed by Nagel. He suggests that, in cases where someone cannot avoid acting wrongly, he should be blamed for acting wrongly, and should feel remorse and guilt. This is the claim that conflicts most sharply with the doctrine that ought implies can. As I have said, what is hardest to believe is that, whatever someone does, or might have done, he deserves to be blamed, and should feel remorse and guilt. Consequentialism does not imply this claim. When Clare saves her child rather than the strangers, she deserves no blame, and she should not feel remorse and guilt. Perhaps she should feel what Williams calls *agent-regret*. Perhaps she should have this feeling when she thinks of the dead strangers whom she could have saved. But this feeling is not remorse or guilt.

C does not imply that, whatever Clare does or might have done, she deserves to be blamed, and should feel remorse and guilt. This is what Williams and Nagel claim about agents who face moral tragedies. If we believe that ought implies can, we may reject this claim. But this would not be a reason to reject C, since it does not imply this claim.

If a Consequentialist rejects these remarks, he must revise his moral theory. Suppose that he concedes that, if we could not possibly always avoid doing what we believe will make the outcome worse, it cannot be claimed that this is what we ought always to do. It cannot be claimed that it is always wrong to do what we believe will make the outcome worse. Since it is not possible that we never act in this way, it cannot always be wrong to act in this way. There must be some cases where, though we act in this way, we are not acting wrongly. According to (C3) it is always wrong to do what we believe will make the outcome worse. A Consequentialist might now abandon (C3) and substitute

(C3') We ought always to avoid doing what we believe will make the outcome worse, *if this is possible in a way that does not itself make the outcome worse*. If this is impossible, we ought to avoid doing what we believe will make the outcome worse, whenever we could have acted differently, in a way that would not have made the outcome worse.

As I have argued, 'impossible' does not here mean 'causally impossible, given our actual desires and dispositions'. It might mean 'causally impossible, whatever our desires and dispositions might have been'. If it would make the outcome worse if we were all pure do-gooders, it is causally impossible that we never do what we believe will make the outcome worse. This would have been causally impossible, whatever our desires and dispositions might have been. Since it is causally impossible, in this sense, that we *never* act in this way, (C3') implies that, when we act in this way, we cannot *always* be acting wrongly. If Consequentialism claims (C3') rather than (C3), it takes a revised form that satisfies the doctrine that ought implies can. This revised version of C meets the objection that appeals to this doctrine.

How much difference does it make if C is revised in this way? Suppose that we all accept (C3'), and that we believe truly that the outcome would be worse if we were all pure do-gooders. The outcome would be better if we had one of many other possible sets of desires and dispositions. Assume next that it is causally possible that we cause ourselves to have, or allow ourselves to keep, one of these other sets of desires and dispositions. (Only on this assumption does this objection to C arise.) (C3') implies that we ought to cause ourselves to have, or to keep, one of these other sets of desires and dispositions. Since it is possible to act in either of these ways, (C3') implies that it would be wrong not to do so.

Assume next that we have one of these other sets of desires and dispositions. Because this is true, we often do what we believe will make the outcome worse. (C3') implies that when we act in this way we are acting wrongly whenever we could have acted differently, in a way that would not have made the outcome worse. Would it have been possible that, in all of these cases, we acted differently, in a way that would not have made the outcome worse? We are not here asking whether this would have been causally possible, given our actual desires and dispositions. We are asking whether this would have been possible, if our desires and dispositions had been different. The answer to this question is No. It would not have been possible for us to have acted differently, in *all* of these cases, in a way that would not have made the outcome worse. We could have acted differently, in *all* of these cases, only if we were all pure do-gooders, and this would have made the outcome worse.

We should now ask, 'Could we have acted differently in *some* of these cases, in a way that would not have made the outcome worse?' The answer is Yes. It is impossible that we always act like pure do-gooders without having the disposition of a pure do-gooder. But it would have been possible for us to have sometimes acted in this way, without having this disposition. If Determinism is not true, we could often have acted in this way. (C3') would then imply that, though we are not always acting wrongly when we act in this way, we are often acting wrongly. By substituting (C3') for (C3) a Consequentialist meets the objection that appeals to the doctrine that ought implies can. And this revision does not make much difference.

7   Sidgwick, p. 490.
8   Sen and Williams, p. 16.
9   'Feeling that the deepest truth I have to tell is by no means "good tidings" ... I would not, if I could ... say anything which would make philosophy – my philosophy – popular.' Sidgwick, pp. 395–6.
10 Williams, p. 135.
11 Williams, p. 135, in the same sentence.
12 Sen and Williams, p. 15.

13   Williams, p. 135.
14   Rawls, pp. 133 and 182, especially footnote 31.

References

Adams, R. M., "Motive Utilitarianism," *The Journal of Philosophy* 73 (1976): 467–81.
Hare, R. M., "Ethical Theory and Utilitarianism," in A. Sen and B. Williams, *Utilitarianism and Beyond* (Cambridge: Cambridge University Press, 1982).
Mackie, J. L., *Ethics* (Harmondsworth: Penguin Books, 1977).
Nagel, Thomas, "War and Massacre," *Philosophy and Public Affairs* 1 (1972): 123–44.
Rawls, John, *A Theory of Justice* (Cambridge, MA: Harvard University Press, 1971).
Regan, Donald, *Utilitarianism and Co-operation* (Oxford: Clarendon Press, 1980).
Sen, Amartya and Bernard Williams, *Utilitarianism and Beyond* (Cambridge: Cambridge University Press, 1982).
Sidgwick, Henry, *The Methods of Ethics* (London: Macmillan, 1967).
Williams, Bernard, "A Critique of Utilitarianism," in J. J. C. Smart and B. Williams, *Utilitarianism: For and Against* (Cambridge: Cambridge University Press, 1973).

9

Alienation, Consequentialism, and the Demands of Morality

Peter Railton

Introduction

Living up to the demands of morality may bring with it alienation – from one's personal commitments, from one's feelings or sentiments, from other people, or even from morality itself. In this article I will discuss several apparent instances of such alienation, and attempt a preliminary assessment of their bearing on questions about the acceptability of certain moral theories. Of special concern will be the question whether problems about alienation show consequentialist moral theories to be self-defeating.

I will not attempt a full or general characterization of alienation. Indeed, at a perfectly general level alienation can be characterized only very roughly as a kind of estrangement, distancing, or separateness (not necessarily consciously attended to) resulting in some sort of loss (not necessarily consciously noticed).[1] Rather than seek a general analysis I will rely upon examples to convey a sense of what is involved in the sorts of alienation with which I am concerned. There is nothing in a word, and the phenomena to be discussed below could all be considered while avoiding the controversial term 'alienation.' My sense, however, is that there is some point in using this formidable term, if only to draw attention to commonalities among problems not always noticed. For example, in the final section of this article I will suggest that one important form of alienation in moral practice, the sense that morality confronts us as an

Peter Railton, "Alienation, Consequentialism, and the Demands of Morality," *Philosophy and Public Affairs* 13, 2 (1984): 134–71.

alien set of demands, distant and disconnected from our actual concerns, can be mitigated by dealing with other sorts of alienation morality may induce. Finally, there are historical reasons, which will not be entered into here, for bringing these phenomena under a single label; part of the explanation of their existence lies in the conditions of modern "civil society," and in the philosophical traditions of empiricism and rationalism – which include a certain picture of the self's relation to the world – that have flourished in it.

Let us begin with two examples.

I. John and Anne and Lisa and Helen

To many, John has always seemed a model husband. He almost invariably shows great sensitivity to his wife's needs, and he willingly goes out of his way to meet them. He plainly feels great affection for her. When a friend remarks upon the extraordinary quality of John's concern for his wife, John responds without any self-indulgence or self-congratulation. "I've always thought that people should help each other when they're in a specially good position to do so. I know Anne better than anyone else does, so I know better what she wants and needs. Besides, I have such affection for her that it's no great burden – instead, I get a lot of satisfaction out of it. Just think how awful marriage would be, or life itself, if people didn't take special care of the ones they love." His friend accuses John of being unduly modest, but John's manner convinces him that he is telling the truth: this is really how he feels.

Lisa has gone through a series of disappointments over a short period, and has been profoundly depressed. In the end, however, with the help of others she has emerged from the long night of anxiety and melancholy. Only now is she able to talk openly with friends about her state of mind, and she turns to her oldest friend, Helen, who was a mainstay throughout. She'd like to find a way to thank Helen, since she's only too aware of how much of a burden she's been over these months, how much of a drag and a bore, as she puts it. "You don't have to thank me. Lisa," Helen replies, "you deserved it. It was the least I could do after all you've done for me. We're friends, remember? And we said a long time ago that we'd stick together no matter what. Some day I'll probably ask the same thing of you, and I know you'll come through. What else are friends for?" Lisa wonders whether Helen is saying this simply to avoid creating feelings of guilt, but Helen replies that she means every word – she couldn't bring herself to lie to Lisa if she tried.

II. What's Missing?

What is troubling about the words of John and Helen? Both show stout character and moral awareness. John's remarks have a benevolent, consequentialist cast, while Helen reasons in a deontological language of duties, reciprocity, and respect. They are not self-centered or without feeling. Yet something seems wrong.

The place to look is not so much at what they say as what they don't say. Think, for example, of how John's remarks might sound to his wife. Anne might have hoped that it was, in some ultimate sense, in part for *her* sake and the sake of their love as such that John pays such special attention to her. That he devotes himself to her because of the characteristically good consequences of doing so seems to leave her, and their relationship as such, too far out of the picture – this despite the fact that these characteristically good consequences depend in important ways on his special relation to her. She is being taken into account by John, but it might seem she is justified in being hurt by the way she is being taken into account. It is as if John viewed her, their relationship, and even his own affection for her from a distant, objective point of view – a moral point of view where reasons must be reasons for any rational agent and so must have an impersonal character even when they deal with personal matters. His wife might think a more personal point of view would also be appropriate, a point of view from which "It's my wife" or "It's Anne" would have direct and special relevance, and play an unmediated role in his answer to the question *"Why* do you attend to her so?"

Something similar is missing from Helen's account of why she stood by Lisa. While we understand that the specific duties she feels toward Lisa depend upon particular features of their relationship, still we would not be surprised if Lisa finds Helen's response to her expression of gratitude quite distant, even chilling. We need not question whether she has strong feeling for Lisa, but we may wonder at how that feeling finds expression in Helen's thinking.[2]

John and Helen both show alienation: there would seem to be an estrangement between their affections and their rational, deliberative selves; an abstract and universalizing point of view mediates their reponses to others and to their own sentiments. We should not assume that they have been caught in an uncharacteristic moment of moral reflection or after-the-fact rationalization; it is a settled part of their characters to think and act from a moral point of view. It is as if the world were for them a fabric of obligations and permissions in which personal considerations deserve recognition only to the extent that, and in the way that, such considerations find a place in this fabric.

To call John and Helen alienated from their affections or their intimates is not of itself to condemn them, nor is it to say that they are experiencing any sort of distress. One may be alienated from something without recognizing this as such or suffering in any conscious way from it, much as one may simply be uninterested in something without awareness or conscious suffering. But alienation is not mere lack of interest: John and Helen are not *uninterested* in their affections or in their intimates; rather, their interest takes a certain alienated form. While this alienation may not itself be a psychological affliction, it may be the basis of such afflictions – such as a sense of loneliness or emptiness – or of the loss of certain things of value – such as a sense of belonging or the pleasures of spontaneity. Moreover, their alienation may cause psychological distress in others, and make certain valuable sorts of relationships impossible.

However, we must be on guard lest oversimple categories distort our diagnosis. It seems to me wrong to picture the self as ordinarily divided into cognitive and affective halves, with deliberation and rationality belonging to the first, and sentiments belonging to the second. John's alienation is not a problem on the boundary of naturally given cognitive and affective selves, but a problem partially constituted by the bifurcation of his psyche into these separate spheres. *John*'s deliberative self seems remarkably divorced from his affections, but not all psyches need be so divided. That there is a cognitive element in affection – that affection is not a mere "feeling" that is a given for the deliberative self but rather involves as well certain characteristic modes of thought and perception – is suggested by the difficulty some may have in believing that John really does love Anne if he persistently thinks about her in the way suggested by his remarks. Indeed, his affection for Anne does seem to have been demoted to a mere "feeling." For this reason among others, we should not think of John's alienation from his affections and his alienation from Anne as wholly independent phenomena, the one the cause of the other.[3] Of course, similar remarks apply to Helen.

III.   The Moral Point of View

Perhaps the lives of John and Anne or Helen and Lisa would be happier or fuller if none of the alienation mentioned were present. But is this a problem for *morality*? If, as some have contended, to have a morality is to make normative judgments from a moral point of view and be guided by them, and if by its nature a moral point of view must exclude considerations that lack universality, then any genuinely moral way of going about life would seem liable to produce the sorts of alienation mentioned above.[4] Thus it would be a conceptual confusion to ask that we never be required by morality to go beyond a personal point of view, since to fail ever to look at things from an impersonal (or nonpersonal) point of view would be to fail ever to *be* distinctively moral – not immoralism, perhaps, but amoralism. This would not be to say that there are not other points of view on life worthy of our attention,[5] or that taking a moral point of view is always appropriate – one could say that John and Helen show no moral defect in thinking so impersonally, although they do moralize to excess. But the fact that a particular morality requires us to take an impersonal point of view could not sensibly be held against it, for that would be what makes it a morality at all.

This sort of position strikes me as entirely too complacent. First, we must somehow give an account of practical reasoning that does not merely multiply points of view and divide the self – a more unified account is needed. Second, we must recognize that loving relationships, friendships, group loyalties, and spontaneous actions are among the most important contributors to whatever it is that makes life worthwhile; any moral theory deserving serious consideration must itself give them serious consideration. As William K. Frankena has written, "Morality is made for man, not man for morality."[6] Moral considerations are often supposed to be overriding in practical reasoning. If we were to find that adopting a particular morality led to irreconcilable conflict with central types of human well-being – as cases akin to John's and Helen's have led some to suspect – then this surely would give us good reason to doubt its claims.[7]

For example, in the closing sentences of *A Theory of Justice* John Rawls considers the "perspective of eternity," which is impartial across all individuals and times, and writes that this is a "form of *thought and feeling* that rational persons can adopt in the world." "Purity of heart," he concludes, "would be to see clearly and act with grace and self-command from this point of view."[8] This may or may not be purity of heart, but it could not be the standpoint of actual life without radically detaching the individual from a range of personal concerns and commitments. Presumably we should not read Rawls as recommending that we adopt this point of view in the bulk of our actions in daily life, but the fact that so purely abstracted a perspective is portrayed as a kind of moral ideal should at least start us wondering.[9] If to be more perfectly moral is to ascend ever higher toward *sub specie aeternitatis* abstraction, perhaps we made a mistake in boarding the moral escalator in the first place. Some of the very "weaknesses" that prevent us from achieving this moral ideal – strong attachments to persons or projects – seem to be part of a considerably more compelling human ideal.

Should we say at this point that the lesson is that we should give a more prominent role to the value of non-alienation in our moral reasoning? That would be too little too late: the problem seems to be the way in which morality asks us to look at things, not just the things it asks us to look at.

IV. The "Paradox of Hedonism"

Rather than enter directly into the question whether being moral is a matter of taking a moral point of view and whether there is thus some sort of necessary connection between being moral and being alienated in a way detrimental to human flourishing, I will consider a related problem the solution to which may suggest a way of steering around obstacles to a more direct approach.

One version of the so-called "paradox of hedonism" is that adopting as one's exclusive ultimate end in life the pursuit of maximum happiness may well prevent one from having certain experiences or engaging in certain sorts of relationships or commitments that are among the greatest sources of happiness.[10] The hedonist, looking around him, may discover that some of those who are less concerned with their own happiness than he is, and who view people and projects less instrumentally than he does, actually manage to live happier lives than he despite his dogged pursuit of happiness. The "paradox" is pragmatic, not logical, but it looks deep nonetheless: the hedonist, it would appear, ought not to be a hedonist. It seems, then, as if we have come across a second case in which mediating one's relations to people or projects by a particular point of view – in this case, a hedonistic point of view – may prevent one from attaining the fullest possible realization of sought-after values.

However, it is important to notice that even though adopting a hedonistic life project may tend to interfere with realizing that very project, there is no such natural exclusion between acting for the sake of another or a cause as such and recognizing how important this is to one's happiness. A spouse who acts for the sake of his mate may know full well that this is a source of deep satisfaction for him – in addition to providing him with reasons for acting internal to it, the relationship may also promote the external goal of achieving happiness. Moreover, while the pursuit of happiness may not be the reason he entered or sustains the relationship, he may also recognize that if it had not seemed likely to make him happy he would not have entered it, and that if it proved over time to be inconsistent with his happiness he would consider ending it.

It might be objected that one cannot really regard a person or a project as an end as such if one's commitment is in this way contingent or overridable. But were this so, we would be able to have very few commitments to ends as such. For example, one could not be committed to both one's spouse and one's child as ends as such, since at most one of these commitments could be overriding in cases of conflict. It is easy to confuse the notion of a commitment to an end *as such* (or *for its own sake*) with that of an *overriding* commitment, but strength is not the same as structure. To be committed to an end as such is a matter of (among other things) whether it furnishes one with reasons for acting that are not mediated by other concerns. It does not follow that these reasons must always outweigh whatever opposing reasons one may have, or that one may not at the same time have other, mediating reasons that also incline one to act on behalf of that end.

Actual commitments to ends as such, even when very strong, are subject to various qualifications and contingencies.[11] If a friend grows too predictable or moves off to a different part of the world, or if a planned life project proves less engaging or practical than one had imagined, commitments and affections naturally change. If a relationship were highly vulnerable to the least change, it would be strained to speak of genuine affection rather than, say, infatuation. But if members of a relationship came to believe that they would be better off without it, this ordinarily would be a non-trivial change, and it is not difficult to imagine that their commitment to the relationship might be contingent in this way but nonetheless real. Of course, a relationship involves a shared history and shared expectations as well as momentary experiences, and it is unusual that affection or concern can be changed overnight, or relationships begun or ended at will. Moreover, the sorts of affections and commitments that can play a decisive role in shaping one's life and in making possible the deeper sorts of satisfactions are not those that are easily overridden or subject to constant reassessment or second-guessing. Thus a sensible hedonist would not forever be subjecting his affections or commitments to egoistic calculation, nor would he attempt to break off a relationship or commitment merely because it might seem to him at a given moment that some other arrangement would make him happier. Commitments to others or to causes as such may be very closely linked to the self, and a hedonist who knows what he's about will not be one who turns on his self at the slightest provocation. Contingency is not expendability, and while some commitments are remarkably non-contingent – such as those of parent to child or patriot to country – it cannot be said that commitments of a more contingent sort are never genuine, or never conduce to the profounder sorts of happiness.[12]

Following these observations, we may reduce the force of the "paradox of hedonism" if we distinguish two forms of hedonism. *Subjective hedonism* is the view that one should adopt the hedonistic point of view in action, that is, that one should whenever possible attempt to determine which act seems most likely to contribute optimally to one's happiness, and behave accordingly. *Objective hedonism* is the view that one should follow that course of action which would in fact most contribute to one's happiness, even when this would involve *not* adopting the hedonistic point of view in action. An act will be called *subjectively hedonistic* if it is done from a hedonistic point of view; an act is *objectively hedonistic* if it is that act, of those available to the agent, which would most contribute to his happiness.[13] Let us call someone a *sophisticated hedonist* if he aims to lead an objectively hedonistic life (that is, the happiest life available to him in the circumstances) and yet is not committed to subjective hedonism. Thus, within the limits of what is psychologically possible, a sophisticated hedonist is prepared to eschew the hedonistic point of view whenever taking this point of view conflicts with following an objectively hedonistic course of action. The so-called paradox of hedonism shows that there will be such conflicts: certain acts or courses of action may be objectively hedonistic only if not subjectively hedonistic. When things are put this way, it seems that the sophisticated hedonist faces a problem rather than a paradox: how to act in order to achieve maximum possible happiness if this is at times – or even often – *not* a matter of carrying out hedonistic deliberations.

The answer in any particular case will be complex and contextual – it seems unlikely that any one method of decision making would always promote thought and action most conducive to one's happiness. A sophisticated hedonist might proceed precisely by looking at the complex and contextual: observing the actual modes of thought and action of those people who are in some ways like himself and who seem most happy. If our assumptions are right, he will find that few such individuals are subjective hedonists; instead, they act for the sake of a variety of ends as such. He may then set out to develop in himself the traits of character, ways of thought, types of commitment, and so on, that seem common in happy lives. For example, if he notes that the happiest people often have strong loyalties to friends, he must ask how he can become a more loyal friend – not merely how he can seem to be a loyal friend (since those he has observed are not happy because they merely seem loyal) – but how he can in fact be one.

Could one really make such changes if one had as a goal leading an optimally happy life? The answer seems to me a qualified *yes*, but let us first look at a simpler case. A highly competitive tennis player comes to realize that his obsession with winning is keeping him from playing his best. A pro tells him that if he wants to win he must devote himself more to the game and its play as such and think less about his performance. In the commitment and concentration made possible by this devotion, he is told, lies the secret of successful tennis. So he spends a good deal of time developing an enduring devotion to many aspects of the activity, and finds it peculiarly satisfying to become so absorbed in it. He plays better, and would have given up the program of change if he did not, but he now finds that he plays tennis more for its own sake, enjoying greater internal as well as external rewards from the sport. Such a person would not keep thinking – on or off the court – "No matter how I play, the only thing I really care about is whether I win!" He would recognize such thoughts as self-defeating, as evidence that his old, unhelpful way of looking at things was returning. Nor would such a person be self-deceiving. He need not hide from himself his goal of winning, for this goal is consistent with his increased devotion to the game. His commitment to the activity is not eclipsed by, but made more vivid by, his desire to succeed at it.

The same sort of story might be told about a sophisticated hedonist and friendship. An individual could realize that his instrumental attitude toward his friends prevents him from achieving the fullest happiness friendship affords. He could then attempt to focus more on his friends as such, doing this somewhat deliberately, perhaps, until it comes more naturally. He might then find his friendships improved and himself happier. If he found instead that his relationships were deteriorating or his happiness declining, he would reconsider the idea. None of this need be hidden from himself: the external goal of happiness reinforces the internal goals of his relationships. The sophisticated hedonist's motivational structure should therefore meet a *counterfactual condition*: he need not always act for the sake of happiness, since he may do various things for their own sake or for the sake of others, but he would not act as he does if it were not compatible with his leading an objectively hedonistic life. Of course, a sophisticated hedonist cannot guarantee that he will meet this counterfactual condition, but only attempt to meet it as fully as possible.

Success at tennis is a relatively circumscribed goal, leaving much else about one's life undefined. Maximizing one's happiness, by contrast, seems all-consuming. Could commitments to other ends survive alongside it? Consider an analogy. Ned needs to make a living. More than that, he needs to make as much money as he can – he has expensive tastes, a second marriage, and children reaching college age, and he does not have extensive means. He sets out to invest his money and his labor in ways he thinks will maximize return. Yet it does not follow that he acts as he does solely for the sake of earning as much as possible.[14] Although it is obviously true that he does what he does because he believes that it will maximize return, this does not preclude his doing it for other reasons as well, for example, for the sake of living well or taking care of his children. This may continue to be the case even if Ned comes to want money for its own sake, that is, if he comes to see the accumulation of wealth as intrinsically as well as extrinsically attractive.[15] Similarly, the stricture that one seek the objectively hedonistic life certainly provides one with considerable guidance, but it does not supply the whole of one's motives and goals in action.

My claim that the sophisticated hedonist can escape the paradox of hedonism was, however, qualified. It still seems possible that the happiest sorts of lives ordinarily attainable are those led by people who would reject even sophisticated hedonism, people whose character is such that if they were presented with a choice between two entire lives, one of which contains less total happiness but nonetheless realizes some other values more fully, they might well knowingly choose against maximal happiness. If this were so, it would show that a sophisticated hedonist might have reason for changing his beliefs so that he no longer accepts hedonism in any form. This still would not refute objective hedonism as an account of the (rational, prudential, or moral) *criterion* one's acts should meet, for it would be precisely in order to meet this criterion that the sophisticated hedonist would change his beliefs.[16]

V.   The Place of Non-Alienation Among Human Values

Before discussing the applicability of what has been said about hedonism to morality, we should notice that alienation is not always a bad thing, that we may not want to overcome all forms of alienation, and that other values, which may conflict with non-alienation in particular cases, may at times have a greater claim on us. Let us look at a few such cases.

It has often been argued that a morality of duties and obligations may appropriately come into play in familial or friendly relationships when the relevant sentiments have given out, for instance, when one is exasperated with a friend, when love is tried, and so on.[17] 'Ought' implies 'can' (or, at least, 'could'), and while it may be better in human terms when we do what we ought to do at least in part out of feelings of love, friendship, or sympathy, there are times when we simply cannot muster these sentiments, and the right thing to do is to act as love or friendship or sympathy would have directed rather than refuse to perform any act done merely from a sense of duty.

But we should add a further role for unspontaneous, morally motivated action: even when love or concern is strong, it is often desirable that people achieve some distance from their sentiments or one another. A spouse may act toward his mate in a grossly overprotective way; a friend may indulge another's ultimately destructive tendencies; a parent may favor one child inordinately. Strong and immediate affection may overwhelm one's ability to see what another person actually needs or deserves. In such cases a certain distance between people or between an individual and his sentiments, and an intrusion of moral considerations into the gap thus created, may be a good thing, and part of genuine affection or commitment. The opposite view, that no such mediation is desirable as long as affection is strong, seems to me a piece of romanticism. Concern over alienation therefore ought not to take the form of a cult of "authenticity at any price."

Moreover, there will occur regular conflicts between avoiding alienation and achieving other important individual goals. One such goal is autonomy. Bernard Williams has emphasized that many of us have developed certain "ground projects" that give shape and meaning to our lives, and has drawn attention to the damage an individual may suffer if he is alienated from his ground projects by being forced to look at them as potentially overridable by moral considerations.[18] But against this it may be urged that it is crucial for autonomy that one hold one's commitments up for inspection – even one's ground projects. Our ground projects are often formed in our youth, in a particular family, class, or cultural background. It may be alienating and even disorienting to call these into question, but to fail to do so is to lose autonomy. Of course, autonomy could not sensibly require that we question all of our values and commitments at once, nor need it require us to be forever detached from what we are doing. It is quite possible to submit basic aspects of one's life to scrutiny and arrive at a set of autonomously chosen commitments that form the basis of an integrated life. Indeed, psychological conflicts and practical obstacles give us occasion for reexamining our basic commitments rather more often than we'd like.

At the same time, the tension between autonomy and non-alienation should not be exaggerated. Part of avoiding exaggeration is giving up the Kantian notion that autonomy is a matter of escaping determination by any contingency whatsoever. Part, too, is refusing to conflate autonomy with sheer independence from others. Both Rousseau and Marx emphasized that achieving control over one's own life requires participation in certain sorts of social relations – in fact, relations in which various kinds of alienation have been minimized.

Autonomy is but one value that may enter into complex trade-offs with non-alienation. Alienation and inauthenticity do have their uses. The alienation of some individuals or groups from their milieu may at times be necessary for fundamental social criticism or cultural innovation. And without some degree of inauthenticity, it is doubtful whether civil relations among people could long be maintained. It would take little ingenuity, but too much of the reader's patience, to construct here examples involving troubling conflicts between non-alienation and virtually any other worthy goal.

VI. Reducing Alienation in Morality

Let us now move to morality proper. To do this with any definiteness, we must have a particular morality in mind. For various reasons, I think that the most plausible sort of morality is consequentialist in form, assessing rightness in terms of contribution to the good. In attempting to sketch how we might reduce alienation in moral theory and practice, therefore, I will work within a consequentialist framework (although a number of the arguments I will make could be made, *mutatis mutandis*, by a deontologist).

Of course, one has adopted no morality in particular even in adopting consequentialism unless one says what the good is. Let us, then, dwell briefly on axiology. One mistake of dominant consequentialist theories, I believe, is their failure to see that things other than subjective states can have intrinsic value. Allied to this is a tendency to reduce all intrinsic values to one – happiness. Both of these features of classical utilitarianism reflect forms of alienation. First, in divorcing subjective states from their objective counterparts, and claiming that we seek the latter exclusively for the sake of the former, utilitarianism cuts us off from the world in a way made graphic by examples such as that of the experience machine, a hypothetical device that can be programmed to provide one with whatever subjective states he may desire. The experience machine affords us decisive subjective advantages over actual life: few, if any, in actual life think they have achieved all that they could want, but the machine makes possible for each an existence that he cannot distinguish from such a happy state of affairs.[19] Despite this striking advantage, most rebel at the notion of the experience machine. As Robert Nozick and others have pointed out, it seems to matter to us what we actually *do* and *are* as well as how life *appears* to us.[20] We see the point of our lives as bound up with the world and other people in ways not captured by subjectivism, and our sense of loss in contemplating a life tied to an experience machine, quite literally alienated from the surrounding world, suggests where subjectivism has gone astray. Second, the reduction of all goals to the purely abstract goal of happiness or pleasure, as in hedonistic utilitarianism, treats all other goals instrumentally. Knowledge or friendship may promote happiness, but is it a fair characterization of our commitment to these goals to say that this is the only sense in which they are ultimately valuable? Doesn't the insistence that there is an abstract and uniform goal lying behind all of our ends bespeak an alienation from these particular ends?

Rather than pursue these questions further here, let me suggest an approach to the good that seems to me less hopeless as a way of capturing human value: a pluralistic approach in which several goods are viewed as intrinsically, non-morally valuable – such as happiness, knowledge, purposeful activity, autonomy, solidarity, respect, and beauty.[21] These goods need not be ranked lexically, but may be attributed weights, and the criterion of rightness for an act would be that it must contribute to the weighted sum of these values in the long run. This creates the possibility of trade-offs among values of the kinds discussed in the previous section. However, I will not stop here to develop or defend such an account of the good and the right, since our task is to show how certain problems of alienation that arise in moral contexts might be dealt with if morality is assumed to have such a basis.

Consider, then, Juan, who, like John, has always seemed a model husband. When a friend remarks on the extraordinary concern he shows for his wife, Juan characteristically responds: "I love Linda. I even *like* her. So it means a lot to me to do things for her. After all we've been through, it's almost a part of me to do it." But his friend knows that Juan is a principled individual, and asks Juan how his marriage fits into that larger scheme. After all, he asks, it's fine for Juan and his wife to have such a close relationship, but what about all the other, needier people Juan could help if he broadened his horizon still further? Juan replies, "Look, it's a better world when people can have a relationship like ours – and nobody could if everyone were always asking themselves who's got the most need. It's not easy to make things work in this world, and one of the best things that happens to people is to have a close relationship like ours. You'd make things worse in a hurry if you broke up those close relationships for the sake of some higher goal. Anyhow, I know that you can't always put family first. The world isn't such a wonderful place that it's OK just to retreat into your own little circle. But still, you need that little circle. People get burned out, or lose touch, if they try to save the world by themselves. The ones who can stick with it and do a good job of making things better are usually the ones who can make that fit into a life that does not make them miserable. I haven't met any real saints lately, and I don't trust people who think they *are* saints."

If we contrast Juan with John, we do not find that the one allows moral considerations to enter his personal life while the other does not. Nor do we find that one is less serious in his moral concern. Rather, what Juan recognizes to be morally required is not by its nature incompatible with acting directly for the sake of another. It is important to Juan to subject his life to moral scrutiny – he is not merely slumped when asked for a defense of his acts above a personal level, he does not *just* say "Of course I take care of her, she's my wife!" or "It's Linda" and refuse to listen to the more impersonal considerations raised by his friend. It is consistent with what he says to imagine that his motivational structure has a form akin to that of the sophisticated hedonist, that is, his motivational structure meets a counterfactual condition: while he ordinarily does not do what he does simply for the sake of doing what's right, he would seek to lead a different sort of life if he did not think his were morally defensible. His love is not a romantic submersion in the other to the exclusion of worldly responsibilities, and to that extent it may be said to involve a degree of alienation from Linda. But this does not seem to drain human value from their relationship. Nor need one imagine that Linda would be saddened to hear Juan's words the way Anne might have been saddened to overhear the remarks of John.[22]

Moreover, because of his very willingness to question his life morally, Juan avoids a sort of alienation not sufficiently discussed – alienation from others, beyond one's intimate ties. Individuals who will not or cannot allow questions to arise about what they are doing from a broader perspective are in an important way cut off from their society and the larger world. They may not be troubled by this in any very direct way, but even so they may fail to experience that powerful sense of purpose and meaning that comes from seeing oneself as part of something larger and more enduring than oneself or one's intimate circle. The search for such a sense of purpose and meaning seems to me ubiquitous – surely much of the impulse to religion, to ethnic or regional identification (most strikingly, in the "rediscovery" of such identities), or to institutional loyalty stems from this desire to see ourselves as part of a more general, lasting, and worthwhile scheme of things.[23] This presumably is part of what is meant by saying that secularization has led to a sense of meaninglessness, or that the decline of traditional communities and societies has meant an increase in anomie. (The sophisticated hedonist, too, should take note: one way to gain a firmer sense that one's life is worthwhile, a sense that may be important to realizing various values in one's own life, is to overcome alienation from others.)

Drawing upon our earlier discussion of two kinds of hedonism, let us now distinguish two kinds of consequentialism. *Subjective consequentialism* is the view that whenever one faces a choice of actions, one should attempt to determine which act of those available would most promote the good, and should then try to act accordingly. One is behaving as subjective consequentialism requires – that is, leading a *subjectively consequentialist life* – to the extent that one uses and follows a distinctively consequentialist mode of decision making, consciously aiming at the overall good and conscientiously using the best available information with the greatest possible rigor. *Objective consequentialism* is the view that the criterion of the rightness of an act or course of action is whether it in fact would most promote the good of those acts available to the agent. Subjective consequentialism, like subjective hedonism, is a view that prescribes following a particular mode of deliberation in action; objective consequentialism, like objective hedonism, concerns the outcomes actually brought about, and thus deals with the question of deliberation only in terms of the tendencies of certain forms of decision making to promote appropriate outcomes. Let us reserve the expression *objectively consequentialist act (or life)* for those acts (or that life) of those available to the agent that would bring about the best outcomes.[24] To complete the parallel, let us say that a *sophisticated consequentialist* is someone who has a standing commitment to leading an objectively consequentialist life, but who need not set special stock in any particular form of decision making and therefore does not necessarily seek to lead a subjectively consequentialist life. Juan, it might be argued (if the details were filled in), is a sophisticated consequentialist, since he seems to believe he should act for the best but does not seem to feel it appropriate to bring a consequentialist calculus to bear on his every act.

Is it bizarre, or contradictory, that being a sophisticated consequentialist may involve rejecting subjective consequentialism? After all, doesn't an adherent of subjective consequentialism also seek to lead an objectively consequentialist life? He may, but then he is mistaken in thinking that this means he should always undertake a distinctively consequentialist deliberation when faced with a choice. To see his mistake, we need only consider some examples.

It is well known that in certain emergencies, the best outcome requires action so swift as to preclude consequentialist deliberation. Thus a sophisticated consequentialist has reason to inculcate in himself certain dispositions to act rapidly in obvious emergencies. The disposition is not a mere reflex, but a developed pattern of action deliberately acquired. A simple example, but it should dispel the air of paradox.

Many decisions are too insignificant to warrant consequentialist deliberation ("Which shoelace should I do up first?") or too predictable in outcome ("Should I meet my morning class today as scheduled or should I linger over the newspaper?"). A famous old conundrum for consequentialism falls into a similar category: before I deliberate about an act, it seems I must decide how much time would be optimal to allocate for this deliberation; but then I must first decide how much time would be optimal to allocate for this time-allocation decision; but before that I must decide how much time would be optimal to allocate for *that* decision; and so on. The sophisticated consequentialist can block this paralyzing regress by noting that often the best thing to do is not to ask questions about time allocation at all; instead, he may develop standing dispositions to give more or less time to decisions depending upon their perceived importance, the amount of information available, the predictability of his choice, and so on. I think we all have dispositions of this sort, which account for our patience with some prolonged deliberations but not others.

There are somewhat more intriguing examples that have more to do with psychological interference than mere time efficiency: the timid, put-upon employee who knows that if he deliberates about whether to ask for a raise he will succumb to his timidity and fail to demand what he actually deserves; the self-conscious man who knows that if, at social gatherings, he is forever wondering how he should act, his behavior will be awkward and unnatural, contrary to his goal of acting naturally and appropriately; the tightrope walker who knows he must not reflect on the value of keeping his concentration; and so on. People can learn to avoid certain characteristically self-defeating lines of thought – just as the tennis player in an earlier example learned to avoid thinking constantly about winning – and the sophisticated consequentialist may learn that consequentialist deliberation is in a variety of cases self-defeating, so that other habits of thought should be cultivated.

The sophisticated consequentialist need not be deceiving himself or acting in bad faith when he avoids consequentialist reasoning. He can fully recognize that he is developing the dispositions he does because they are necessary for promoting the good. Of course, he cannot be preoccupied with this fact all the while, but then one cannot be *preoccupied* with anything without this interfering with normal or appropriate patterns of thought and action.

To the list of cases of interference we may add John, whose all-purpose willingness to look at things by subjective consequentialist lights prevents the realization in him and in his relationships with others of values that he would recognize to be crucially important.

Bernard Williams has said that it shows consequentialism to be in grave trouble that it may have to usher itself from the scene as a mode of decision making in a number of important areas of life.[25] Though I think he has exaggerated the extent to which we would have to exclude consequentialist considerations from our lives in order to avoid disastrous results, it is fair to ask: If maximizing the good were in fact to require that consequentialist reasoning be *wholly* excluded, would this refute consequentialism? Imagine an all-knowing demon who controls the fate of the world and who visits unspeakable punishment upon man to the extent that he does not employ a Kantian morality. (Obviously, the demon is not himself a Kantian.) If such a demon existed, sophisticated consequentialists would have reason to convert to Kantianism, perhaps even to make whatever provisions could be made to erase consequentialism from the human memory and prevent any resurgence of it.

Does this possibility show that objective consequentialism is self-defeating? On the contrary, it shows that objective consequentialism has the virtue of not blurring the distinction between the *truth-conditions* of an ethical theory and its *acceptance-conditions* in particular contexts, a distinction philosophers have generally recognized for theories concerning other subject matters. It might be objected that, unlike other theories, ethical theories must meet a condition of publicity, roughly to the effect that it must be possible under all circumstances for us to recognize a true ethical theory as such and to promulgate it publicly without thereby violating that theory itself.[26] Such a condition might be thought to follow from the social nature of morality. But any such condition would be question-begging against consequentialist theories, since it would require that one class of actions – acts of adopting or promulgating an ethical theory – *not* be assessed in terms of their consequences. Moreover, I fail to see how such a condition could emanate from the social character of morality. To prescribe the adoption and promulgation of a mode of decision making regardless of its consequences seems to me radically detached from human concerns, social or otherwise. If it is argued that an ethical theory that fails to meet the publicity requirement could under certain conditions endorse a course of action leading to the abuse and manipulation of man by man, we need only reflect that no psychologically possible decision procedure can guarantee that its widespread adoption could never have such a result. A "consequentialist demon" might increase the amount of abuse and manipulation in the world in direct proportion to the extent that people act according to the categorical imperative. Objective consequentialism (unlike certain deontological theories) has valuable flexibility in permitting us to take consequences into account in assessing the appropriateness of certain modes of decision making, thereby avoiding any sort of self-defeating decision procedure worship.

A further objection is that the lack of any direct link between objective consequentialism and a particular mode of decision making leaves the view too vague to provide adequate guidance in practice. On the contrary, objective consequentialism sets a definite and distinctive criterion of right action, and it becomes an empirical question (though not an easy one) which modes of decision making should be employed and when. It would be a mistake for an objective consequentialist to attempt to tighten the connection between his criterion of rightness and any particular mode of decision making: someone who recommended a particular mode of decision making regardless of consequences would not be a hard-nosed, non-evasive objective consequentialist, but a self-contradicting one.

VII.   Contrasting Approaches

The seeming "indirectness" of objective consequentialism may invite its confusion with familiar indirect consequentialist theories, such as rule-consequentialism. In fact, the subjective/objective distinction cuts across the rule/act distinction, and there are subjective and objective forms of both rule- and act-based theories. Thus far, we have dealt only with subjective and objective forms of act-consequentialism. By contrast, a *subjective rule*-consequentialist holds (roughly) that in deliberation we should always attempt to determine which act, of those available, conforms to that set of rules general acceptance of which would most promote the good; we then should attempt to perform this act. An *objective rule*-consequentialist sets actual conformity to the rules with the highest acceptance value as his criterion of right action, recognizing the possibility that the best set of rules might in some cases – or even always – recommend that one not perform rule-consequentialist deliberation.

Because I believe this last possibility must be taken seriously, I find the objective form of rule-consequentialism more plausible. Ultimately, however, I suspect that rule-consequentialism is untenable in either form, for it could recommend acts that (subjectively or objectively) accord with the best set of rules even when these rules are *not* in fact generally accepted, and when as a result these acts would have devastatingly bad consequences. "Let the rules with greatest acceptance utility be followed, though the heavens fall!" is no more plausible than *"Fiat justitia, ruat coelum!"* – and a good bit less ringing. Hence, the arguments in this article are based entirely upon act-consequentialism.

Indeed, once the subjective/objective distinction has been drawn, an act-consequentialist can capture some of the intuitions that have made rule- or trait-consequentialism appealing.[27] Surely part of the attraction of these indirect consequentialisms is the idea that one should have certain traits of character, or commitments to persons or principles, that are sturdy enough that one would at least sometimes refuse to forsake them even when this refusal is known to conflict with making some gain – perhaps small – in total utility. Unlike his subjective counterpart, the objective act-consequentialist is able to endorse characters and commitments that are sturdy in just this sense.

To see why, let us first return briefly to one of the simple examples of Section VI. A sophisticated act-consequentialist may recognize that if he were to develop a standing disposition to render prompt assistance in emergencies without going through elaborate act-consequentialist deliberation, there would almost certainly be cases in which he would perform acts worse than those he would have performed had he stopped to deliberate, for example, when his prompt action is misguided in a way he would have noticed had he thought the matter through. It may still be right for him to develop this disposition, for without it he would act rightly in emergencies still less often – a quick response is appropriate much more often than not, and it is not practically possible to develop a disposition that would lead one to respond promptly in exactly those cases where this would have the best results. While one can attempt to cultivate dispositions that are responsive to various factors which might indicate whether promptness is of greater importance than further thought, such refinements have their own costs and, given the limits of human resources, even the best cultivated dispositions will sometimes lead one astray. The objective act-consequentialist would thus recommend cultivating dispositions that will sometimes lead him to violate his own criterion of right action. Still, he will not, as a trait-consequentialist would, shift his criterion and say that an act is right if it stems from the traits it would be best overall to have (given the limits of what is humanly achievable, the balance of costs and benefits, and so on). Instead, he continues to believe that an act may stem from the dispositions it would be best to have, and yet be wrong (because it would produce worse consequences than other acts available to the agent in the circumstances).[28]

This line of argument can be extended to patterns of motivation, traits of character, and rules. A sophisticated act-consequentialist should realize that certain goods are reliably attainable – or attainable at all – only if people have well-developed characters; that the human psyche is capable of only so much self-regulation and refinement; and that human perception and reasoning are liable to a host of biases and errors. Therefore, individuals may be more likely to act rightly if they possess certain enduring motivational patterns, character traits, or *prima facie* commitments to rules in addition to whatever commitment they have to act for the best. Because such individuals would not consider consequences in all cases, they would miss a number of opportunities to maximize the good; but if they were instead always to attempt to assess outcomes, the overall result would be worse, for they would act correctly less often.[29]

We may now strengthen the argument to show that the objective act-consequentialist can approve of dispositions, characters, or commitments to rules that are sturdy in the sense mentioned above, that is, that do not merely supplement a commitment to act for the best, but sometimes override it, so that one knowingly does what is contrary to maximizing the good. Consider again Juan and Linda, whom we imagine to have a commuting marriage. They normally get together only every other week, but one week she seems a bit depressed and harried, and so he decides to take an extra trip in order to be with her. If he did not travel, he would save a fairly large sum that he could send OXFAM to dig a well in a drought-stricken village. Even reckoning in Linda's uninterrupted malaise, Juan's guilt, and any ill effects on their relationship, it may be that for Juan to contribute the fare to OXFAM would produce better consequences overall than the unscheduled trip. Let us suppose that Juan knows this, and that he could stay home and write the check if he tried. Still, given Juan's character, he in fact will not try to perform this more beneficial act but will travel to see Linda instead. The objective act-consequentialist will say that Juan performed the wrong act on this occasion. Yet he may also say that if Juan had had a character that would have led him to perform the better act (or made him more inclined to do so), he would have had to have been less devoted to Linda. Given the ways Juan can affect the world, it may be that if he were less devoted to Linda his overall contribution to human well-being would be less in the end, perhaps because he would become more cynical and self-centered. Thus it may be that Juan should have (should develop, encourage, and so on) a character such that he sometimes knowingly and deliberately acts contrary to his objective consequentialist duty. Any other character, of those actually available to him, would lead him to depart still further from an objectively consequentialist life. The issue is not whether staying home would *change* Juan's character – for we may suppose that it would not – but whether he would in fact decide to stay home if he had that character, of those available, that would lead him to perform the most beneficial overall sequence of acts. In some cases, then, there will exist an objective act-consequentialist argument for developing and sustaining characters of a kind Sidgwick and others have thought an act-consequentialist must condemn.[30]

VIII.   Demands and Disruptions

Before ending this discussion of consequentialism, let me mention one other large problem involving alienation that has seemed uniquely troubling for consequentialist theories and that shows how coming to terms with problems of alienation may be a social matter as well as a matter of individual psychology. Because consequentialist criteria of rightness are linked to maximal contribution to the good, whenever one does not perform the very best act one can, one is "negatively responsible" for any shortfall in total well-being that results. Bernard Williams has argued that to accept such a burden of responsibility would force most of us to abandon or be prepared to abandon many of our most basic individual commitments, alienating ourselves from the very things that mean the most to us.[31]

To be sure, objective act-consequentialism of the sort considered here is a demanding and potentially disruptive morality, even after allowances have been made for the psychological phenomena thus far discussed and for the difference between saying an act is wrong and saying that the agent ought to be blamed for it. But just *how* demanding or disruptive it would be for an individual is a function – as it arguably should be – of how bad the state of the world is, how others typically act, what institutions exist, and how much that individual is capable of doing. If wealth were more equitably distributed, if political systems were less repressive and more responsive to the needs of their citizens, and if people were more generally prepared to accept certain responsibilities, then individuals' everyday lives would not have to be constantly disrupted for the sake of the good.

For example, in a society where there are no organized forms of disaster relief, it may be the case that if disaster were to strike a particular region, people all over the country would be obliged to make a special effort to provide aid. If, on the other hand, an adequate system of publicly financed disaster relief existed, then it probably would be a very poor idea for people to interrupt their normal lives and attempt to help – their efforts would probably be uncoordinated, ill-informed, an interference with skilled relief work, and economically disruptive (perhaps even damaging to the society's ability to pay for the relief effort).

By altering social and political arrangements we can lessen the disruptiveness of moral demands on our lives, and in the long run achieve better results than free-lance good-doing. A consequentialist theory is therefore likely to recommend that accepting negative responsibility is more a matter of supporting certain social and political arrangements (or rearrangements) than of setting out individually to save the world. Moreover, it is clear that such social and political changes cannot be made unless the lives of individuals are psychologically supportable in the meanwhile, and this provides substantial reason for rejecting the notion that we should abandon all that matters to us as individuals and devote ourselves solely to net social welfare. Finally, in many cases what matters most is *perceived* rather than actual demandingness or disruptiveness, and this will be a relative matter, depending upon normal expectations. If certain social or political arrangements encourage higher contribution as a matter of course, individuals may not sense these moral demands as excessively intrusive.

To speak of social and political changes is, of course, to suggest eliminating the social and political preconditions for a number of existing projects and relationships, and such changes are likely to produce some degree of alienation in those whose lives have been disrupted. To an extent such people may be able to find new projects and relationships as well as maintain a number of old projects and relationships, and thereby avoid intolerable alienation. But not all will escape serious alienation. We thus have a case in which alienation will exist whichever course of action we follow – either the alienation of those who find the loss of the old order disorienting, or the continuing alienation of those who under the present order cannot lead lives expressive of their individuality or goals. It would seem that to follow the logic of Williams' position would have the unduly conservative result of favoring those less alienated in the present state of affairs over those who might lead more satisfactory lives if certain changes were to occur. Such conservativism could hardly be warranted by a concern about alienation if the changes in question would bring about social and political preconditions for a more widespread enjoyment of meaningful lives. For example, it is disruptive of the ground projects of many men that women have begun to demand and receive greater equality in social and personal spheres, but such disruption may be offset by the opening of more avenues of self-development to a greater number of people.

In responding to Williams' objection regarding negative responsibility, I have focused more on the problem of disruptiveness than the problem of demandingness, and more on the social than the personal level. More would need to be said than I am able to say here to come fully to terms with his objection, although some very general remarks may be in order. The consequentialist starts out from the relatively simple idea that certain things seem to matter to people above all else. His root conception of moral rightness is therefore that it should matter above all else whether people, insofar as possible, actually realize these ends.[32] Consequentialist moralities of the sort considered here undeniably set a demanding standard, calling upon us to do more for one another than is now the practice. But this standard plainly does not require that most people lead intolerable lives for the sake of some greater good: the greater good is empirically equivalent to the best possible lives for the largest possible number of people.[33] Objective consequentialism gives full expression to this root intuition by setting as the criterion of rightness actual contribution to the realization of human value, allowing practices and forms of reasoning to take whatever shape this requires. It is thus not equivalent to requiring a certain, alienated way of thinking about ourselves, our commitments, or how to act.

Samuel Scheffler has recently suggested that one response to the problems Williams raises about the impersonality and demandingness of consequentialism could be to depart from consequentialism at least far enough to recognize as a fundamental moral principle an agent-centered prerogative, roughly to the effect that one is not always obliged to maximize the good, although one is always permitted to do so if one wishes. This prerogative would make room for agents to give special attention to personal projects and commitments. However, the argument of this article, if successful, shows there to be a firm place in moral practice for prerogatives that afford such room even if one accepts a fully consequentialist fundamental moral theory.[34]

IX. Alienation from Morality

By way of conclusion, I would like to turn to alienation from morality itself, the experience (conscious or unconscious) of morality as an external set of demands not rooted in our lives or accommodating to our perspectives. Giving a convincing answer to the question "Why should I be moral?" must involve diminishing the extent that morality appears alien.

Part of constructing such an answer is a matter of showing that abiding by morality need not alienate us from the particular commitments that make life worthwhile, and in the previous sections we have begun to see how this might be possible within an objective act-consequentialist account of what morality requires. We saw how in general various sorts of projects or relationships can continue to be a source of intrinsic value even though one recognizes that they might have to undergo changes if they could not be defended in their present form on moral grounds. And again, knowing that a commitment is morally defensible may well deepen its value for us, and may also make it possible for us to feel part of a larger world in a way that is itself of great value. If our commitments are regarded by others as responsible and valuable (or if we have reason to think that others should so regard them), this may enhance the meaning or value they have for ourselves, while if they are regarded by others as irresponsible or worthless (especially, if we suspect that others regard them so justly), this may make it more difficult for us to identify with them or find purpose or value in them. Our almost universal urge to rationalize our acts and lives attests our wish to see what we do as defensible from a more general point of view. I do not deny that bringing a more general perspective to bear on one's life may be costly to the self – it may cause reevaluations that lower self-esteem, produce guilt, alienation, and even problems of identity. But I do want to challenge the simple story often told in which there is a personal point of view from which we glimpse meanings which then vanish into insignificance when we adopt a more general perspective. In thought and action we shuttle back and forth from more personal to less personal standpoints, and both play an important role in the process whereby purpose, meaning, and identity are generated and sustained.[35] Moreover, it may be part of mature commitments, even of the most intimate sort, that a measure of perspective beyond the personal be maintained.

These remarks about the role of general perspectives in individual lives lead us to what I think is an equally important part of answering the question "Why should I be moral?": reconceptualization of the terms of the discussion to avoid starting off in an alienated fashion and ending up with the result that morality still seems alien. Before pursuing this idea, let us quickly glance at two existing approaches to the question.

Morality may be conceived of as in essence selfless, impartial, impersonal. To act morally is to subordinate the self and all contingencies concerning the self's relations with others or the world to a set of imperatives binding on us solely as rational beings. We should be moral, in this view, because it is ideally rational. However, morality thus conceived seems bound to appear as alien in daily life. "Purity of heart" in Rawls' sense would be essential to acting morally, and the moral way of life would appear well removed from our actual existence, enmeshed as we are in a web of "particularistic" commitments – which happen to supply our *raisons d'être.*

A common alternative conception of morality is not as an elevated purity of heart but as a good strategy for the self. Hobbesian atomic individuals are posited and appeal is made to game theory to show that payoffs to such individuals may be greater in certain conflict situations – such as reiterated prisoners' dilemmas – if they abide by certain constraints of a moral kind (at least, with regard to those who may reciprocate) rather than act merely prudentially. Behaving morally, then, may be an advantageous policy in certain social settings. However, it is not likely to be the *most* advantageous policy in general, when compared to a strategy that cunningly mixes some compliance with norms and some non-compliance; and presumably the Hobbesian individual is interested only in maximal self-advantage. Yet even if we leave aside worries about how far such arguments might be pushed, it needs to be said that morality as such would confront such an entrepreneurial self as an alien set of demands, for central to morality is the idea that others' interests must sometimes be given weight for reasons unrelated to one's own advantage.

Whatever their differences, these two apparently antithetical approaches to the question "Why should I be moral?" have remarkably similar underlying pictures of the problem. In these pictures, a presocial, rational, abstract individual is the starting point, and the task is to construct proper interpersonal relations out of such individuals. Of course, this conceit inverts reality: the rational individual of these approaches is a social and historical *product.* But that is old hat. We are not supposed to see this as any sort of history, we are told, but rather as a way of conceptualizing the questions of morality. Yet why when conceptualizing are we drawn to such asocial and ahistorical images? My modest proposal is that we should keep our attention fixed on society and history at least long enough to try recasting the problem in more naturalistic terms.[36]

As a start, let us begin with individuals situated in society, complete with identities, commitments, and social relations. What are the ingredients of such identities, commitments, and relations? When one studies relationships of deep commitment – of parent to child, or wife to husband – at close range, it becomes artificial to impose a dichotomy between what is done for the self and what is done for the other. We cannot decompose such relationships into a vector of self-concern and a vector of other-concern, even though concern for the self and the other are both present. The other has come to figure in the self in a fundamental way – or, perhaps a better way of putting it, the other has become a reference point of the self. If it is part of one's identity to be the parent of Jill or the husband of Linda, then the self has reference points beyond the ego, and that which affects these reference points may affect the self in an unmediated way.[37] These reference points do not all fall within the circle of intimate relationships, either. Among the most important constituents of identities are social, cultural, or religious ties – one is a Jew, a Southerner, a farmer, or an alumnus of Old Ivy. Our identities exist in relational, not absolute space, and except as they are fixed by reference points in others, in society, in culture, or in some larger constellation still, they are not fixed at all.[38]

There is a worthwhile analogy between meaning in lives and meaning in language. It has been a while since philosophers have thought it helpful to imagine that language is the arrangement resulting when we hook our private meanings up to a system of shared symbols. Meaning, we are told, resides to a crucial degree in use, in public contexts, in referential systems – it is possible for the self to use a language with meanings because the self is embedded in a set of social and historical practices. But ethical philosophers have continued to speak of the meaning of life in surprisingly private terms. Among recent attempts to give a foundation for morality, Nozick's perhaps places greatest weight on the idea of the meaning of life, which he sees as a matter of an individual's "ability to regulate and guide [his] life in accordance with some overall conception [he] chooses to accept," emphasizing the idea that an individual creates meaning through choice of a life plan; clearly, however, in order for choice to play a self-defining role, the options among which one chooses must already have some meaning independent of one's decisions.[39]

It is not only "the meaning of life" that carries such presuppositions. Consider, for example, another notion that has played a central role in moral discourse: respect. If the esteem of others is to matter to an individual those others must themselves have some significance to the individual; in order for their esteem to constitute the sought-after respect, the individual must himself have some degree of respect for them and their judgment.[40] If the self loses significance for others, this threatens its significance even for itself; if others lose significance for the self, this threatens to remove the basis for self-significance. It is a commonplace of psychology and sociology that bereaved or deracinated individuals suffer not only a sense of loss owing to broken connections with others, but also a loss in the solidity of the self, and may therefore come to lose interest in the self or even a clear sense of identity. Reconstructing the self and self-interest in such cases is as much a matter of constructing new relations to others and the world as it is a feat of self-supporting self-reconstruction. Distracted by the picture of a hypothetical, presocial individual, philosophers have found it very easy to assume, wrongly, that in the actual world concern for oneself and one's goals is quite automatic, needing no outside support, while a direct concern for others is inevitably problematic, needing some further rationale.

It does not follow that there is any sort of categorical imperative to care about others or the world beyond the self as such. It is quite possible to have few external reference points and go through life in an alienated way. Life need not have much meaning in order to go on, and one does not even have to care whether life goes on. We cannot show that moral skepticism is necessarily irrational by pointing to facts about meaning, but a naturalistic approach to morality need no more refute radical skepticism than does a naturalistic approach to epistemology. For actual people, there may be surprisingly little distance between asking in earnest "Why should I take any interest in anyone else?" and asking "Why should I take any interest in myself?"[41] The proper response to the former is not merely to point out the indirect benefits of caring about things beyond the self, although this surely should be done, but to show how denying the significance of anything beyond the self may undercut the basis of significance for the self. There is again a close, but not exact parallel in language: people can get along without a language, although certainly not as well as they can with it; if someone were to ask "Why should I use my words the same way as others?" the proper response would not only be to point out the obvious benefits of using his words in this way, but also to point out that by refusing to use words the way others do he is undermining the basis of meaning in his own use of language.

These remarks need not lead us to a conservative traditionalism. We must share and preserve meanings in order to have a language at all, but we may use a common language to disagree and innovate. Contemporary philosophy of language makes us distrust any strict dichotomy between meaning, on the one hand, and belief and value, on the other; but there is obviously room within a system of meanings for divergence and change on empirical and normative matters. Language itself has undergone considerable change over the course of history, coevolving with beliefs and norms without in general violating the essential conditions of meaningfulness. Similarly, moral values and social practices may undergo change without obliterating the basis of meaningful lives, so long as certain essential conditions are fulfilled. (History does record some changes, such as the uprooting of tribal peoples, where these conditions were not met, with devastating results.)

A system of available, shared meanings would seem to be a precondition for sustaining the meaningfulness of individual lives in familiar sorts of social arrangements. Moreover, in such arrangements identity and self-significance seem to depend in part upon the significance of others to the self. If we are prepared to say that a sense of meaningfulness is a precondition for much else in life, then we may be on the way to answering the question "Why should I be moral?" for we have gone beyond pure egocentrism precisely by appealing to facts about the self.[42] Our earlier discussions have yielded two considerations that make the rest of the task of answering this question more tractable. First, we noted in discussing hedonism that individual lives seem most enjoyable when they involve commitments to causes beyond the self or to others as such. Further, we remarked that it is plausible that the happiest sorts of lives do not involve a commitment to hedonism even of a sophisticated sort. If a firm sense of meaningfulness is a precondition of the fullest happiness, this speculation becomes still more plausible. Second, we sketched a morality that began by taking seriously the various forms of human non-moral value, and then made room for morality in our lives by showing that we can raise moral questions without thereby destroying the possibility of realizing various intrinsic values from particular relationships and activities. That is, we saw how being moral might be compatible (at least in these respects) with living a desirable life. It would take another article, and a long one, to show how these various pieces of the answer to "Why should I be moral?" might be made less rough and fitted together into a more solid structure. But by adopting a non-alienated starting point – that of situated rather than presocial individuals – and by showing how some of the alienation associated with bringing morality to bear on our lives might be avoided, perhaps we have reduced the extent to which morality seems alien to us by its nature.

Notes

1 The loss in question need not be a loss of something of value, and *a fortiori* need not be a bad thing overall: there are some people, institutions, or

cultures alienation from which would be a boon. Alienation is a more or less troubling phenomenon depending upon what is lost; and in the cases to be considered, what is lost is for the most part of substantial value. It does not follow, as we will see in Section V, that in all such cases alienation is a bad thing on balance. Moreover, I do not assume that the loss in question represents an actual *decline* in some value as the result of a separation coming into being where once there was none. It seems reasonable to say that an individual can experience a loss in being alienated from nature, for example, without assuming that he was ever in communion with it, much as we say it is a loss for someone never to receive an education or never to appreciate music. Regrettably, various relevant kinds and sources of alienation cannot be discussed here. A general, historical discussion of alienation may be found in Richard Schacht, *Alienation* (Garden City, NY: Doubleday, 1971).

2   This is not to say that no questions arise about whether Helen's (or John's) feelings and attitudes constitute the fullest sort of affection, as will be seen shortly.

3   Moreover, there is a sense in which someone whose responses to his affections or feelings are characteristically mediated by a calculating point of view may fail to know himself fully, or may seem in a way unknowable to others, and this "cognitive distance" may itself be part of his alienation. I am indebted here to Allan Gibbard.

4   There is a wide range of views about the nature of the moral point of view and its proper role in moral life. Is it necessary that one actually act on universal principles, or merely that one be willing to universalize the principles upon which one acts? Does the moral point of view by its nature require us to consider everyone alike? Here I am using a rather strong reading of the moral point of view, according to which taking the moral point of view involves universalization and the equal consideration of all.

5   A moral point of view theorist might make use of the three points of view distinguished by Mill: the moral, the aesthetic, and the sympathetic. "The first addresses itself to our reason and conscience; the second to our imagination; the third to our human fellow-feeling," from "Bentham," reprinted in *John Stuart Mill: Utilitarianism and Other Writings*, ed. Mary Warnock (New York: New American Library, 1962), p. 121. What is morally right, in his view, may fail to be "loveable" (e.g., a parent strictly disciplining a child) or "beautiful" (e.g., an inauthentic gesture). Thus, the three points of view need not concur in their positive or negative assessments. Notice, however, that Mill has divided the self into three realms, of "reason and conscience," of "imagination," and of "human fellow-feeling"; notice, too, that he has chosen the word 'feeling' to characterize human affections.

6   William K. Frankena, *Ethics*, 2d ed. (Englewood Cliffs, NJ: Prentice-Hall, 1973), p. 116. Moralities that do not accord with this dictum – or a modified version of it that includes all sentient beings – might be deemed alienated in a Feuerbachian sense.

7   Mill, for instance, calls the moral point of view "unquestionably the first and most important," and while he thinks it the error of the moralizer (such as Bentham) to elevate the moral point of view and "sink the [aesthetic and sympathetic] entirely," he does not explain how to avoid such a result if the moral point of view is to be, as he says it ought, "paramount." See his "Bentham," pp. 121f.

    Philosophers who have recently raised doubts about moralities for such reasons include Bernard Williams, in "A Critique of Utilitarianism," in J. J. C. Smart and B. Williams, *Utilitarianism: For and Against* (Cambridge: Cambridge University Press, 1973), and Michael Stocker, in "The Schizophrenia of Modern Ethical Theories," *Journal of Philosophy* 73 (1976): 453–66.

8   John Rawls, *A Theory of Justice* (Cambridge: Harvard University Press, 1971), p. 587, emphasis added.

9   I am not claiming that we should interpret all of Rawls' intricate moral theory in light of these few remarks. They are cited here merely to illustrate a certain tendency in moral thought, especially that of a Kantian inspiration.

10 This is a "paradox" for individual, egoistic hedonists. Other forms the "paradox of hedonism" may take are social in character: a society of egoistic hedonists might arguably achieve less total happiness than a society of more benevolent beings; or, taking happiness as the sole social goal might lead to a less happy society overall than could exist if a wider range of goals were pursued.

11 This is not to deny that there are indexical components to commitments.

12 It does seem likely to matter just what the commitment is contingent upon as well as just how contingent it is. I think it is an open question whether commitments contingent upon the satisfaction of egoistic hedonist criteria are of the sort that might figure in the happiest sorts of lives ordinarily available. We will return to this problem presently.

    Those who have had close relationships often develop a sense of *duty* to one another that may outlast affection or emotional commitment, that is, they may have a sense of obligation to one another that is less contingent than affection or emotional commitment, and that should not simply be confused with them. If such a sense of obligation is in conflict with self-interest, and if it is a normal part of the most satisfying sorts of close relationships, then this may pose a problem for the egoistic hedonist.

13 A few remarks are needed. First, I will say that an act is available to an agent if he would succeed in performing it if he tried. Second, here and elsewhere in this article I mean to include quite "thick" descriptions of actions, so that it may be part of an action that one perform it with a certain intention or goal. In the short run (but not so much the long run) intentions, goals, motives, and the like are usually less subject to our deliberate control than overt behavior – it is easier to say "I'm sorry" than to say it and mean it. This, however, is a fact about the relative availability of acts to the agent at a given time, and should not dictate what is to count as an act. Third, here and

elsewhere I ignore for simplicity's sake the possibility that more than one course of action may be maximally valuable. And fourth, for reasons I will not enter into here, I have formulated objective hedonism in terms of actual outcomes rather than expected values (relative to the information available to the agent). One could make virtually the same argument using an expected value formulation.

14   Michael Stocker considers related cases in "Morally Good Intentions," *The Monist* 54 (1970): 124–41. I am much indebted to his discussion.

15   There may be a parallelism of sorts between Ned's coming to seek money for its own sake and a certain pattern of moral development: what is originally sought in order to live up to familial or social expectations may come to be an end in itself.

  It might be objected that the goal of earning as much money as possible is quite unlike the goal of being as happy as possible, since money is plainly instrumentally valuable even when it is sought for its own sake. But happiness, too, is instrumentally valuable, for it may contribute to realizing such goals as being a likeable or successful person.

16   An important objection to the claim that objective hedonism may serve as the *moral* criterion one's acts should meet, even if this means not believing in hedonism, is that moral principles must meet a *publicity* condition. I will discuss this objection in Section VI.

17   See, for example, Stocker, "The Schizophrenia of Modern Ethical Theories."

18   Williams, "Critique."

19   At least one qualification is needed: the subjective states must be psychologically possible. Perhaps some of us desire what are, in effect, psychologically impossible states.

20   Robert Nozick, *Anarchy, State, and Utopia* (New York: Basic Books, 1974), pp. 42ff.

21   To my knowledge, the best-developed method for justifying claims about intrinsic value involves thought-experiments of a familiar sort, in which, for example, we imagine two lives, or two worlds, alike in all but one respect, and then attempt to determine whether rational, well-informed, widely-experienced individuals would (when vividly aware of both alternatives) be indifferent between the two or have a settled preference for one over the other. Since no one is ideally rational, fully informed, or infinitely experienced, the best we can do is to take more seriously the judgments of those who come nearer to approximating these conditions. Worse yet: the best we can do is to take more seriously the judgments of those we *think* better approximate these conditions. (I am not supposing that facts or experience somehow entail values, but that in rational agents, beliefs and values show a marked mutual influence and coherence.) We may overcome some narrowness if we look at behavior and preferences in other societies and other epochs, but even here we must rely upon interpretations colored by our own beliefs and values. Within the confines of this article I must leave unanswered a host of deep and

troubling questions about the nature of values and value judgments. Suffice it to say that there is no reason to think that we are in a position to give anything but a tentative list of intrinsic goods.

It becomes a complex matter to describe the psychology of intrinsic value. For example, should we say that one values a relationship of solidarity, say, a friendship, *because it is* a friendship? That makes it sound as if it were somehow instrumental to the realization of some abstract value, friendship. Surely this is a misdescription. We may be able to get a clearer idea of what is involved by considering the case of happiness. We certainly do not value a particular bit of experienced happiness because it is instrumental in the realization of the abstract goal, happiness – we value the experience for its own sake because it is a happy experience. Similarly, a friendship is itself the valued thing, the thing of a valued kind. Of course, one can say that one values friendship and therefore seeks friends, just as one can say one values happiness and therefore seeks happy experiences. But this locution must be contrasted with what is being said when, for example, one talks of seeking *things that make one happy.* Friends are not "things that make one achieve friendship" – they partially constitute friendships, just as particular happy experiences partially constitute happiness for an individual. Thus taking friendship as an intrinsic value does not entail viewing particular friendships instrumentally.

22   If one objects that Juan's commitment to Linda is lacking because it is contingent in some ways, the objector must show that the *kinds* of contingencies involved would destroy his relationship with Linda, especially since moral character often figures in commitments – the character of the other, or the compatibility of a commitment with one's having the sort of character one values – and the contingencies in Juan's case are due to his moral character.

23   I do not mean to suggest that such identities are always matters of choice for individuals. Quite the reverse, identities often arise through socialization, prejudice, and similar influences. The point rather is that there is a very general phenomenon of identification, badly in need of explanation, that to an important extent underlies such phenomena as socialization and prejudice, and that suggests the existence of certain needs in virtually all members of society – needs to which identification with entities beyond the self answers.

Many of us who resist raising questions about our lives from broader perspectives do so, I fear, not out of a sense that it would be difficult or impossible to lead a meaningful life if one entertained such perspectives, but rather out of a sense that our lives would not stand up to much scrutiny therefrom, so that leading a life that *would* seem meaningful from such perspectives would require us to change in some significant way.

24   Although the language here is causal – 'promoting' and 'bringing about' – it should be said that the relation of an act to the good need not always be causal. An act of learning may non-causally involve coming to have knowledge (an intrinsic good by my reckoning) as well as contributing causally to

later realizations of intrinsic value. Causal consequences as such do not have a privileged status. As in the case of objective hedonism, I have formulated objective consequentialism in terms of actual outcomes (so-called "objective duty") rather than expected values relative to what is rational for the agent to believe ("subjective duty"). The main arguments of this article could be made using expected value, since the course of action with highest expected value need not in general be the subjectively consequentialist one. See also notes 13 and 21.

Are there any subjective consequentialists? Well, various theorists have claimed that a consequentialist must be a subjective consequentialist in order to be genuine – see Williams, "Critique," p. 135, and Rawls, *Theory of Justice*, p. 182.

25   Williams, "Critique," p. 135.

26   For discussion of a publicity condition, see Rawls, *Theory of Justice*, pp. 133, 177–82, 582. The question whether a publicity condition can be justified is a difficult one, deserving fuller discussion than I am able to give it here.

27   For an example of trait-consequentialism, see Robert M. Adams, "Motive Utilitarianism," *Journal of Philosophy* 73 (1976): 467–81.

28   By way of contrast, when Robert Adams considers application of a motive-utilitarian view to the ethics of actions, he suggests "conscience utilitarianism," the view that "we have a *moral duty* to do an act, if and only if it would be demanded of us by the most useful kind of conscience we could have," "Motive Utilitarianism," p. 479. Presumably, this means that it would be morally wrong to perform an act contrary to the demands of the most useful sort of conscience. I have resisted this sort of redefinition of rightness for actions, since I believe that the most useful sort of conscience may on occasion demand of us an act that does not have the best overall consequences of those available, and that performing this act would be wrong.

Of course, some difficulties attend the interpretation of this last sentence. I have assumed throughout that an act is available to an agent if he would succeed in performing it if he tried. I have also taken a rather simple view of the complex matter of attaching outcomes to specific acts. In those rare cases in which the performance of even one exceptional (purportedly optimizing) act would completely undermine the agent's standing (optimal) disposition, it might not be possible after all to say that the exceptional act would be the right one to perform in the circumstances. (This question will arise again shortly.)

29   One conclusion of this discussion is that we cannot realistically expect people's behavior to be in strict compliance with the counterfactual condition even if they are committed sophisticated consequentialists. At best, a sophisticated consequentialist tries to meet this condition. But it should be no surprise that in practice we are unlikely to be morally ideal. Imperfections in information alone are enough to make it very improbable that individuals will lead objectively consequentialist lives. Whether or when to *blame*

people for real or apparent failures to behave ideally is, of course, another matter.

Note that we must take into account not just the frequency with which right acts are performed, but the actual balance of gains and losses to overall well-being that results. Relative frequency of right action will settle the matter only in the (unusual) case where the amount of good at stake in each act of a given kind – for example, each emergency one comes across – is the same.

30   In *The Methods of Ethics*, bk. IV, chap. v, sec, 4, Sidgwick discusses "the Ideal of character and conduct" that a utilitarian should recognize as "the sum of excellences or Perfections," and writes that "a Utilitarian must hold that it is always wrong for a man knowingly to do anything other than what he believes to be most conducive to Universal Happiness" (p. 492). Here Sidgwick is uncharacteristically confused – and in two ways. First, considering act-by-act evaluation, an objective utilitarian can hold that an agent may simply be wrong in believing that a given course of action is most conducive to universal happiness, and therefore it may be right for him knowingly to do something other than this. Second, following Sidgwick's concern in this passage and looking at enduring traits of character rather than isolated acts, and even assuming the agent's belief to be correct, an objective utilitarian can hold that the ideal character for an individual, or for people in general, may involve a willingness knowingly to act contrary to maximal happiness when this is done for the sake of certain deep personal commitments. See Henry Sidgwick, *The Methods of Ethics*, 7th ed. (New York: Dover, 1966), p. 492.

It might be thought counterintuitive to say, in the example given, that it is not right for Juan to travel to see Linda. But it must be kept in mind that for an act-consequentialist to say that an action is not right is not to say that it is without merit, only that it is not the very best act available to the agent. And an intuitive sense of the rightness of visiting Linda may be due less to an evaluation of the act itself than to a reaction to the sort of character a person would have to have in order to stay home and write a check to OXFAM under the circumstances. Perhaps he would have to be too distant or righteous to have much appeal to us – especially in view of the fact that it is his spouse's anguish that is at stake. We have already seen how an act-consequentialist may share this sort of character assessment.

31   Williams, "Critique," sec. 3.

32   I appealed to this "root conception" in rejecting rule-consequentialism in Section VII. Although consequentialism is often condemned for failing to provide an account of morality consistent with respect for persons, this root conception provides the basis for a highly plausible notion of such respect. I doubt, however, that any fundamental ethical dispute between consequentialists and deontologists can be resolved by appeal to the idea of respect for persons. The deontologist has his notion of respect – e.g., that we not use people in certain ways – and the consequentialist has *his* – e.g., that the good of every person has an equal claim upon us, a claim unmediated by any

notion of right or contract, so that we should do the most possible to bring about outcomes that actually advance the good of persons. For every consequentially justified act of manipulation to which the deontologist can point with alarm there is a deontologically justified act that fails to promote the well-being of some person(s) as fully as possible to which the consequentialist can point, appalled. Which notion takes "respect for persons" more seriously? There may be no non-question-begging answer, especially once the consequentialist has recognized such things as autonomy or respect as intrinsically valuable.

33   The qualification 'empirically equivalent to' is needed because in certain empirically unrealistic cases, such as utility monsters, the injunction "Maximize overall realization of human value" cannot be met by improving the lives of as large a proportion of the population as possible. However, under plausible assumptions about this world (including diminishing marginal value) the equivalence holds.

34   For Scheffler's view, see *The Rejection of Consequentialism: A Philosophical Investigation of the Considerations Underlying Rival Moral Conceptions* (Oxford: Clarendon Press, 1982). The consequentialist may also argue that at least some of the debate set in motion by Williams is more properly concerned with the question of the relation between moral imperatives and imperatives of rationality than with the content of moral imperatives as such. (See note 42.)

35   For example, posterity may figure in our thinking in ways we seldom articulate. Thus, nihilism has seemed to some an appropriate response to the idea that mankind will soon destroy itself. "Everything would lose its point" is a reaction quite distinct from "Then we should enjoy ourselves as much as possible in the meantime," and perhaps equally comprehensible.

36   I do not deny that considerations about pay-offs of strategies in conflict situations may play a role in cultural or biological evolutionary explanations of certain moral sentiments or norms. Rather, I mean to suggest that there are characteristic sorts of abstractions and simplifications involved in game-theoretic analysis that may render it blind to certain phenomena crucial for understanding morality and its history, and for answering the question "Why should I be moral?" when posed by actual individuals.

37   Again we see the inadequacy of subjectivism about values. If, for example, part of one's identity is to be Jill's parent, then should Jill cease to exist, one's life could be said to have lost some of its purpose even if one were not aware of her death. As the example of the experience machine suggested earlier, there is an objective side to talk about purpose.

38   Here I do not have in mind identity in the sense usually at stake in discussions of personal identity. The issue is not identity as principle of individuation, but as *experienced*, as a sense of self – the stuff actual identity crises are made of.

39   Nozick, *Anarchy*, p. 49. (I ignore here Nozick's more recent remarks about the meaning of life in his *Philosophical Explanations* [Cambridge: Harvard Uni-

versity Press, 1981].) The notion of a "rationally chosen life plan" has figured
prominently in the literature recently, in part due to Rawls' use of it in characterizing the good (see Rawls, *Theory of Justice*, ch. VII, "Goodness as Rationality"). Rawls' theory of the good is a complex matter, and it is difficult
to connect his claims in any direct way to a view about the meaning of life.
However, see T. M. Scanlon, "Rawls' Theory of Justice," *University of Penn-
sylvania Law Review* 121 (1973): 1020–69, for an interpretation of Rawls in
which the notion of an individual as above all a rational chooser – more committed to maintaining his status as a rational agent able to adopt and modify
his goals than to any particular set of goals – functions as the ideal of a person
implicit in Rawls' theory. On such a reading, we might interpolate into the
original text the idea that meaning derives from autonomous individual
choice, but this is highly speculative. In any event, recent discussions of
rationally chosen life plans as the bearers of ultimate significance or value do
not appear to me to do full justice to the ways in which lives actually come
to be invested with meaning, especially since some meanings would have to
be presupposed by any rational choice of a plan of life.

40 To be sure, this is but one of the forms of respect that are of importance to
moral psychology. But as we see, self-respect has a number of interesting
connections with respect for, and from, others.

41 This may be most evident in extreme cases. Survivors of Nazi death camps
speak of the effort it sometimes took to sustain a will to survive, and of the
importance of others, and of the sense of others, to this. A survivor of
Treblinka recalls, "In our group we shared everything; and at the moment
one of the group ate something without sharing it, we knew it was the beginning of the end for him." (Quoted in Terrence Des Pres, *The Survivor: An
Anatomy of Life in the Death Camps* [New York: Oxford University Press, 1976],
p. 96.) Many survivors say that the idea of staying alive to "bear witness," in
order that the deaths of so many would not escape the world's notice, was
decisive in sustaining their own commitment to survival.

42 One need not be a skeptic about morality or alienated from it in any general
sense in order for the question "Why should I be moral?" to arise with great
urgency. If in a given instance doing what is right or having the best sort of
character were to conflict head-on with acting on behalf of a person or a
project that one simply could not go against without devastating the self, then
it may fail to be reasonable from the agent's standpoint to do what is right.
It is always *morally* wrong (though not always morally blameworthy) to fail
to perform morally required acts, but in certain circumstances that may be
the most reasonable thing to do – not because of some larger moral scheme,
but because of what matters to particular individuals. Therefore, in seeking
an answer to "Why should I be moral?" I do not assume that it must always
be possible to show that the moral course of action is ideally rational or
otherwise optimal from the standpoint of the agent. (I could be more specific
here if I had a clearer idea of what rationality is.) It would seem ambitious

enough to attempt to show that, in general, there are highly desirable lives available to individuals consistent with their being moral. While we might hope for something stronger, this could be enough – given what can also be said on behalf of morality from more general viewpoints – to make morality a worthy candidate for our allegiance as individuals.

It should perhaps be said that on an objective consequentialist account, being moral need not be a matter of consciously following distinctively moral imperatives, so that what is at stake in asking "Why should I be moral?" in connection with such a theory is whether one has good reason to lead one's life in such a way that an objective consequentialist criterion of rightness is met as nearly as possible. In a given instance, this criterion might be met by acting out of a deeply felt emotion or an entrenched trait of character, without consulting morality or even directly in the face of it. This, once more, is an indication of objective consequentialism's flexibility: the idea is to *be* and *do* good, not necessarily to *pursue* goodness.

10

Bayesian Decision Theory and Utilitarian Ethics

John C. Harsanyi

One of the great intellectual achievements of the twentieth century is the Bayesian theory of rational behavior under risk and uncertainty. Many economists, however, are still unaware of how strong the case really is for Bayesian theory, and many more fail to appreciate the far-reaching implications the Bayesian concept of rationality has for ethics and welfare economics. The purpose of this paper is to argue that the Bayesian rationality postulates are absolutely inescapable criteria of rationality for policy decisions; and to point out that these Bayesian rationality postulates, together with a hardly controversial Pareto optimality requirement, entail *utilitarian ethics* as a matter of mathematical necessity.

I. The Bayesian Rationality Postulates

In discussing the criteria for rational behavior, I will distinguish behavior under certainty, under risk, and under uncertainty. Certainty obtains when we can predict the actual outcome of any action we can take. Risk obtains when we know at least the objective probabilities associated with alternative possible outcomes. Finally, uncertainty obtains when even these objective probabilities are partly or wholly unknown to us (or are possibly even undefined).

In the case of certainty, I will assume that each individual chooses among various alternative situations, where each situation is

John C. Harsanyi, "Bayesian Decision Theory and Utilitarian Ethics," *The American Economic Review* 68 (1978): 223–8.

characterized by finitely many economic and noneconomic variables, such as his holdings of different commodities, including money, his health, his social position, his social relationships, etc., as well as by similar economic and noneconomic variables affecting other individuals in the society. Thus, mathematically, any situation can be regarded as a point in a finite-dimensional (say, r-dimensional) Euclidean space E^r.

In the case of risk and of uncertainty, an individual's choices can be modeled as choices among different lotteries whose "prizes" are situations, that is, points in E^r. A lottery can be described as

(1) $$L = (A_1 \mid e_1, \ldots, A_k \mid e_k, \ldots, A_K \mid e_K)$$

indicating that this lottery L will yield prizes $A_1, \ldots, A_K$, depending on which one of K mutually exclusive and exhaustive events $e_1, \ldots, e_K$ occurs. These events $e_1, \ldots, e_K$ will be called conditioning events. Mathematically, any event e_k ($k = 1, \ldots, K$) can be regarded as a measurable subset of the space Ω of all possible "states of the world." A lottery L will be called a risky or an uncertain lottery, depending on whether the decision maker does or does not know the objective probability $p_k = Prob\ (e_k)$ associated with every event e_k ($k = 1, \ldots, K$) used in this lottery L.

In analyzing the behavior of any individual i ($i = 1, \ldots, n$), strict preference by him will be denoted by $>_i$ and nonstrict preference including indifference, or equivalence, by $\geqq_i$.

Rational behavior by a given individual i under certainty can be characterized by two rationality postulates:

1. *Complete preordering.* The nonstrict preferences of this individual i establish a complete preordering over the space E^r of all possible situations (or over some suitable closed subset of E^r).
2. *Continuity.* Suppose that the sequence $A_1, A_2, \ldots$, of situations converges to a particular situation A_0, and that another sequence $B_1, B_2, \ldots$, of situations converges to B_0, with $A_k \geqq_i B_k$ for all k. Then, $A_0 \geqq_i B_0$.

For convenience I will call these two postulates the *basic utility axioms.* Using these two axioms, we can characterize rational behavior as follows.

THEOREM 1: *Utility Maximization. If an individual's preferences satisfy the two basic utility axioms, then his behavior will be equivalent to maximizing a well-defined (ordinal) utility function.*[1] (For proof, see Gerard Debreu, pp. 55–9.)

To characterize rational behavior under risk and under uncertainty, we need two additional rationality postulates:

3. *Probabilistic equivalence.* Let

(2) $$L = (A_1 | e_1, \ldots, A_K | e_K)$$

and

$$L^* = (A_1 | e_1^*, \ldots, A_K | e_K^*)$$

and suppose that the decision maker knows the objective probabilities associated with events $e_1, \ldots, e_K$ as well as with events $e_1^*, \ldots, e_K^*$, and knows that these probabilities satisfy

(3) $$Prob(e_k) = Prob(e_k^*) \quad \text{for } k = 1, \ldots, K$$

Then he will be indifferent between lotteries L and L^*.

In other words, a rational individual will be indifferent between two risky lotteries if these yield him the same prizes with the same probabilities – even if the two lotteries use quite different physical processes to generate these possibilities. Note that this postulate implies von Neumann and Morgenstern's postulate on compound lotteries: that a rational individual will be indifferent between a two-stage lottery and a one-stage lottery if both offer the same prizes with the same probabilities.

4. *Sure-thing principle.* Suppose that $A_k^* >_i A_k$ for $k = 1, \ldots, K$. Then

(4) $$(A_1^* | e_1, \ldots, A_K^* | e_K) \geqq_i (A_1 | e_1, \ldots, A_K | e_K)$$

In other words, other things being equal, a rational individual will not prefer a lottery yielding less desirable prizes over a lottery yielding more desirable prizes. Note that the sure-thing principle is essentially identical with the game-theoretical principle that a rational individual will avoid using any (weakly or strongly) dominated strategy.

Obviously, both postulates 3 and 4 are extremely compelling rationality requirements. But they are subject to two qualifications.

(i) Both postulates presuppose that the utility $U(A_k)$ of any prize A_k is independent of its conditioning event e_k. This requirement can always be satisfied by suitable definition of the prizes. For example, the utility of an umbrella depends on whether it is raining or not (and whether there is a heavy rain or a light rain). Therefore, it would be inappropriate to make an umbrella a prize of a lottery when the nature of the weather is the conditioning event; rather, we must redefine the prize as staying dry, or as getting slightly wet, or as getting very wet – since, as a rule, the utilities associated with these prizes can be assessed without knowing the weather, etc.

(ii) More importantly, both postulates (and especially postulate 3) presuppose that the decision maker has no specific utility or disutility for gambling as such, that is, for the nervous tension and the other psychological experiences directly connected with gambling. In other words, the two postulates assume that the decision maker will take a purely *result-oriented* attitude toward lotteries, and will derive all his utility and disutility from the prizes he may or may not win through these lotteries, rather than from the act of gambling itself.

Clearly, this assumption is seldom, if ever, satisfied in the case of gambling done primarily for entertainment. For example, people who gamble in a casino will usually do this because they are attracted by the nervous tension associated with gambling; and since the latter may strongly depend on the details of the physical process used to produce the relevant probabilities, they may be far from indifferent to the nature of this physical process. (For example, they may not at all be indifferent between participating in a one-stage lottery and participating in a probabilistically equivalent two-stage lottery.)

On the other hand, it is natural to expect that, in making important policy decisions, responsible decision makers will take a result-oriented attitude toward risk taking. This is probably a reasonably realistic descriptive prediction; and it is certainly an obvious normative rationality requirement as well as a moral requirement: responsible business executives using their shareholders' money, and responsible political leaders acting on behalf of their constituents, are expected to do their utmost to achieve the best possible results, rather than to gratify their own personal desire for nervous tension (or for avoiding nervous tension). Even clearer is the obligation of taking a purely result-oriented attitude in making important moral decisions.

Thus, we can conclude that while postulates 3 and 4 have little application to gambling done for entertainment, they are very basic rationality requirements for all serious policy decisions as well as for personal moral decisions.

II. Expected-Utility Maximization

The main conclusion of Bayesian theory is that a rational decision maker under risk and under uncertainty will act in such a way as to maximize his expected utility; or, equivalently, that he will assess the utility of any lottery to him as being equal to its expected utility (expected-utility theorem). Different authors have used different axioms to derive this theorem, and some of these axioms had somewhat questionable intuitive plausibility.[2] It can be shown, however, that for deriving the theorem, all we need, apart from the two basic probability axioms, are the probabilistic equivalence postulate and the sure-thing principle, both of which represent absolutely compelling rationality requirements for serious policy decisions.

THEOREM 2: *Expected-Utility. If an individual's preferences satisfy postulates 1, 2, 3, and 4, then he will have a (cardinal) utility function U_i such that assigns, to any lottery L of form (1), a utility equal to its expected utility, that is, equal to the quantity*

$$(5) \qquad U_i(L) = \sum_{k=1}^{K} p_k U_i(A_k)$$

where p_k ($k = 1, \ldots, K$) is the probability associated with the conditioning event e_k. More specifically, if L is a risky lottery, then p_k must be interpreted as the objective probability $p_k = Prob(e_k)$ of this event e_k; whereas if L is an uncertain lottery, then p_k must be interpreted as the subjective probability $p_k = Prob_i^*(e_k)$ that the decision maker chooses to assign to this event e_k.[3]

Property (5) is called the expected-utility property, and any utility function U_i possessing this property is called a von Neumann-Morgenstern utility function. For short reference, I will call postulates 1, 2, 3, and 4 the Bayesian rationality postulates.[4]

III.   An Axiomatic Foundation for Utilitarian Morality

Now I propose to show that the Bayesian rationality postulates, together with a very natural Pareto optimality requirement, logically entail a utilitarian ethic.

According to Theorems 1 and 2, the behavior of a rational individual i ($i = 1, \ldots, n$) would be equivalent to that resulting from the maximization of the expected value of some cardinal utility function U_i expressing his *personal* preferences. In the case of most individuals, these personal preferences will not be completely selfish; but usually they will give greater weight to his own personal interests and to the interests of his family, friends, and other associates, than to the interests of complete strangers.

Yet, there are situations where an individual's behavior will not be guided by his more or less self-centered personal preferences, but rather will be guided by much more impartial and impersonal criteria. We expect that judges and other public officials will be guided in their official capacities by some notions of public interest and of impartial justice; and, more importantly, every individual will have to be guided by certain impartial and impersonal criteria when he is trying to make a moral value judgment. Indeed, by definition, any evaluative judgment based on biased, partial, and personal criteria will not be a moral value judgment at all, but rather will be a mere judgment of personal preference.

I will describe the criteria guiding an individual when he is honestly trying to make an impartial and impersonal moral value judgment as this individual's moral preferences.

In view of Theorems 1 and 2, if the moral preferences of an individual i satisfy certain consistency requirements, then his moral value judgments will be such as if he tried to maximize a special utility function expressing these moral preferences. This utility function will be called his social welfare function W_i.

I now propose to show that a rational individual's social welfare function must be a positive linear combination of all individuals' utility functions. I will assume that society consists of n individuals. Consider the social welfare function of individual j. The following three axioms will be used:

Axiom a: Individual rationality. The personal preferences of *all* n individuals satisfy the four Bayesian rationality postulates.

Axiom b: Rationality of moral preferences. The moral preferences of individual j satisfy the four Bayesian rationality postulates.

Axiom c: Pareto optimality. Suppose that at least *one* of the n individuals personally prefers social situation A over social situation B, and that none of the other individuals personally prefers B over A. Then, individual j will morally prefer A over B.

Axiom a is an obvious rationality requirement. So is Axiom b: it expresses the principle that an individual making a moral value judgment must follow, if possible, even higher standards of rationality than an individual merely pursuing his personal interests. Thus, if rationality requires that each individual should follow the Bayesian rationality postulates in his personal life as postulate 1 asserts, then he must even more persistently follow these rationality postulates when he is making moral value judgments.[5] While Axioms a and b are rationality requirements, Axiom c is a moral principle – but it is surely a rather noncontroversial moral principle.

In view of Theorem 2, Axiom a implies that the personal preferences of each individual i can be represented by a von Neumann-Morgenstern (vN-M) utility function U_i, whereas Axiom b implies that the moral preferences of individual j can be represented by a social welfare function W_j which likewise has the nature of a vN-M utility function. Finally, the three axioms together imply the following theorem.

THEOREM 3: *Linearity of the social welfare function. The social welfare function* W_j *of individual j must be a real-valued function over all social situations A, and must have the mathematical form*

(6) $$W_j(A) = \sum_{i=1}^{n} \alpha_i U_i(A)$$

with α_i *strictly positive for* $i = 1, \ldots, n$

For the proof, see the author (1955, pp. 313–14).[6]

Note that the proof of Theorem 3 does not assume the possibility of interpersonal utility comparisons. The theorem will remain valid even if such comparisons are not admitted. Of course, if such comparisons are ruled out, then the coefficients α_i will have to be based completely on individual j's personal – and more or less arbitrary – value judgments.

On the other hand, if interpersonal utility comparisons (or at least interpersonal comparisons of utility differences) are admitted, then our three axioms can be supplemented by a fourth axiom:

Axiom d: Equal treatment of all individuals. Individual j's social welfare function W_j will assign equal weights to the utility functions $U_1, \ldots, U_n$ of the n individuals when these utility functions are expressed in equal utility units.

Using this axiom, we can infer that in (6) we must have

(7) $$\alpha_1 = \ldots = \alpha_n$$

IV. The Equiprobability Model for Moral Value Judgments

The axiomatic analysis of Section III has the advantage that it uses only extremely weak philosophical assumptions: it derives utilitarian ethics from two rationality requirements and one very natural moral requirement. However, if we are willing to accept somewhat stronger philosophical commitments, then we can obtain a somewhat stronger form of Theorem 3 (to the effect that the social welfare function must be the arithmetic mean of all individual utilities). What is more important, we can achieve deeper philosophical insights into the nature of moral value judgments.

I have argued that moral value judgments must be based on impartial and impersonal criteria. Now I propose to give a more specific formal definition for this requirement of impartiality and of impersonality.

Suppose individual *j* expresses a value judgment about the relative merits of one possible social situation *A* as against another possible social situation *B*. How do we know whether he expresses a genuine moral value judgment, based on impartial and impersonal considerations? He would certainly satisfy our impartiality and impersonality requirements if he did not know how his choice between *A* and *B* would affect him personally and, in particular, if he did not know what his own social position would be in situations *A* and *B*. More specifically, let us assume he would think that in either situation he would have the same probability $1/n$ to occupy any one of the *n* possible social positions – and, indeed, to be put in the place of any one of the *n* individuals in the society. Then, he would clearly satisfy the impartiality and impersonality requirements to the fullest possible degree. I will call this assumption the equiprobability model of moral value judgments.

Obviously, this equiprobability model cannot be taken literally. When individual *j* makes a value judgment as to the relative merits of situations *A* and *B*, he will often have quite a good idea of the actual social position he would have in each situation; and he will certainly know his own personal identity. Nevertheless, his judgment as to the relative merits of situations *A* and *B* will qualify as a genuine moral value judgment as long as he at least makes a serious attempt to *disregard* these morally irrelevant pieces of information in making this judgment.

If we apply Theorem 2 to this equiprobability model, then we obtain the following theorem.

THEOREM 4: *The social welfare function as an arithmetic mean of all individual utilities. Suppose that individual j follows the Bayesian rationality postulates. Then, under the equiprobability model, he will make his moral value judgments in such a way as to maximize the social welfare function:*

(8) $$W_j(A) = \frac{1}{n} \sum_{i=1}^{n} U_i(A)$$

The theorem follows from the fact that under the equiprobability model, *j*'s expected utility will be given by the right-hand member of (8).

Unlike Theorem 3, Theorem 4, as well as the equiprobability model itself, does presuppose the possibility of interpersonal comparisons of utility differences (utility increments).

To sum up, we have found that the Bayesian rationality postulates, together with a Pareto optimality requirement, logically entail utilitarian ethics (Theorem 3) – even if interpersonal utility comparisons are not admitted. But, in actual fact, as I have tried to show elsewhere (see the author, 1977a), there are no valid arguments against such comparisons. Yet, once such comparisons are admitted, the logical connection between Bayesian theory and utilitarian morality becomes even more obvious (Theorem 4).

Notes

1 For some purposes it may be desirable to define rational behavior without requiring that it should satisfy the continuity postulate (postulate 2). It can be shown that if a given individual's preferences satisfy at least the complete preordering postulate (postulate 1), then his behavior will be equivalent to lexicographically maximizing a certain utility vector.

2 For example, Leonard Savage's Postulate 4 directly assumes that the decision maker will act on the basis of consistent *qualitative* subjective probabilities (i.e., he will consistently act on the opinion that some events are more likely to occur than not to occur, while other events are more likely not to occur than to occur). In my own view, consistency in the use of qualitative or quantitative subjective probabilities should not be assumed as an axiom, but rather should be inferred from some more basic – and, one may hope, more compelling – axioms. This is the approach taken by F. J. Anscombe and Robert J. Aumann.

3 Owing to space limitations, the proof has been omitted. But see my working paper.

4 As M. Hausner has shown, we can obtain a weaker form of the expected-utility theorem without using postulate 2: if an individual's preferences satisfy at least postulates 1, 3, and 4, then his behavior will be equivalent to lexicographically maximizing the expected value of a certain utility vector.

5 Axiom b, and, in particular, the assumption that people's moral preferences should satisfy the sure-thing principle, was criticized by Peter Diamond. As I have tried to show in my 1975 paper, his criticism is invalid.

6 In view of Hausner's results, a weaker form of Theorem 3 will remain true even if, in Axioms a and b, we redefine the Bayesian rationality postulates so as to omit postulate 2 (the continuity postulate). In this case both the quantities U_i and the quantity W_j will have to be reinterpreted as lexicographically ordered utility vectors.

References

F. J. Anscombe and R. J. Aumann, "A Definition of Subjective Probability," *Annals Math. Statist.*, March 1963, 34, 199–205.

Gerard Debreu, *Theory of Value*, New York 1959.

P. Diamond, "Cardinal Welfare, Individualistic Ethics, and Interpersonal Comparison of Utility: Comment," *J. Polit. Econ.*, Oct. 1967, 75, 765–6.

J. C. Harsanyi, "Cardinal Welfare, Individualistic Ethics, and Interpersonal Comparisons of Utility," *J. Polit. Econ.*, Aug. 1955, 63, 309–21.

——, "Nonlinear Social Welfare Functions," *Theory Decn.*, 1975, 6, 311–32.

——, (1977a) "Morality and the Theory of Rational Behavior," *Soc. Res.*, Winter 1977, 44, 623–56.

——, (1977b) "Bayesian Decision Theory," work. paper no. CP-404, Center Res. Manage. Sci., University of California-Berkeley 1977.

M. Hausner, "Multidimensional Utilities," in Robert M. Thrall et al., eds., *Decision Processes*, New York 1954, 167–80.

Leonard J. Savage, *The Foundations of Statistics*, New York 1954.

11

Toward a Credible Form
of Utilitarianism

Richard B. Brandt

Introduction

This paper is an attempt to formulate, in a tolerably precise way, a type
of utilitarian ethical theory which is not open to obvious and catastrophic
objections. It is not my aim especially to advocate the kind of view finally
stated, although I do believe it is more acceptable than any other type of
utilitarianism.

Utilitarianism is a topic discussed by contemporary moralists in either,
or both, of two contexts. One of these contexts is that of traditional normative discussion of the correct answer to such questions as "What do all
right actions have in common?" Many linguistically oriented philosophers do not believe such questions are a proper subject for philosophical discussion, but noncognitivists in metaethics can, as well as anyone
else, consistently defend (or criticize) a utilitarian normative ethic, not
claiming that such a theory is strictly true but nevertheless offering arguments of a kind.

Utilitarianism also plays a substantial part in contemporary meta-
ethical discussions. If you ask some philosophers what can count as a
good or valid reason for an ethical judgment, you may be told that some
kind of utilitarian reason – inference from good consequences to rightness
– is one kind, or even the only kind. This view may be supported by
urging that this is the kind of reasoning people actually do use, or by

Richard B. Brandt, "Toward a Credible Form of Utilitarianism, *Morality and the
Language of Conduct*, Hector-Neri Castañeda and George Nakhnikian, eds.
(Detroit, MI: Wayne State University Press, 1965), pp. 107–43.

saying that this is the kind of reasoning used in reflective moments by people whom we should count as reliable moral judges. Alternatively, it may be argued that this kind of reasoning is the kind that should be used – regardless of whether it is used – in view of the function of ethical reasoning and conscience in society, or in view of what counts as a "moral judgment" or as "moral reasoning" or as "justified ethical reasoning."

Discussions of utilitarianism in these two contexts are not as different as might at first appear. If some kind of utilitarian reasoning can be shown to be what reflective people do use, or if it can be shown to be the kind all ought to use, then presumably utilitarianism as a normative position – as the one "valid" principle in normative ethics – can be established, in the way we can expect to establish such things in ethics.

The formulation of utilitarianism I shall work out in this paper, then, can be viewed in either of two ways, corresponding with the persuasions of the reader. It can be viewed as a candidate for the status of normative "truth," or, for the noncognitivist, for whatever status is in his theory the analogue of truth in cognitivist theories. Or it can be viewed as a way of thinking or reasoning, as a rule of valid inference – the central theme either of considerations which play a role in the ethical inferences of reliable moral judges, or of considerations which would play a certain role in ethical thinking if we thought as we ought to do, in view of the functions (etc.) of ethical discourse. One way of putting the contrast is this: we can view our formulation either as a candidate for the status of being a true principle of normative ethics or as a rule for valid inferences in ethics. I am not, incidentally, suggesting that it is a merely terminological matter which view we take of it; I think it is *not* merely this, since the kinds of reasoning used to support one view may be quite different from those used to support the other view. My point is that the theory I wish to discuss may properly be considered in either light, and that the difficulties I shall raise are difficulties which must be taken seriously by philosophers who discuss utilitarianism in either of these contexts. Mostly, I shall talk for convenience as if utilitarianism were a normative principle; but everything I say, and all the difficulties I consider, can just as well be placed in the context of metaethical discussion.

The view to be discussed is a form of "rule-utilitarianism." This terminology must be explained. I call a utilitarianism "act-utilitarianism" if it holds that the rightness of an act is fixed by the utility of *its* consequences, as compared with those of other acts the agent might perform instead. Act-utilitarianism is hence an atomistic theory: the value of the effects of a single act on the world is decisive for its rightness. "Rule-utilitarianism," in contrast, applies to views according to which the rightness of an act is not fixed by *its* relative utility, but by conformity with general rules or principles; the utilitarian feature of these theories consists in the fact that the correctness of these rules or principles is fixed in some way by the utility of their general acceptance. In contrast with the atomism of act-utilitarianism, rule-utilitarianism is in a sense an organic theory: the rightness of individual acts can be ascertained only by assessing a whole social policy.

Neither form of utilitarianism is necessarily committed on the subject of what counts as "utility": not on the meaning or function of such phrases as "maximize intrinsic good," and not on the identity of intrinsic goods – whether enjoyments, or states of persons, or states of affairs, such as equality of distribution.

In recent years, types of rule-utilitarianism have been the object of much interest.[1] And for good reason. Act-utilitarianism, at least given the assumptions about what is valuable which utilitarians commonly make, has implications which it is difficult to accept.[2] It implies that if you have employed a boy to mow your lawn and he has finished the job and asks for his pay, you should pay him what you promised only if you cannot find a better use for your money. It implies that when you bring home your monthly pay-check you should use it to support your family and yourself only if it cannot be used more effectively to supply the needs of others. It implies that if your father is ill and has no prospect of good in his life, and maintaining him is a drain on the energy and enjoyments of others, then, if you can end his life without provoking any public scandal or setting a bad example, it is your positive duty to take matters into your own hands and bring his life to a close. A virtue of rule-utilitarianism, in at least some of its forms, is that it avoids at least some of such objectionable implications.

In the present paper I wish to arrive at a more precise formulation of a rule-utilitarian type of theory which is different from act-utilitarianism and which is not subject to obvious and catastrophic difficulties. To this end I shall, after an important preliminary discussion, begin by considering two formulations, both supported by distinguished philosophers, which, as I shall show, lead us in the wrong direction. This discussion will lead to a new formulation devised to avoid the consequences of the first theories. I shall then describe three problems which the new theory seems to face, and consider how – by amendments or otherwise – these difficulties may be met.

1.   Utilitarianism as a Theory About the Objectively Right

Before we can proceed there is a preliminary issue to be settled. It is generally agreed that utilitarianism is a proposal about which acts are *right* or *wrong*. Unfortunately it is also widely held – although this is a matter of dispute – that these terms are used in several senses. Hence, in order to state the utilitarian thesis clearly, we must identify which sense of these words (if there is more than one) we have in mind. Utilitarianism may be clearly false in all of its forms if it is construed as a universal statement about which acts are right or wrong, in some of the senses in which these words are, or at least are supposed to be, used.

It is plausible to say that "wrong" is sometimes used in a sense equivalent to "morally blameworthy" or "reprehensible," in a sense which implies the propriety of disapproval of the agent for his deed. Now, if utilitarianism is understood as a theory about right and wrong actions in this sense, I believe it is an indefensible theory in all its forms. For we have good reason to think that whether an act is wrong in this sense depends in part on such things as whether the agent sincerely believed he was doing his duty, whether the temptation to do what he did was so strong that only a person of very unusual firmness of will would have succeeded in withstanding it, and whether the agent's action was impulsive and provoked, or deliberate and unprovoked. If whether an act is wrong depends in part on any one of these factors, then it is difficult to see how the utilitarian thesis that rightness or wrongness is in some sense a function of utility can be correct.

We can, however, construe utilitarianism as a thesis about which acts are right or wrong in some other sense. It may, for instance, be taken as a theory about which acts are right or wrong in a forward-looking sense, which I shall call the "objective" sense. But what is this sense? It is by no means easy to say; and we must be careful not to describe some alleged sense of these words which in fact they never bear in common speech at all. Let me explain this possible second sense by means of an example.

Consider Eisenhower's position at the summit conference in 1960. Khrushchev demanded that Eisenhower apologize, as a condition for negotiation. Let us suppose that Eisenhower proceeded to ask himself the moral question, "What is the morally right thing for me to do now? Is it my moral obligation to apologize or to refuse to apologize?" Clearly, it would seem, this is a question he might have asked himself, whether he did or not. Obviously, if he did try to answer this question, he must have considered many things. One thing he must have considered was the state of Khrushchev's mind. Did Khrushchev really think there had been a breach of faith, an affront to the Russian people, which in decency called for at least an apology? Was Khrushchev really willing to negotiate for peace if only this – which might relieve some political pressures at home – were done? Everything considered, would an apology, however personally distasteful (and perhaps politically unfortunate, at home), markedly promote the cause of peace? Let us suppose that Eisenhower surveyed these points as carefully as possible with his advisers and came to a conclusion on them. And let us suppose that he then moved to a moral conclusion. Presumably his conclusion (if he raised the moral question) was that it was not his duty to apologize, that on the contrary it was his duty *not* to apologize. But surely in a complex situation of this sort he must have put his conclusion in a qualified way; he must have said something like, "*Probably* it is my duty not to apologize." And, conceivably, he might some day change his mind about this, and say to himself, "It was my duty to apologize; my judgment then was mistaken." I think we shall all agree that he might well have expressed himself in this qualified way and that he might later revise his judgment in the manner suggested.

The crucial thing about understanding the sense in which "duty" (or "wrong") is here being used is whether the qualifying "probably" is introduced or whether the revision conceding a "mistake" may be made, for one reason or for another. Does he say "probably" because he does not and cannot know Khrushchev's real state of mind? Does he say a "mistake" was made because, as it turns out, Khrushchev's state of mind was really different from what at the time he supposed it to be? If the answer to these questions is affirmative, then evidently duty depends, at least to some extent, on what the facts really are and not merely on what one thinks they are, even after careful consultation with advisers. But if the answer is negative, then it is open to one to say that the qualification and mistakes come in only because it is so difficult to *balance* different considerations, and that what is one's duty does not depend on what the facts really are, but only on what one thinks they are, at least after properly careful reflection and investigation.

If we answer these questions in the affirmative and consequently say that "duty" is sometimes used in a sense such that whether something is one's duty depends on what the facts really are, then we are conceding that the word (and, presumably, "right" and "wrong" and "moral obligation") is sometimes used in an "objective" sense – the sense in which G. E. Moore thought it was sometimes used when he wrote *Ethics* and *Principia Ethica*. And if so, it is not entirely stupid to propose, as Moore did, that furthermore, an act is right, in that objective sense of "right," if and only if its *actual* consequences, whether foreseeable at the time or not, are such that the performance of the act produces at least as much intrinsic good as could be produced by any other act the agent could perform instead. It is this sense of these terms – the sense in which duty (etc.) depends on what the facts really are and not on what the agent thinks about them – which I am terming the "objective" sense. I shall construe utilitarianism as a proposal about which acts are right or wrong in this objective sense.

It would be foolish, however, to say that it is quite *obvious* that the answer to the above questions is in the affirmative; and consequently it would be foolish to affirm without doubt that there is a sense of "duty" in which duty depends on what the facts are and not on what the agent thinks they are – and much more foolish to affirm without doubt that there is *no* sense of "duty" in which duty depends, not on the facts, but on what the agent thinks the facts are, at least after properly careful investigation.

Philosophers who think these words have no "objective" sense at all, or who at least think there is still a third sense of these terms, over and above the two I have sketched, probably can mostly be said to think that these words are used in what we may call the "subjective" sense – and either that this is their only sense or that it is one ordinary sense. They do not agree among themselves about what this sense is. Some of them hold that "right" (etc.) is sometimes so used that – if I may identify their conception by my own terminology, which, of course, some of them would not accept – an act is right in that sense if and only if it would have been right in my objective sense, if the facts had really been what the agent thought they were, or at least would have thought they were if he had investigated properly. What is one's duty, on this view, depends on what the agent thinks about the facts – or would think if he investigated properly – not on what the facts really are. Naturally, if one has this (alleged) sense of "duty" or "right" in mind when formulating the principle of utilitarianism, one will say the principle is that an act is right if and only if the agent *thinks* – or would think, if he investigated properly – it will maximize utility (or have some such relation to utility). Or, perhaps, the principle will say that an act is right if and only if it will maximize expectable utility, or something of the sort.

The question whether there is an objective sense, or a subjective sense, or perhaps both such senses, is a difficult one. Although I think it plausible to suppose there is an "objective" sense, I do feel doubt about the matter. I propose, nevertheless, to discuss utilitarianism as a theory about right and wrong in this sense. I do so for several reasons. First, there are many philosophers who think there is such a sense, and an examination of utilitarianism construed in this way "speaks to their condition."[3]

Second, even if there were no such ordinary sense of "right," we could define such a sense by reference to the "subjective" sense of "right" (assuming there is one); and it so happens that we could say all the things that we have occasion to say in ethics by using this defined "objective" sense of "right" and also terms like "blameworthy" and "reprehensible." We could say "all we have occasion to say" in the sense that any statement we make, and think important, could be put in terms of this vocabulary. Third, it is important to see how types of rule-utilitarian theory fare if they are construed as theories about which acts are right or wrong in this sense. Doubtless sometimes writers on this topic have not kept clearly in mind just which sense of "right" they were talking about; it is useful to see what difficulties arise *if* they are to be taken as talking of what is right or wrong in the objective sense. Finally, an assessment of utilitarianisms as theories about which acts are objectively right will enable us to make at least some assessments of utilitarianisms as theories about which acts are subjectively right, in view of the logical connection indicated above between "right" in the objective sense and "right" in the subjective sense.

2. Accepted Rules vs. Justifiable Rules as the Test of Rightness

It is convenient to begin by taking as our text some statements drawn from an interesting article by J. O. Urmson. In this paper, Urmson suggested that John Stuart Mill should be interpreted as a rule-utilitarian; and Urmson's opinion was that Mill's view would be more plausible if he were so interpreted. Urmson summarized the possible rule-utilitarian interpretation of Mill in four propositions, of which I quote the first two:

A. A particular action is justified as being right [in the sense of being morally obligatory] by showing that it is in accord with [is required by] some moral rule. It is shown to be wrong by showing that it transgresses some moral rule.
B. A moral rule is shown to be correct by showing that the recognition of that rule promotes the ultimate end.[4]

Urmson's first proposition could be taken in either of two ways. When it speaks of a "moral rule," it may refer to an *accepted* moral rule, presumably one accepted in the society of the agent. Alternatively, it may refer to a *correct* moral rule, presumably one the recognition of which

214 Richard B. Brandt

promotes the ultimate end. If we ask in which way the proposed theory should be taken, in order to arrive at a defensible theory, part of the answer is that qualifications are going to be required, whichever way we take it. I think it more worthwhile and promising, however, to try to develop it in the second interpretation.

Various philosophers would make the opposite judgment about which interpretation is the more promising. And there is much to be said for their view, in particular the following points. First, we shall probably all agree that the moral rules accepted in a community often do fix real obligations on members of the community. For example, among ourselves it is taken for granted that primary responsibility for caring for an old man falls on his children, although in special cases it could fall elsewhere. On the other hand, suppose that our social system contained the rule – as that of the Hopi actually does – that this responsibility falls primarily on the children of a man's sisters, again with exceptions for special cases. It seems clear that in a social system like ours the children do have responsibility for their father, whereas in a social system like that of the Hopi they do not – the responsibility belongs to the children of the sisters. There are complications, to be sure; but in general we must say that when an institutional system specifies that responsibility falls in a certain place, then on the whole and with some exceptions and qualifications, that is where it really does lie. Any theory which denies this is mistaken; and if our second theory is to be plausible, it must be framed so as to imply this. Second, I think we should concede that if two persons are debating whether some act is right and one of them is able to show that it infringes on the accepted moral code of the community, the "burden of proof" passes to the other party. The fact that it is generally believed that a certain kind of action is wrong is prima facie evidence that it is wrong; it is up to persons who disagree to show their hand. Third, if a conscientious man is deliberating whether he is morally obligated to do a certain thing which he does not wish to do, I believe he will generally feel he must do this thing, even if he thinks that a correct moral code would not require him to, provided he concludes that many or most persons in his community would conclude otherwise. The reason for this is partly, I think, that a conscientious man will take pains to avoid even the appearance of evil; but the reason is also that a conscientious man will wish to make substantial allowances for the fact that he is an interested party and might have been influenced by his own preferences in his thinking about his obligations. He will therefore tend to hold himself to the received code when this is to his disadvantage.

Nevertheless, it is extremely difficult to defend Urmson's rule interpreted in this way, even when we hedge it with qualifications, as, for example, Toulmin did. In the first place, people do not *think* that anything like this is true; they think they are assessing particular cases by reference to objectively valid principles which they happen to know, and not simply by reference to a community code. Notice how we do not find it surprising that people with unusual moral principles, such as the immorality of killing and violence in all circumstances, come to distinctive conclusions about their own particular obligations, by no means drawing their particular moral judgments from the code of the community. The whole tradition emphasizing the role of conscience in moral thinking is contrary to the view that socially accepted principles are crucial for deciding what is right or wrong. In the second place, we frequently judge ourselves to have moral obligations either when we don't know what the community "standards" are, or when we think that in all probability there is no decided majority one way or the other: for instance, with respect to sexual behavior, or to declaration, to revenue officers, of articles purchased abroad or of one's personal income. Surely we do not think that in such situations the proper judgment of particular cases is that they are morally indifferent? Third, and perhaps most important, we sometimes judge that we have an obligation when we know that the community thinks we don't; and we sometimes think an act is right when the community thinks it wrong. For instance, we may judge that we have an obligation to join in seeking presidential clemency for a convicted Communist spy whom we regard as having received an unduly severe sentence because of mass hysteria at the time of his trial, although we know quite well that the communal code prescribes no favors for Communists. Again, we may think it not wrong to work on the Sabbath, marry a divorced person, perform a medically necessary abortion, or commit suicide, irrespective of general disapproval in our group. Were these things *ever* objectively wrong, in view of being proscribed – even unanimously – by the community of the agent? (It may be replied that the "code" does not legislate for complex matters of these sorts, but only for more basic things, like Ross's list of prima facie obligations. But it is not clear what can be the basis for this distinction; the acts in question may be prohibited by law and would be reported by a visiting anthropologist as proscribed by the code.)

One might argue that the existence of an accepted moral rule is not sufficient to make particular actions wrong or obligatory but is a necessary condition. To say this, however, is to say that men have no obligation to rise above the commonplace morals of their times. Whereas in fact we do not think it right for men to be cruel to animals or to slaves in a society which condones this.

We cannot well say in advance that no thesis like Urmson's can play an important part in a defensible theory of morals, if it is interpreted in this first way. But the difficulties are surely enough to encourage experimenting with versions of the second interpretation. Let us turn to this.

For a start, we might summarize the gist of Urmson's proposal, construed in the second way, as follows: "An act is right if and only if it conforms with that set of moral rules, the recognition of which would have significantly desirable consequences." A somewhat modified version of this is what I shall be urging.

One minor amendment I wish to make immediately. I think we should replace the second clause by the expression, "the recognition of which would have the *best* consequences." This amendment may be criticized on the ground that the business of moral rules is with commanding or prohibiting actions whose performance or omission would be quite harmful if practiced widely, but not to require actions which just maximize benefits, especially if the benefit concerns only the agent. It may be said, then, that the amendment I propose is possibly a clue to *perfect* behavior but not to right behavior. But this objection overlooks an important point. We must remember that it is a serious matter to have a moral rule at all, for moral rules take conduct out of the realm of preference and free decision. So, for the recognition of a certain moral rule to have good consequences, the benefits of recognition must outweigh the costliness of restricting freedom. Therefore, to recognize a moral rule restricting self-regarding behavior will rarely have the best consequences; rules of prudence should normally not be moral rules. Again, my proposal implies that moral rules will require services for other people only when it is better to have such services performed from a sense of obligation than not performed at all; so the amendment does not commit us to saying that it is morally obligatory to perform minor altruistic services for others.

But why insist on the amendment? The reason is that the original, as I stated it (but not necessarily as Urmson intended it), is insufficiently comparative in form. The implication is that a rule is acceptable so long as it is significantly better than no regulation at all. But the effect of this is tolerantly to accept a great many rules which we should hardly regard as morally acceptable. Consider promises. There are various possible rules about when promises must be kept. One such possible rule is to require keeping *all* promises, absolutely irrespective of unforeseeable and uncontemplated hardships on the promisee. Recognition of this rule might have good consequences as compared with no rule at all. Therefore it seems to satisfy the unamended formula. Many similar rules would satisfy it. But we know of another rule – the one we recognize – with specifications about allowable exceptions, which would have much better consequences. If we are utilitarian in spirit, we shall want to endorse such a rule but not both of these rules; and the second one is much closer to our view about what our obligations are. The amendment in general endorses as correct many rules which command our support for parallel reasons, and refuses to endorse many others which we reject for parallel reasons.

3.   A Specious Rule-Utilitarianism

I shall now digress briefly, in order to bring out the importance of avoiding a form of rule-utilitarianism which seems to differ only insignificantly from our above initial suggestion, and which at first seems most attractive. It is worthwhile doing so, partly because two very interesting and important papers developing a rule-utilitarian theory may be construed as falling into the trap I shall describe.[5] I say only that they "may be" so construed because their authors are possibly using somewhat different concepts and, in particular, may not be thinking of utilitarianism as a thesis about right and wrong in the objective sense.

Suppose that we wrote, instead of the above suggested formulation, the following: "An act is right if and only if it conforms with that set of moral rules, general conformity with which would have best consequences." This phrasing is a bit vague, however, so let us expand it to this: "An act is right if and only if it conforms with that set of general prescriptions for action such that, if everyone always did, from among all the things which he could do on a given occasion, what conformed with these prescriptions, then at least as much intrinsic good would be produced as by conformity with any other set of general prescriptions." This sounds very like our above formulation. It is, however, different in a very important way: for its test of whether an act is right, or a general rule correct, is what would happen if people *really all did act* in a certain way. The test is not the consequences of recognizing a rule, or of acting with such a rule in mind; the test as stated does not require that people do, or even can, think of or formulate, much less apply the rule of a moral code. What is being said is simply that a rule is correct, and corresponding conduct right, if it would have best consequences for everyone actually to act, for whatever reason, in accordance with the rule. Of course, one of the consequences to be taken into account may be the fact that expectations of conduct according to the rule might be built up, and that people could count on conforming behavior.

This theory is initially attractive. We seem to be appealing to it in our moral reasoning when we say, "You oughtn't to do so-and-so, because if everybody in your circumstances did this, the consequences would be bad."

Nevertheless, the fact is that this theory – however hard it may be to see that it does – has identically the same consequences for behavior as does act-utilitarianism. And since it does, it is a mistake to advocate it as a theory preferable to act-utilitarianism, as some philosophers may have done. Let us see how this is.

Let us ask ourselves: What would a set of moral prescriptions be like, such that general conformity with it, in the sense intended, would have the best consequences? The answer is that the set would contain just one rule, the prescription of the *act-utilitarian*: "Perform an act, among those open to you, which will have at least as good consequences as any other." There cannot be a moral rule, conformity with which could have better consequences than this one. If it really is true that doing a certain thing will have the very best consequences in the long run, everything considered, of all the things I can do, then there is nothing better I can do than this. If everyone always did the very best thing it was possible for him to do, the total intrinsic value produced would be at a maximum. Any act which deviated from this principle would produce less good than some other act which might have been performed. It is clear, then, that the moral rule general conformity with which would produce most good is a rule corresponding to the principle of act-utilitarianism. The two theories, then, have identical consequences for behavior. I am, of course, not at all suggesting that everyone *trying* to produce the best consequences will have the same consequences as everyone *trying* to follow some different set of rules – or that everyone trying to follow some different set of rules may not have better consequences than everyone trying just to produce the best consequences. Far from it. What I am saying is that *succeeding* in producing the best consequences is a kind of success which cannot be improved upon. And it is this which is in question, when we are examining the formula we are now looking at.

To say that succeeding in producing the best consequences cannot be improved upon is consistent with admitting that what will in fact have the best consequences, in view of what other people in fact have done or will do, may be different from what would have had the best consequences if other people were to behave differently from the way in which they did or will do. The behavior of others is part of the context relevant for determining the effects of a given act of any agent.

It may be thought that this reasoning is unfair to this rule-utilitarian view. For what this theory has in mind, it may be said, is rules forbidding classes of actions described in ways other than by reference to their utility – rules forbidding actions like lies, adultery, theft, etc. So, it may be said, the principle of act-utilitarianism is not even a competitor for the position of one of the rules admitted by this theory.

My reply to this objection is twofold. In the first place, it would be rather foolish to suppose that any system of moral rules could omit rules about doing good, rules about doing what will maximize utility. Surely we do wish to include among our rules one roughly to the effect that, if we have the opportunity to do a great deal of good for others at little cost, we should do it. And also a rule to the effect that we should avoid harming others. It is no accident that W. D. Ross's list of seven prima facie obligations contains four which refer to doing good, in one way or another. But the point would still stand even if we ignore this fact. For suppose we set about to describe a set of rules, none of which is explicitly to prescribe *doing good*, but general conformity with which will maximize utility. Now obviously, the set of rules in question will be that set which prescribes, by descriptions which make no reference to having good consequences, exactly that very class of actions which would also be prescribed by the act-utilitarian principle. And one can find a set of rules which will prescribe exactly this class of acts without referring to utility. We can find such a set, because every member of the class of acts prescribed by the act-utilitarian principle will have some other property *on account of which* it will maximize utility in the circumstances. Every act, that is to say, which maximizes utility does so because of some doubtless very complex property that it has. As a result, we can set up a system of prescriptions for action which refer to these complex properties, such that our system of rules will prescribe exactly the set of acts prescribed by the act-utilitarian principle. The set of rules may be enormously long and enormously complex. But this set of rules will have the property of being that set, general conformity with which will maximize utility. And the acts prescribed will be identical with the acts prescribed by the act-utilitarian principle. So, again, the prescriptions for conduct of this form of rule-utilitarianism are identical with those of the act-utilitarian theory.

4. Rule-Utilitarianism: A Second Approximation

The whole point of the preceding remarks has been to focus attention on the point that a rule-utilitarianism like Urmson's is different from act-utilitarianism only when it speaks of something like *"recognition* of a rule having the best consequences" instead of something like "*conformity* with a certain rule having the best consequences." With this in mind, we can see clearly one of the virtues of Urmson's proposal, which we interpreted as being: "An act is right if and only if it conforms with that set of moral rules, *the recognition of which* would have the best consequences."

But, having viewed the difficulties of a view verbally very similar to the above, we are now alert to the fact that the formulation we have suggested is itself open to interpretations that may lead to problems. How may we construe Urmson's proposal, so that it is both unambiguous and credible? Of course we do not wish to go to the opposite extreme and take "recognition of" to mean merely "doffing the hat to" without attempt to practice. But how shall we take it?

I suggest the following as a second approximation.

First, let us speak of a set of moral rules as being "learnable" if people of ordinary intelligence are able to learn or absorb its provisions, so as to believe the moral propositions in question in the ordinary sense of "believe" for such contexts.[6] Next, let us speak of "the adoption" of a moral code by a person as meaning "the learning and belief of its provisions (in the above sense) and conformity of behavior to these to the extent we may expect people of ordinary conscientiousness to conform their behavior to rules they believe are principles about right or obligatory behavior." Finally, let us, purely arbitrarily and for the sake of brevity, use the phrase "maximizes intrinsic value" to mean "would produce at least as much intrinsic good as would be produced by any relevant alternative action." With these stipulations, we can now propose, as a somewhat more precise formulation of Urmson's proposal, the following rule-utilitarian thesis: "An act is right if and only if it conforms with that learnable set of rules, the adoption of which by everyone would maximize intrinsic value."

This principle does not at all imply that the rightness or wrongness of an act is contingent upon the agent's having *thought about* all the complex business of the identity of a set of ideal moral rules; it asserts, rather, that an act is right if and only if it *conforms* to such a set of rules, regardless of what the agent may think. Therefore the principle is not disqualified from being a correct principle about what is objectively right or wrong, in Moore's sense; for it makes rightness and wrongness a matter of the facts, and totally independent of what the agent thinks is right, or of what the agent thinks about the facts, or of the evidence the agent may have, or of what is probably the case on the basis of this evidence.

An obvious merit of this principle is that it gives expression to at least part of our practice or procedure in trying to find out what is right or wrong. For when we are in doubt about such matters, we often try to think out how it would work in practice to have a moral code which prohibited or permitted various actions we are considering. We do not, of course, ordinarily do anything as complicated as try to think out the *complete* ideal moral code; we are content with considering whether certain specific injunctions relevant to the problem we are considering might be included in a good and workable code. Nevertheless, we are prepared to admit that the whole ideal code is relevant. For if someone shows us that a specific injunction which we think would be an acceptable part of a moral code clearly would not work out in view of other provisions necessary to an ideal code, we should agree that a telling point had been made and revise our thinking accordingly.

In order to get a clearer idea of the kind of "set of rules" (with which right actions must conform) which could satisfy the conditions this rule-utilitarian principle lays down, let us note some general features such a set presumably would have. First, it would contain rules giving directions for recurrent situations which involve conflicts of human interests. Presumably, then, it would contain rules rather similar to W. D. Ross's list of prima facie obligations: rules about the keeping of promises and contracts, rules about debts of gratitude such as we may owe to our parents, and, of course, rules about not injuring other persons and about promoting the welfare of others where this does not work a comparable hardship on us. Second, such a set of rules would not include petty restrictions; nor, at least for the most part, would it contain purely prudential rules. Third, the rules would not be very numerous; an upper limit on quantity is set by the ability of ordinary people to learn them. Fourth, such a set of rules would not include unbearable demands; for their inclusion would only serve to bring moral obligation into discredit. Fifth, the set of rules adoption of which would have the best consequences could not leave too much to discretion. It would make concessions to the fact that ordinary people are not capable of perfectly fine discriminations, and to the fact that, not being morally perfect, people of ordinary conscientiousness will have a tendency to abuse a moral rule where it suits their interest. We must remember that a college dormitory rule like "Don't play music at such times or in such a way as to disturb the study or sleep of others" would be ideally flexible if people were perfect; since they aren't, we have to settle for a rule like "No music after 10 P.M." The same thing is true for a moral code. The best moral code has to allow for the fact that people are what they are; it has to be less flexible and less efficient than a moral code that was to be adopted by perfectly wise and perfectly conscientious people could be.

Should we think of such a moral code as containing only prescriptions for situations likely to arise in *everyone's* life – rules like "If you have made a promise, then . . ." or "If you have a parent living, then treat him thus-and-so"? Or should we think of it as containing distinct sets of prescriptions for *different roles or statuses*, such as "If you are a policeman, then . . ." or "If you are a physician, then . . ."? And if the ideal code is to contain different prescriptions for different roles and statuses, would it not be so complex that it could not be learned by people of ordinary intelligence? The answer to these questions is that the rule-utilitarian is not committed, by his theory, to the necessity of such special codes, although I believe he may well admit their desirability – admit, for instance, that it is a good thing for a physician to carry a rule in his mental kit, specially designed to answer the question, "Shall I treat a patient who does not pay his bill?" In any case, our rule-utilitarian theory can *allow* for such special rules. Nor is there a difficulty in the fact that people of normal intelligence could hardly learn all these special sets of rules. For we can mean, by saying that a code can be "learned" by people of ordinary intelligence, that any person can learn all the rules relevant to the problems *he* will face. A rule-utilitarian will not, of course, have in mind a moral code which in some part is secret – for instance, lawyers having a moral code known only to themselves, a code which it would be harmful for others to know about. For surely in the long run it could not have best consequences for a society to have a moral code, perhaps granting special privileges to some groups, which could not stand the light of public knowledge.

5.   First Problem: Moral Codes for an Imperfect Society

Our "second approximation" to a rule-utilitarian principle has proposed that an act is right if and only if it conforms with the requirements of a learnable moral code, the adoption of which by *everyone* would maximize utility – and meaning by "adoption of a code" the learning and belief that the code lays down the requirements for moral behavior, and conformity to it to the extent we may expect from people of *ordinary conscientiousness*.

The italicized words in the preceding paragraph indicate two respects in which the proposed test of rightness in a sense departs from reality. In actuality moral codes are not subscribed to by everybody in all particulars: there is virtual unanimity on some items of what we call "the code of the community" (such as the prohibition of murder and incest), but on other matters there is less unanimity (in the United States, the "code" permits artificial birth-control measures despite disapproval by many Catholics), and it is a somewhat arbitrary matter to decide when the disagreement has become so general that we ought not to speak of something as part of the code of the community at all. There is probably some measure of disagreement on many or most moral matters in most modern communities (and, surely, in at least many primitive communities). Furthermore, our proposal, in an effort to be definite about the degree of commitment involved in the "adoption" of a code, spoke of an "ordinary conscientiousness." This again departs from reality. Ordinary conscientiousness may be the exception: many people are extremely, perhaps even overly conscientious; at the other extreme, some people act as if they have developed no such thing as a conscience at all. It is characteristic of actual communities that there is a wide range in degrees of conscientiousness.

As a result of these departures from reality, our test for rightness savors a bit of the utopian. We are invited to think of different worlds, each populated by people of "ordinary conscientiousness," all of whom are inoculated with a standard moral code. We are to decide whether given types of action are right or wrong by considering which of these hypothetical communities would realize a maximum of value.

There is force in the proposal. In fact, if we are thinking of sponsoring some ideal, this conception is a useful one for appraising whatever ideal we are considering. Just as we might ask whether large military establishments or a capitalist economy would be suitable for the ideal community of the future, so we can ask whether certain features of our present moral code would be suitable in such a community. It may be that such a conception should play a large role in deciding what ultimate ideals we should espouse.

Nevertheless, this conception may, from its very framework, necessarily be unsuitable for deciding the rightness of actions in the real world. It appears that, in fact, this is the case with both of the features mentioned above.

First, the proposal is to test rightness by the desirability of a rule in a moral code among people of ordinary conscientiousness. Now, in a community composed of people of ordinary conscientiousness we do not have to provide for the contingency of either saints or great sinners. In particular, we do not have to provide for the occurrence of people like Adolf Hitler. In such a community, presumably, we could get along with a minimal police force, perhaps an unarmed police force. Similarly, it would seem there would be no value in a moral prescription like "Resist evil men." In the community envisaged, problems of a certain sort would presumably not arise, and therefore the moral code need not have features designed to meet those problems. Very likely, for instance, a moral code near to that of extreme pacifism would work at least as well as a code differing in its non-pacifism.

More serious is the flaw in the other feature: that the test of rightness is to be compatibility with the requirements of the moral code, adoption of which *by everyone* would maximize utility. The trouble with this is that it permits behavior which really would be desirable if everyone agreed, but which might be objectionable and undesirable if not everyone agreed. For instance, it may well be that it would have the best consequences if the children are regarded as responsible for an elderly parent who is ill or needy; but it would be most unfortunate if the members of a Hopi man's native household – primarily his sisters and their families – decided that their presently recognized obligation had no standing on this account, since the result would be that as things now stand, no one at all would take the responsibility. Again, if everyone recognized an obligation to share in duties pertaining to national defense, it would be morally acceptable to require this legally; but it would hardly be morally acceptable to do so if there are pacifists who on moral grounds are ready to die rather than bear arms. And similarly for other matters about which there are existing and pronounced moral convictions.

It seems clear that some modification must be made if our rule-utilitarian proposal is to have implications consistent with the moral convictions of thoughtful people. Unfortunately it is not clear just what the modification should be. The one I am inclined to adopt is as follows. First, we must drop that part of our conception which assumes that people in our hypothetical societies are of ordinary conscientiousness. We want to allow for the existence of both saints and sinners and to have a moral code to cope with them. In order to do this, we had better move closer to Urmson's original suggestion. We had better drop the notion of "adoption" and replace it by his term "recognition," meaning by "recognition by all" simply "belief by all that the rules formulate moral requirements." Second, we must avoid the conception of the acceptance of all the rules of a given moral code by *everybody* and replace it by something short of this, something which does not rule out the problems created by actual convictions about morals. Doing so means a rather uneasy compromise, because we cannot sacrifice the central feature of the rule-utilitarian view, which is that the rightness of an act is to be tested by whether it conforms with rules the (somehow) general acceptance of which would maximize utility. The compromise I propose is this: that the test whether an act is right is whether it is compatible with that set of rules which, were it to replace the moral commitments of members of the *actual society* at the time, *except where there are already fairly decided moral convictions*, would maximize utility.

The modified theory, then, is this: "An act is right if and only if it conforms with that learnable set of rules, the recognition of which as morally binding, roughly at the time of the act, by all actual people insofar as these rules are not incompatible with existing fairly decided moral commitments, would maximize intrinsic value."[7]

The modification has the effect that whether an act is right depends to some extent on such things as (1) how large a proportion of the actual population is conscientious and (2) what are the existing fairly decided moral beliefs at the time. This result is not obviously a mistake.

6. Second Problem: Conflicts of Rules

The objection is sure to be raised against any rule-utilitarian theory of the general sort we are considering that the whole conception is radically misconceived. For the theory proposes that what makes an act right is its conformity to the set of rules, recognition of which would maximize utility; and it is proposed that if we are in serious doubt whether an action would be right, we should ask ourselves whether it would conform with a utility-maximizing set of rules. Now, the objection will run, the very conception of such a set of rules evaporates, or else appears to involve contradictions, when we try to get it in sharp focus. The very idea of a set of rules simple enough to be learned and different from act-utilitarianism, and at the same time sufficiently comprehensive and precise to yield directions for conduct in every situation which may arise, is an impossible dream.

The reason is that moral problems are often quite complex. There are pros and cons – obligations and counter-obligations – which have to be weighed delicately. For instance, a promise that has been made to do something is normally a point in favor of saying that doing it is obligatory; but just how much force the promise will have depends on various circumstances, such as when it was made, how solemnly it was made, whether it was fully understood by both parties, etc. The force of these circumstances cannot be stated and weighed by any set of rules. There is a moral to be drawn, it may be said, from W. D. Ross's theory of prima facie obligations: Ross could provide no general direction for what to do when prima facie obligations conflict; he had to leave the resolution of such conflicts to conscience or intuition. So, in general, no code simple enough to be written down and learned (and different from act-utilitarianism) can prescribe what is right in complex cases.

The difficulty is obviously a serious one. If the very concept of a complete code, the recognition of which would maximize utility, cannot be explained in detail, then the proposal that the rightness of every action is fixed by its conformity with the provisions of such a code must be abandoned.

What must be done to meet this charge? Of course, it cannot be demanded that we actually produce the ideal moral code for our society, or even a complete code of which the correct code might be supposed to be a variation. What can be fairly demanded is that we describe classes of rules or elements which may be expected in the ideal code, and that we make clear, in the course of this description, that the rules constituting the classes are simple enough to be learned, and that a person who had learned the rules of the several classes would be in a position to give an answer to all moral questions – or at least as definite an answer as can reasonably be expected. We may suppose that, if the theory is to be plausible, these classes of rules will be familiar – that they will be rules which thoughtful people do use in deciding moral issues. Let us see what can be said.

It is clear that a complete moral code must contain rules or principles of more than one level. The lowest level will consist of rules devised to cover familiar recurrent situations, presumably rather like those proposed by Ross in his formulation of prima facie obligations. Thus, it will contain rules like "Do not injure conscious beings," "Do what you have promised to do," etc. On reflection, we can see that such rules must be qualified in two ways. First, each of them must conclude with an exceptive clause something like "except as otherwise provided in this code." But second, they must be more complex than our samples; as Ross well knew, such simple rules do not state accurately what we think are our prima facie obligations – and presumably such rules are not the rules it would maximize welfare to have recognized as first-order rules. Consider for instance the rule I have suggested about promises. It is too simple, for we do not seriously believe that *all* promises have even a prima facie claim to be fulfilled; nor would it be a good thing for people to think they ought. For instance, we think there is no obligation at all to keep a promise made on the basis of deliberate misrepresentation by the promisee; and it is to the public interest that we should think as we do. Just as the law of contracts lists various types of contracts which it is against the public interest for the courts to enforce, so there are types of promises the fulfillment of which we do not think obligatory, and a moral requirement to fulfill them would be contrary to the public interest. The lowest-level group of rules, then, will include one about promise-keeping which will state explicitly which types of promises must be kept except when some more stringent obligation intervenes. And the same for the other basic moral rules.

I do not know if anyone would contend that it would be impossible to write down an exact statement formulating our total prima facie obligations – the kinds of considerations which to some extent make a moral claim on agents. I do not know if anyone would say that in principle we cannot state exactly the list of prima facie obligations it would maximize utility for everyone to feel. Whether or not anyone does say that a list of exact prima facie obligations cannot be stated, I know of no solid argument which can be put forward to show that this is the case. I do not believe a satisfactory list *has* been provided (Ross's statement being quite abbreviated), but I know of no sound reason for thinking that it cannot be. It would not, I think, be an impossible inquiry to determine what is the total set of distinct fundamental prima facie obligations people in fact do recognize in their moral thinking.

A set of first-level rules, however, is not enough. For moral perplexities arise most often where there are conflicts of prima facie obligations, where there would be conflicts of the first-level moral rules. If the rule-utilitarian theory is to work, it must provide for the resolution of such perplexities. How can this be done?

The problem can be partially met by supposing that a complete moral code will contain second-level rules specifically prescribing for conflicts of the basic rules. One second-level rule might be: "Do not injure anyone solely in order to produce something good, unless the good achieved be substantially greater than the injury." In fact we already learn and believe rules roughly of this kind. For instance, Ross suggested in *The Right and the Good* that we think there is normally a stronger obligation to avoid injury to others than to do good or to keep one's promises. A moral code can contain some such second-order rules without intolerable complexity.

But such rules will hardly be numerous enough to solve all the problems. And the rule we stated was not precise: it used the vague phrase "substantially greater," which is clear enough, in context, to decide for many situations, but it is by no means precise enough to legislate for all. I think, therefore, that if the very conception of a set of rules simple enough to be learned and adequate to adjudicate all possible cases is to be intelligible, it must be possible to formulate a consistent and plausible "remainder-rule," that is, a top-level rule giving adequate directions for all cases for which the lower-level rules do not prescribe definitely enough or for which their prescriptions are conflicting. We are not here called upon to identify the correct remainder-rule – although we know that the rule-utilitarian theory is that the correct one is the one the recognition of which (etc.) would do most good. What we are called upon to do is to sketch out what such a rule might well be like.

It is worthwhile to mention two possibilities for a remainder-rule.[8] First, such a rule might specify that all cases not legislated for by other clauses in the code be decided simply on the basis of comparative utility of consequences. For such cases, then, the remainder-rule would prescribe exactly what the act-utilitarian principle prescribes. Second (and I think this possibility the more interesting), the remainder-rule might be: "One is obligated to perform an action if and only if a person who knew the relevant facts and had them vividly in mind, had been carefully taught the other rules of this code, and was uninfluenced by interests beyond those arising from learning the code, would feel obligated to perform that action." Such a rule could decide cases not legislated for by the remainder of the code only if the explicit rules were taught so as to be connected with different degrees of *felt obligation*. In some cases such an association could be established by the very content of the rule, for instance, in the case of a rule stating that there is an obligation not to injure others, and that the obligation increases in strength with the amount of injury involved. Another example is that of second-level rules about the priorities of first-level rules. In other cases the association might be fixed simply by the relative insistence or firmness of the teachers, with respect to the rule in question. As a result of the rules being taught in this way, conscientious people would have established in them hesitations, of different degrees of strength, to do certain sorts of things – in other words, a sense of obligation to do or avoid certain things, the sense having different force for different things. Therefore, when persons so trained were faced with a situation in which lower-order rules gave conflicting directions (and where no higher-order rule assigned an explicit priority), they would hesitate to resolve the problem in various ways because of the built-in sense of obligation. Now, the proposed remainder-rule would in effect be a somewhat qualified prescription to take whatever course of action would leave morally well-trained people least dissatisfied. (I imagine that something like this is what Ross had in mind when he said that in complex situations one must rely on one's intuition.) The rule-utilitarian proposal is, of course, that the correct degree of felt obligation to be associated with a rule is, like the order of priorities expressed in the second-level rules, fixed by the relative utilities of the various possible arrangements – partly the utilities of the adjudications of complex cases by the remainder-rule.

It is after all possible, then, for a moral code different from act-utilitarianism to be simple enough to be learned and still able to decide for all problems which may arise.

7. Third Problem: Relativity to the Agent's Society

One final complication may be needed in the rule-utilitarian proposal. In place of saying that the rightness of an act is fixed by conformity with the prescriptions of the moral code, the recognition of which as morally binding by people (etc.) *everywhere* would maximize intrinsic good, we might say that the rightness of an act is fixed by conformity with the prescriptions of that moral code, the recognition of which as morally binding by people *in the agent's society* would maximize intrinsic good. This kind of complication should be avoided if possible, because it is difficult to assign a definite meaning to the phrase "in the agent's society." We should notice, incidentally, that it is *not* suggested that the test be the maximizing of intrinsic good only in the agent's society; such a thesis would promise quite dubious consequences.

A modification of this sort would admit a kind of relativism into ethics. For, while it is consistent with the rule-utilitarian principle itself being correct for everyone, it has the consequence that an act might be right in one society which would be wrong in another society. For instance, it might be a moral obligation for a man to support his elderly father in one society, but not his obligation in another society. Most philosophers, however, would probably view this kind of relativism as innocuous, since such differences in obligation could occur only when conditions in the two societies were different in such a way that recognition of one rule by one society would have best consequences, and recognition of a different rule by another society would also have best consequences.

But is there any reason for adopting this complicating feature? Why not say that, if a moral code is valid for anybody it is valid for everybody? Surely, it will be said, *some* moral rules are universally valid – perhaps, for instance, a rule forbidding a person from causing another pain merely in order to give himself pleasure. And if so, perhaps we can go on, with Ross, to say that the fundamental principles of obligation are universally true, although their application in special circumstances may give rise to an *appearance* of society-bound rules. For instance, Ross would say that "Keep your promises" is universally a true and important first-level rule. But in some places a thing is promised with certain mutually-understood but not explicitly stated conditions, while in other places the implicit conditions are different. As a result, the conduct required, in view of the explicit promise, by the universally valid principle is different in different societies. Or again, "Thou shalt not steal" or "Thou shalt not commit adultery" might be construed as universally valid injunctions, the first being not to take property which, according to the institutions of the society, is recognized as belonging to another, and the second, not to have sexual relations with any person if either party is, according to the custom of the society, the marriage partner of another. All fundamental moral principles, then, may be thought to have intersocietal validity; only the specific conduct enjoined or prohibited may vary from one society to another because of local conditions.

This view, however, faces serious difficulties. In order to bring these into focus, let us consider an example: the obligations of a father to his children. In the United States, I believe, it is thought that a father should see to it – within the limits of his financial capacities – that his children receive a good education, enjoy physical and mental health, and have some security against unforeseeable catastrophes. Contrast this with a society, like that of the Hopi, in which responsibility for children falls primarily on a household, "household" being defined primarily by blood-ties with the mother. In this situation, responsibility for children is primarily a problem for the mother and her blood relatives. (The factual accuracy of these assertions is not, I believe, a material consideration.) In the United States, the father is generally charged with responsibility for bringing the welfare, or prospects of welfare, of his children up to a certain rough minimum; in the Hopi society this responsibility falls roughly on other persons, although the father may share in it as far as affection dictates. Correspondingly, in the United States grown children have responsibility for their father, whereas among the Hopi the responsibility for the father belongs elsewhere – not on a man's own children but on the household of the father, the one to which he belongs through blood-ties with his mother and siblings.

I take it nobody is going to argue that fathers in the United States do not have the obligations they are generally thought to have, or that Hopi fathers do have obligations which are generally thought to fall elsewhere. (There may be some exceptions to this.) Therefore, if there is to be a *universal* moral rule locating obligations for the welfare of children, it will be one which roughly places it, at least for the present, where it is recognized to be in these societies. What kind of rule might this be? It is hard to say. Very possibly there is uniformity of assignment of such responsibilities in societies with a certain kind of social structure, and hence one could conceivably state a general rule prescribing that fathers do certain things in societies of a specified sociological description. It is doubtful, however, whether such a rule is simple enough to be learned. Moreover, social structures may be too much organic wholes to permit even such generalizations; if so, in respect of some kinds of conduct there can be no general, intersocietally valid moral rule at all.

There is another way of putting much the same point. Instead of asking whether we can frame a general rule which will have implications for particular societies coincident with what we should want to say are the actual locations of responsibilities in these societies, we might ask whether any universal rules can be framed, recognition of which as morally binding would have consequences comparably as good as local rules, devised on the basis of examination of individual institutional structures as a whole. Is the universality of moral rules to be so sacrosanct that we shall not recognize a moral rule as binding on a given society unless it can be viewed as a special case of some universally valid rule? A person who wishes to make utility the test of moral rules will, I think, wish to make the utility of local rules his test.

It may be supposed that the example of family obligations is untypically complex. But to do so would be a mistake. The responsibilities of physicians and teachers – or professional men in general – to the individuals whom they serve pose similar difficulties. So do the ethics of borrowing and the charging of interest. It is possible that the broad outlines of prohibited and required behavior will be rather similar in all societies. But when we come to the fine points – the exceptions, the qualifications, the priorities – we are in for difficulties if we must defend the view that statable universal rules are the best ones for everybody to feel bound by, or that they conform to serious opinions about the location of obligations in various types of society. This, I think, has been the conclusion of various "self-realizationist" philosophers like A. MacBeath and C. A. Campbell.

Let us then consider (without necessarily insisting that it be adopted) the view that the rightness of an act is fixed by conformity with the prescriptions of that moral code, the recognition of which as morally binding by people (etc.) *in the agent's society* would maximize intrinsic good. Can we propose a meaning of "in the agent's society" sufficiently definite that we can say the proposal is at least a clear one?

How shall we identify "the society" of the agent? This question could have been answered fairly simply in much earlier times when all societies were rather clearly demarcated atomic units, although when we remember the relationships of the *kula* reported by Malinowski, we can see that matters were not always so simple even among primitive peoples. The question is difficult in a modern civilization. What is a Columbia

University professor who lives in the suburbs to count as his "society"? The faculty club? His suburb? New York City? The state of New York? Any choice seems a bit arbitrary. Or suppose Khrushchev makes a promise to Eisenhower. What society should we bear in mind as the one the utility of a set of rules in which sets the standard of right and wrong?

Very tentatively, I am inclined to suggest that we understand the "society of an agent" in the following way. An individual, I suggest, may live in several "moral worlds," and the rules for these several moral worlds may be different. For one thing, he is a member of a succession of local groups, each one more inclusive than the last: the local community, the metropolitan area, etc. Now a good part of one's life is lived as a resident, a neighbor, a citizen. Insofar as moral problems arise as part of one's life in this capacity, the problem is to be settled by reference to the rules best for the geographical community. How wide a geographical community should we pick? The best answer seems to be: the largest area over which common rules can be adopted without loss of utility. If it were costly in utility to apply to a borough the rules which were the best for the metropolitan area, then we had better consider our case in the light of rules useful for the smaller group. But a person has other roles besides that of citizen and neighbor. One may be a member of groups which transcend the local community – perhaps nation-wide associations, class, or caste. Most important, perhaps, are transactions resulting from the institutional involvement of the participants; for example, business transactions involving corporations or unions, or the affairs of the church, or educational affairs, or the activities of the press or radio. In these cases a segment of the life-relations of the individuals involved consists in their interactions with others who have the same role or who participate in the same institution. In such cases, I suggest that the moral rules governing behavior should be the rules adoption of which by the relevant group (for example, the group participating in a given institution) would be best, as governing the transactions of that group. It may be, of course, that we do not need some of these complications, that there is no need to distinguish the rules for businessmen in dealing with each other or with a union from the ones properly followed in one's relations with wife and neighbor.[9]

8. Concluding Remarks

The principle with which we end is this: "An act is right if and only if it conforms with that learnable set of rules the recognition of which as morally binding – roughly at the time of the act – by everyone in the society of the agent, except for the retention by individuals of already formed and decided moral convictions, would maximize intrinsic value."[10]

I wish to make three final comments on this principle.

First, one may ask whether a set of moral rules which would maximize intrinsic value in the way described would necessarily be a *just* set of rules. Surely, if the rules are not just, conformity with them will by no means guarantee that an action is right. A further inquiry must be made about whether additional requirements are needed to assure that moral rules are just. It may be that, as I have suggested elsewhere, none is called for if equality of some sort is an intrinsic good.

Second, if the proposed principle is correct, we can give at least a partial answer to a person who asks *why* he ought to perform actions he is obligated to perform, if they conflict with his self-interest. Perhaps a person who asks such a question is merely confused, and his query not worth our attention. But we can say to him that one reason for meeting his obligation is that by doing so he plays the game of living according to the rules which will maximize welfare. And this will be, at least partially, a satisfying answer to a man who is activated by love or sympathy or respect directed at other sentient beings generally.

Finally, some reflections on the employment of the principle. It is, perhaps, obvious that it is not necessary to advocate that everyone always bear the rule-utilitarian principle in mind in deciding what he ought to do. Not that it would be harmful – beyond the waste of time – to do so; for it is obvious that the clear moral obligations are prescribed by the principle. For example, only an instant's thought is required to see that it is socially useful to recognize the rule that solemn promises should be kept – doubtless with some qualifications. The rule's employment is important, however, in analyzing more difficult cases, in making clear whether a given moral rule should be qualified in a certain way. Of course, it would be foolish to suggest that application of the principle is an easy road to the resolution of moral problems. It may very often be that after most careful reflection along the lines suggested, the most that can be said is that a given action is probably the one which the principle requires. If so, if we accept the principle, we can go on to say that this action is probably the right one.

Notes

1   In one form or another its plausibility has been urged by J. O. Urmson, Kurt Baier, J. D. Mabbott, Stephen Toulmin, R. F. Harrod, Kai Neilsen, A. MacBeath, C. A. Campbell, Jonathan Harrison, Marcus Singer, and, to some extent, John

Rawls and P. H. Nowell-Smith. Mabbott has expressed the opinion that the essence of it is to be found in Francis Hutcheson.

2   In this paper I propose to ignore that form of act-utilitarianism which proposes to close the gap between what seems to be right and the implications of act-utilitarianism, by asserting that such things as promise-keeping are intrinsically good. This form of theory has most recently been defended by Oliver Johnson in his *Rightness and Goodness* (The Hague: Martinus Nijhoff, 1959).

I am inclined to agree that there are some intrinsically good things which are not states of persons – for instance, equality of distribution of welfare. But act-utilitarians require to count further things – such as specific traits of character like truthfulness, or complexes like the-keeping-of-a-promise – as intrinsically good in order to square with reasonable convictions about what is right or wrong. But surely it is contrary to the spirit of utilitarianism to decide the issue, say, whether a promise should be kept by appeal to such intrinsic values. One would have thought the utilitarian would test the merits of traits of character like truthfulness by examining whether they have good consequences rather than decide that there is an obligation to tell the truth by considering the intrinsic goodness of truthfulness. Should not the issue of the intrinsic goodness of truthfulness wait upon reasoning to show that it is a good thing to tell the truth? One who denies this is far from traditional utilitarian thought. In any case, can we seriously claim that the-keeping-of-a-promise is an intrinsic good? It would be absurd to hold that we can add to the value of the world by the simple device of making promises and then keeping them, irrespective of what is effected by the keeping of them. Presumably, then, what is held is rather that the-breaking-of-a-promise is intrinsically bad. But how will it be shown that precisely this is intrinsically bad? Suppose I promise to do something no one wants done, and everyone is greatly relieved when I fail to perform. Is this intrinsically evil?

The kind of utilitarianism I propose here to discuss is one with narrower commitments about what is intrinsically good – one which does not claim that specific kinds of action or specific traits of character (like truthfulness or fidelity) are intrinsically good or bad. This kind of utilitarianism is worth assessment even if my reasons for ignoring other types are unsound.

3   Notice that such philosophers are not refuted by the mere consideration that sometimes we say "is right" and not "is probably right" even when we know we lack evidence about some facts that might be relevant to what is right in the objective sense. It would be a mistake to infer from such usage that we are not employing "right" in the objective sense. For, in general, we are entitled to make any assertion roundly without the qualifying word "probable" if we know of no definite grounds for questioning the truth of the assertion.

4   J. O. Urmson, "The Interpretation of the Philosophy of J. S. Mill," *Philosophical Quarterly*, III (1953), 33–9.

5   These articles are: J. Harrison, "Utilitarianism, Universalization, and Our

Duty to be Just," *Proceedings of the Aristotelian Society*, Vol. LIII (1952–53), pp. 105–34; and R. F. Harrod, "Utilitarianism Revised," *Mind*, n.s. XLV (1936), 137–56.

6 To say that a moral code can be learned by a person is not to say he can learn to *recite* it. It is enough if he learns it well enough to recall the relevant rule when stimulated by being in a context to which it is relevant, Learning a moral code is thus like learning a complex route into a large city: we may not be able to draw it or explain to others what it is, but when we drive it and have the landmarks before us, we remember each turn we are to make.

7 This formulation is rather similar in effect to one suggested to me by Wilfrid Sellars. (I have no idea whether he now inclines toward it, or whether he ever did lean toward it strongly.) This is: "An act is right if and only if it conforms with that set of rules the *teaching of which* to the society of the agent, at the time of the action, would maximize welfare." This formulation is simpler, but it has its own problems. Teaching to which and how many individuals? By whom? With what skill and means? We should remember that it may be unwise to teach children the rules that are best for adults and that it may sometimes be desirable to teach ideals which are more extreme than we want people actually to live by, e.g., those of the Sermon on the Mount.

8 It will probably be clear why the remainder-rule cannot simply be the rule-utilitarian principle itself. For the rule-utilitarian principle states that an act is right if and only if it conforms with the rules of a certain kind of code. If one of the rules of the code were the rule-utilitarian principle, it would contain reference to a code which presumably would itself contain again the rule-utilitarian principle, and so on ad infinitum.

9 The above discussion shows that the theory that what is right is behavior conforming with the *accepted* rules of the agent's society has complications which have not been adequately discussed.

10 As the principle now stands, a given individual might have to learn several codes, corresponding to his several roles in society.

12

Motive Utilitarianism

Robert Adams

Philosophers have written much about the morality of traits of character, much more about the morality of actions, and much less about the morality of motives. [By "motives" here I mean principally wants and desires, considered as giving rise, or tending to give rise to actions. A desire, if strong, stable, and for a fairly general object (e.g., the desire to get as much money as possible), may perhaps constitute a trait of character; but motives are not in general the same, and may not be as persistent, as traits of character.] Utilitarian theories form a good place to begin an investigation of the relation between the ethics of motives and the ethics of actions, because they have a clear structure and provide us with familiar and comprehensible, if not always plausible, grounds of argument. I believe that a study of possible treatments of motives in utilitarianism will also shed light on some of the difficulties surrounding the attempt to make the maximization of utility the guiding interest of ethical theory.

I

What would be the motives of a person morally perfect by utilitarian standards? It is natural to suppose that he or she would be completely controlled, if not exclusively moved, by the desire to maximize utility. Isn't this ideal of singlemindedly optimific motivation demanded by the principle of utility, if the principle, as Bentham puts it, "states the greatest happiness of all those whose interest is in question, as being the right and proper, and only right and proper and universally desirable, end of human action"?[1]

Robert Adams, "Motive Utilitarianism," *The Journal of Philosophy* 73 (1976): 467–81.

But there is a good utilitarian objection to such singlemindedness: it is not in general conducive to human happiness. As Sidgwick says, "Happiness [general as well as individual] is likely to be better attained if the extent to which we set ourselves consciously to aim at it be carefully restricted."[2] Suggestions of a utilitarian theory about motivation that accommodates this objection can be found in both Bentham and Sidgwick.

The test of utility is used in different theories to evaluate different objects. It is applied to acts in act utilitarianism and to roles, practices, and types of action in the various forms of rule utilitarianism. In the view about motives stated in the first paragraph above, the test is not applied at all: nothing is evaluated for its utility, but perfect motivation is identified with an all-controlling desire to maximize utility. The test of utility could be applied in various ways in the evaluation of motives.

It could be applied directly to the motives themselves, and is so applied by Bentham, when he says,

> If they [motives] are good or bad, it is only on account of their effects: good, on account of their tendency to produce pleasure, or avert pain: bad, on account of their tendency to produce pain, or avert pleasure. (*Introduction*, 102)

Alternatively, we could apply the test directly to objects of desire and only indirectly to the desires, saying that the best motives are desires for the objects that have most utility. Sidgwick seems to take this line when he says,

> While yet if we ask for a final criterion of the comparative value of the different objects of men's enthusiastic pursuit, and of the limits within which each may legitimately engross the attention of mankind, we shall none the less conceive it to depend upon the degree in which they respectively conduce to Happiness. (*Methods*, 406)

Or we could apply the test of utility to the acts to which motives give rise (or are likely to give rise) and, thence, indirectly to the motives; the best motives would be those productive of utility-maximizing acts.[3]

Another approach, also endorsed by Bentham, is to evaluate motives by the intentions to which they give rise: "A motive is good, when the intention it gives birth to is a good one; bad, when the intention is a bad one" (*Introduction*, 120). The value of an intention to do an act, he regards as depending, in turn, on whether "the consequences of the act, had they proved what to the agent they seemed likely to be, *would* have been of a beneficial nature" or the opposite (*Introduction*, 93). This approach seems inconsistent with Bentham's insistence that the test of utility must be applied to everything that is to be evaluated – that

> Strictly speaking, nothing can be said to be good or bad, but either in it-self; which is the case only with pain or pleasure: or on account of its effects; which is the case only with things that are the causes or preventives of pain and pleasure. (*Introduction*, 87; cf. 102)

Bentham would presumably defend the evaluating of intentions by the utility of expected consequences of the intended act rather than the utility of the intentions themselves in the same way that he defends a similar method of evaluating dispositions. That is, he would appeal to the assumption "that in the ordinary course of things the consequences of actions commonly turn out conformable to intentions" (*Introduction*, 133), so that there is no practical difference between the utility of the intention and the utility of the expected consequences of the intended action. This assumption is plausible as regards the short-term consequences of our actions, though even there it yields at best a very rough equivalence between utility of intentions and utility of expected consequences. It is wildly and implausibly optimistic as regards our ability to foresee the long-term consequences of our actions.[4]

Bentham similarly regards the evaluating of motives by the value of intentions arising from them as consistent with (or even practically equi-valent to) a direct application of the test of utility to motives, on the ground that the intention resulting from a motive is responsible for "the most material part of [the motive's] effects" (*Introduction*, 120). His posi-tion will still be inconsistent, however, unless he maintains (falsely, I believe) that the resulting intentions to act are responsible for *all* the relevant effects of having a motive.

If the moral point of view, the point of view from which moral evalu-ations are made, is dominated by concern for the maximization of human happiness, then it seems we must revert to the thesis that the test of utility is to be applied directly to everything, including motives. This is the con-clusion toward which the following argument from Sidgwick tends:

> Finally, the doctrine that Universal Happiness is the ultimate *standard* must not be understood to imply that Universal Benevolence is the only right or always best *motive* of action. For . . . if experience shows that the general happiness will be more satisfactorily attained if men frequently act from other motives than pure universal philanthropy, it is obvious that these other motives are reasonably to be preferred on Utilitarian principles. (*Methods*, 413)

Accordingly, the theory that will be my principal subject here is that one pattern of motivation is morally better than another to the extent that the former has more utility than the latter. The morally perfect person, on this view, would have the most useful desires, and have them in exactly the most useful strengths; he or she would have the most useful among the patterns of motivation that are causally possible for human beings.[5] Let us call this doctrine *motive utilitarianism*.

II

It is distinct, both theoretically and practically, from act utilitarianism. It can be better, by motive-utilitarian standards, to have a pattern of motivation that will lead one to act wrongly, by act-utilitarian standards, than to have a motivation that would lead to right action. Even if there is no difference in external circumstances, the motivational pattern that leads to more useful actions is not necessarily the more useful of two motivational patterns, on the whole. For the consequences of any acts one is thereby led to perform are not always the only utility-bearing consequences of being influenced, to a given degree, by a motive.[6]

This can be seen in the following fictitious case. Jack is a lover of art who is visiting the cathedral at Chartres for the first time. He is greatly excited by it, enjoying it enormously, and acquiring memories which will give him pleasure for years to come. He is so excited that he is spending much more time at Chartres than he had planned, looking at the cathedral from as many interior and exterior angles, and examining as many of its details, as he can. In fact, he is spending too much time there, from a utilitarian point of view. He had planned to spend only the morning, but he is spending the whole day; and this is going to cause him considerable inconvenience and unpleasantness. He will miss his dinner, do several hours of night driving, which he hates, and have trouble finding a place to sleep. On the whole, he will count the day well spent, but some of the time spent in the cathedral will not produce as much utility as would have been produced by departing that much earlier. At the moment, for example, Jack is studying the sixteenth to eighteenth century sculpture on the stone choir screen. He is enjoying this less than other parts of the cathedral, and will not remember it very well. It is not completely unrewarding, but he would have more happiness on balance if he passed by these carvings and saved the time for an earlier departure. Jack knows all this, although it is knowledge to which he is not paying much attention. He brushes it aside and goes on looking at the choir screen because he is more strongly interested in seeing, as nearly as possible, everything in the cathedral than in maximizing utility. This action of his is therefore wrong by act-utilitarian standards, and in some measure intentionally so. And this is not the only such case. In the course of the day he knowingly does, for the same reason, several other things that have the same sort of act-utilitarian wrongness.

On the other hand, Jack would not have omitted these things unless he had been less interested in seeing everything in the cathedral than in maximizing utility. And it is plausible to suppose that if his motivation had been different in that respect, he would have enjoyed the cathedral much less. It may very well be that his caring more about seeing the cathedral than about maximizing utility has augmented utility, through enhancing his enjoyment, by more than it has diminished utility through leading him to spend too much time at Chartres. In this case his motivation is right by motive-utilitarian standards, even though it causes him to do several things that are wrong by act-utilitarian standards.

Perhaps it will be objected that the motive utilitarian should say that Jack ought indeed to have been as interested in the cathedral as he was, but ought to have been even more interested in maximizing utility. Thus he would have had as much enjoyment from the more rewarding parts of the cathedral, according to the objector, but would not have spent too much time on the less rewarding parts. The weak point in this objection is the assumption that Jack's enjoyment of the things he would still have seen would not be diminished in these circumstances. I think, and I take it that Sidgwick thought too,[7] that a great concern to squeeze out the last drop of utility is likely to be a great impediment to the enjoyment of life. Therefore it seems plausible to suppose that from a motive-utilitarian point of view Jack ought not only to have been as strongly interested in seeing the cathedral as he was, but also to have been as weakly interested in maximizing utility as he was.

In describing this case I have been treating the maximization of utility as a unitary end which Jack might have pursued for its own sake. Perhaps it will be suggested that, although an all-controlling desire for that end would have diminished utility by dulling Jack's enjoyment, he could have had undimmed enjoyment without wrong action if he had had the maximization of utility as an *inclusive end* – that is, if he had been moved by desire for more particular ends for their own sakes, but in exact proportion to their utility.[8] But this suggestion is not plausible. While he is in the cathedral Jack's desire to see everything in it is stronger, and his desire for the benefits of an early departure is weaker, than would be proportionate to the utility of those ends. And a stronger desire for an early departure would probably have interfered with his enjoyment just as much as a stronger desire for utility maximization as such. We are likely in general to enjoy life more if we are often more interested in the object of an enthusiastic pursuit, and less concerned about other ends, than would be proportionate to their utility. It follows that failing (to some extent) to have utility maximization as an inclusive end is often right by motive-utilitarian standards, and may be supposed to be so in Jack's case.

In order to justify the view that motive utilitarianism implies something practically equivalent to act utilitarianism one would have to show that the benefits that justify Jack's motivation by motive-utilitarian standards also justify his spending time on the choir screen by act-utilitarian standards. But they do not. For they are not consequences of his spending time there, but independent consequences of something that caused, or manifested itself in, his spending time there. It is not that deciding to devote only a cursory inspection to the choir screen would have put him in the wrong frame of mind for enjoying the visit. It is rather that, being in the right frame of mind for enjoying the visit, he could not bring himself to leave the choir screen as quickly as would have maximized utility.

III

The act utilitarian may try to domesticate motive utilitarianism, arguing (A) that motive utilitarianism is merely a theorem of act utilitarianism, and denying (B) that behavior like Jack's inspection of the choir screen, if resulting from obedience to the dictates of motive utilitarianism, can properly be called wrong action.

(A) Since act utilitarianism implies that one ought to do whatever has most utility, it implies that, other things equal, one ought to foster and promote in oneself those motives which have most utility. And that, it may be claimed, is precisely what motive utilitarianism teaches.

(B) Jack was once, let us suppose, an excessively conscientious act utilitarian. Recognizing the duty of cultivating more useful motives in himself, he took a course of capriciousness training, with the result that he now stands, careless of utility, before the choir screen. It would be unfair, it may be argued, to regard what Jack is now doing as a wrong action by utilitarian standards. Rather, we must see it as only an inescapable part of a larger, right action, which began with his enrolling for capriciousness training – just as we do not say that a person rightly jumped from a burning building, saving his life, but wrongly struck the ground, breaking his leg. It is unreasonable, on this view, to separate, for moral evaluation, actions that are causally inseparable.

Both of these arguments are to be rejected. The second (B) involves deep issues about the individuation of actions and the relation between causal determination and moral responsibility. It seems clear enough, however, that Jack's staying at the choir screen is separable from his earlier efforts at character reform in a way that striking the ground is not separable from jumping out of a building. Once you have jumped, it is no longer in your power to refrain from striking the ground, even if you want to. If you are sane and well informed about the situation, you have only one choice to make: to jump or not to jump. There is no further choice about hitting the ground, and therefore it is inappropriate to separate the impact from the leap, as an object of moral evaluation. But even after Jack has taken capriciousness training, it is still in his power to leave the choir screen if he wants to; it is just that he does not want to. His choice to stay and examine it is a new choice, which he did not make, years ago, when he decided to reform. He did decide then to become such that he would sometimes make nonutilitarian choices, but it may not even have occurred to him then that he would ever be in Chartres. It seems perfectly appropriate to ask whether the choice that he now makes is morally right or wrong.

It is plausible, indeed, to say that Jack is not acting wrongly in acting on the motivation that he has rightly cultivated in himself. But I think that is because it is plausible to depart from act utilitarianism at least so far as to allow the rightness or wrongness of Jack's action in this case to depend partly on the goodness or badness of his motive, and not solely on the utility of the act. It is noteworthy in this connection that it would be no less plausible to acquit Jack of wrongdoing if he had always been as easygoing as he now is about small increments of utility, even though there would not in that case be any larger action of character reform, of which Jack's present scrutiny of the choir screen could be regarded as an inescapable part.

A similar irrelevant emphasis on doing something about one's own motivational patterns also infects the attempt (A) to derive motive utilitarianism from act utilitarianism. Motive utilitarianism is not a theorem of act utilitarianism, for the simple reason that motive utilitarianism is not about what motives one ought to foster and promote, or *try* to have, but about what motives one ought to *have*. There is a preconception to be overcome here which threatens to frustrate from the outset the development of any independent ethics of motives. I refer to the assumption that "What should I (try to) do?" is *the* ethical question, and that we are engaged in substantive *ethical* thinking only insofar as we are considering *action*-guiding principles.[9] If we hold this assumption, we are almost bound to read "What motives should I have?" as "What motives should I try to develop and maintain in myself?"

There are other questions, however, that are as fundamental to ethics as "What should I do?" It is characteristic of moral as opposed to pragmatic thinking that, for example, the question, "Have I lived well?" is of interest for its own sake. In pragmatic self-appraisal that question is of interest only insofar as the answer may guide me toward future successes. If I am personally concerned, in more than this instrumental way, and not just in curiosity, about whether I have lived well, my concern is not purely pragmatic, but involves at least a sense of style, if not of morality.

If the question is "Have I lived well?" the motives I have *had* are relevant, and not just the motives I have *tried* to have. If I tried to have the right motive, but nonetheless had the wrong one – if I tried to love righteousness and my neighbors, but failed and did my duty out of fear of hellfire for the most part – then I did not live as well as I would have lived if I had *had* the right motive.

Suppose, similarly, that Martha is an overscrupulous utilitarian, completely dominated by the desire to maximize utility. She has acted rightly, by act-utilitarian standards, just as often as she could. Among her right actions (or attempts at right action) are many *attempts* to become strongly interested in particular objects – more strongly, indeed, than is proportionate to their utility. For she realizes that she and her acquaintances would be happier if she had such interests. But all these attempts have failed.

Mary, on the other hand, has not had to work on herself to develop such nonutilitarian interests, but has always had them; and, largely because of them, her motivational patterns have had more utility, on the whole, than Martha's. The motive utilitarian will take this as a reason (not necessarily decisive) for saying that Martha has *lived less well* than Mary. This censure of Martha's motives is not derivable from act utilitarianism, for her actions have been the best that were causally possible for her. (If you are tempted to say that Martha's conscientiousness is better than Mary's more useful motives, you are experiencing a reluctance to apply the test of utility to motives.)

IV

I have argued that right action, by act-utilitarian standards, and right motivation, by motive-utilitarian standards, are incompatible in some cases. It does not immediately follow, but it may further be argued, that act utilitarianism and motive utilitarianism are incompatible theories.

One argument for this conclusion is suggested, in effect, by Bernard Williams. He does not formulate or discuss motive utilitarianism, but he holds that it is inconsistent of J. J. C. Smart, following Sidgwick, "to present direct [i.e., act] utilitarianism as a doctrine merely about justification and not about motivation." Williams's argument is,

> There is no distinctive place for *direct* utilitarianism unless it is, within fairly narrow limits, a doctrine about how one should decide what to do. This is because its distinctive doctrine is about what acts are right, and, especially for utilitarians, the only distinctive interest or point of the question what acts are right, relates to the situation of deciding to do them. (*op. cit.*, 128)

The doctrine about motives that Williams believes to be implied by act utilitarianism is presumably the doctrine, discarded at the beginning of my present essay, that one ought always to be controlled by the desire or purpose of maximizing utility. And this doctrine, if conjoined with plausible empirical beliefs illustrated in section II above, is inconsistent with motive utilitarianism.

There are two questionable points in Williams's argument. One is the claim that for utilitarians the only use of the question, What acts are right? is for guidance in deciding what to do. He defends this claim, arguing that "utilitarians in fact are not very keen on people blaming themselves, which they see as an unproductive activity," and that they therefore will not be interested in the question, "Did he (or I) do the right thing?" (124). I am not convinced by this defense. Blame is a self-administered negative reinforcement which may perhaps cause desirable modifications of future behavior. The retrospective question about the evaluation of one's action is a question in which one can hardly help taking an interest if one has a conscience; one who desires to act well will naturally desire to *have* acted well. And the desire to act well, at least in weighty matters, will surely be approved on motive-utilitarian grounds.

But suppose, for the sake of argument, we grant Williams that the point of act-utilitarian judgments, when they have a point, is to guide us in deciding what to do. His argument still rests on the assumption that the act utilitarian is committed to the view that it is generally useful to ask what acts are right, and that one ought always or almost always to be interested in the question. Why should the act utilitarian be committed to this view? If he is also a motive utilitarian, he will have reason to say that, although it is indeed useful to be guided by utilitarian judgments in actions of great consequence, it is sometimes better to be relatively uninterested in considerations of utility (and so of morality). "For everything there is a season and a time for every matter under heaven: . . . a time to kill, and a time to heal; a time to break down, and a time to build up," said the Preacher (Ecclesiastes 3:1, 3 RSV). The act-and-motive utilitarian adds, "There is a time to be moral, and a time to be amoral." (The act-and-motive utilitarian is one who holds both act and motive utilitarianism as *theories*. He does not, for he cannot, always satisfy the demands of both theories in his acts and motives.)

Perhaps it will be objected that this reply to Williams overlooks the utility of conscientiousness. Conscience is, in part, a motive: the desire to act or live in accordance with moral principles. If the moral principles are mainly sound, it is so useful a motive that it is important, from a motive-utilitarian standpoint, not to undermine it. This consideration might make a motive utilitarian reluctant to approve the idea of "a time to be amoral," lest such "moral holidays" weaken a predominantly useful conscience.

The question facing the act-and-motive utilitarian at this point is, what sort of conscience has greatest utility. We have seen reason to believe that an act-utilitarian conscience that is scrupulous about small increments of utility would have bad effects on human happiness, smothering many innocent enjoyments in a wet blanket of excessive earnestness. A more useful sort of conscience is probably available to the act-and-motive utilitarian. It would incorporate a vigorous desire to *live well*, in terms of the over-all utility of his life, but not necessarily to *act rightly* on every occasion. Having such a conscience, he would be strongly concerned (1) not to act in ways gravely detrimental to utility, and (2) not to be in a bad motivational state. If he performs a mildly unutilitarian action as an inevitable consequence of the most useful motivation that he can have, on the other hand, he is still living as well as possible, by his over-all utilitarian standards; and there is no reason why such action should undermine his determination to live well. A conscience of this sort seems as possible, and at least as likely to be stable, as a conscience that insists on maximizing utility in every action. Thus the act-and-motive utilitarian has good motive-utilitarian reasons for believing that he should sometimes be, in relation to his act-utilitarian principles, amoral.

V

But this conclusion may be taken, quite apart from Williams's argument, as grounds for thinking that act utilitarianism and motive utilitarianism are incompatible in the sense that holding the latter ought reasonably to prevent us from holding the former as a *moral* theory. The incompatibility has to do with moral seriousness. The problem is not just that one cannot *succeed* in living up to the ideals of both theories simultaneously. It is rather that the motive utilitarian is led to the conclusion that it is morally better on many occasions to be so motivated that one will not even *try* to do what one ought, by act-utilitarian standards, to do. If the act-and-motive utilitarian accepts this conclusion, however, we must wonder whether all his act-utilitarian judgments about what one ought to do are really judgments of *moral* obligation. For it is commonly made a criterion for a theory's being a theory of *moral* obligation, that it claim a special seriousness for its judgments of obligation. By this criterion, act utilitarianism cannot really be a theory of moral obligation (as it purports to be) if it is conjoined with the view that some of its dictates should be taken as lightly as motive utilitarianism would lead us to think they should be taken.

This argument depends on the triviality of any reasonable human interest in some of the obligations that act utilitarianism would lay on us. And the triviality is due to the totalitarian character of act utilitarianism, to its insistence that, as Sidgwick puts it, "it is *always* wrong for a man knowingly to do *anything* other than what he believes to be most conducive to Universal Happiness" (*Methods*, 492, italics mine).

Without this triviality a conflict between the ethics of actions and the ethics of motives need not destroy the seriousness of either. Maybe *no* plausible comprehensive ethical theory can avoid all such conflicts. Are there *some* circumstances in which it is best, for example, in the true morality of motives, to be unable to bring oneself to sacrifice the happiness of a friend when an important duty obliges one, in the true morality of actions, to do so? I don't know. But if there are, the interests involved, on both sides, are far from trivial, and the seriousness of both moralities can be maintained. If one fails to perform the important duty, one ought, seriously, to feel guilty; but one could not do one's duty in such a case without having a motivation of which one ought, seriously, to be ashamed. The situation presents a tragic inevitability of moral disgrace.

There are, accordingly, two ways in which the utilitarian might deal with the argument if he has been trying to combine act and motive utilitarianism and accepts the view I have urged on him about the kind of conscience it would be most useful to have. (A) He could simply acknowledge that he is operating with a modified conception of moral obligation, under which a special seriousness attaches to some but not all moral obligations.[10] He would claim that his use of "morally ought" nonetheless has enough similarity, in other respects, to the traditional use, to be a reasonable extension of it.

(B) The other, to my mind more attractive, way is to modify the act-utilitarian principle, eliminating trivial obligations, and limiting the realm of duty to actions that would be of concern to a conscience of the most useful sort. Under such a limitation it would not be regarded as morally wrong, in general, to fail to maximize utility by a *small* margin. One's relatively uninfluential practical choices would be subject to moral judgment only indirectly, through the motive-utilitarian judgment on the motives on which one acted (and perhaps a character-utilitarian judgment on the traits of character manifested by the action). Some acts, however, such as shoplifting in a dime store or telling inconsequential lies, would still be regarded as wrong even if only slightly detrimental in the particular case, because it is clear that they would be opposed by the most useful sort of conscience. I leave unanswered here the question whether a conscience of the most useful kind would be offended by some acts that maximize utility – particularly by some utility-maximizing violations of such rules as those against stealing and lying. If the answer is affirmative, the position we are considering would have approximately the same practical consequences as are commonly expected from rule utilitarianism. This position – that we have a *moral duty* to do an act, if and only if it would be demanded of us by the most useful kind of conscience we could have – may be called "conscience utilitarianism," and is a very natural position for a motive utilitarian to take in the ethics of actions.

The moral point of view – the point of view from which moral judgments are made – cannot safely be defined as a point of view in which the test of utility is applied directly to all objects of moral evaluation. For it is doubtful that the most useful motives, and the most useful sort of conscience, are related to the most useful acts in the way that the motives, and especially the kind of conscience, regarded as right must be related to the acts regarded as right in anything that is to count as a morality. And therefore it is doubtful that direct application of the test of utility to everything results in a system that counts as a morality.

VI

Considered on its own merits, as a theory in the ethics of motives, which may or may not be combined with some other type of utilitarianism in the ethics of actions, how plausible is motive utilitarianism? That is a question which we can hardly begin to explore in a brief paper, because of the variety of forms that the theory might assume, and the difficulty of stating some of them. The exploration might start with a distinction between individualistic and universalistic motive utilitarianism, analogous to the distinction between act and rule utilitarianism.

Individualistic motive utilitarianism holds that a person's motivation on any given occasion is better, the greater the utility of *his* having it on *that* occasion. This seemed to Bentham, on the whole, the least unsatisfactory view about the moral worth of motives:

> The only way, it should seem, in which a motive can with safety and propriety be styled good or bad, is with reference to its effects *in each individual instance*. (*Introduction*, 120, italics mine)

This doctrine seems liable to counterexamples similar to those which are commonly urged against act utilitarianism. An industrialist's greed, a general's bloodthirstiness, may on some occasions have better consequences on the whole than kinder motives would, and even predictably so. But we want to say that they remain worse motives.

Universalistic motive utilitarianism is supposed to let us say this, but is difficult to formulate. If we try to state it as the thesis that motives are better, the greater the utility of *everybody's* having them on *all* occasions, we implausibly ignore the utility of diversity in motives. A more satisfactory view might be that a motivation is better, the greater the average probable utility of *anyone's* having it on *any* occasion. This formulation gives rise to questions about averaging: do we weigh equally the utility of a motive on all the occasions when it could conceivably occur, or do we have some formula for weighing more heavily the occasions when it is more likely to occur? There are also difficult issues about the relevant description of the motive. One and the same concrete individual motive might be described correctly as a desire to protect Henry Franklin, a desire to protect (an individual whom one knows to be) one's spouse, a desire to protect (an individual whom one knows to be) the chief executive of one's government, and a desire to protect (an individual whom one knows to be) a betrayer of the public trust; these motive types surely have very different average utilities. If one makes the relevant description of the motive too full, of course, one risks making universalistic motive utilitarianism equivalent to individualistic.[11] If the description is not full enough, it will be hard to get any determination of average utility at all. Bentham's principal effort, in his discussion of the ethics of motives, is to show, by a tiresome profusion of examples, that the application of the test of utility to sorts of motive yields no results, because "there is no sort of motive but may give birth to any sort of action" (*Introduction*, 128);

his argument depends on the use of very thin descriptions of sorts of motive.

The doctrine that a type of motive is better, the greater the utility of commending or fostering it in a system of moral education, might seem to be another version of universalistic motive utilitarianism, but is not a form of motive utilitarianism at all. For in it the test of utility is directly applied not to motives or types of motive, but to systems of moral education.

I am not convinced (nor even inclined to believe) that any purely utilitarian theory about the worth of motives is correct. But motive utilitarian considerations will have some place in any sound theory of the ethics of motives, because utility, or conduciveness to human happiness (or more generally, to the good), is certainly a great advantage in motives (as in other things), even if it is not a morally decisive advantage.

Notes

1 Jeremy Bentham, *An Introduction to the Principles of Morals and Legislation* (New York: Hafner, 1961) (referred to hereafter as *Introduction*, with page number), p. 1*n*.
2 Henry Sidgwick, *The Methods of Ethics*, seventh edition (New York: Dover, 1966) (referred to hereafter as *Methods*, with page number), p. 405.
3 This too may find some support in Sidgwick. Cf. *Methods*, 493, on the praise of motives conceived to prompt to felicific conduct.
4 Also, as Gregory Kavka has pointed out to me, the utility of *having* an intention (e.g., to retaliate if attacked) may be quite different from the utility (actual or expected) of *acting* on it. I shall be making a similar point about motives, below.
5 It is difficult to say what is meant by the question, whether a certain pattern of motivation is causally possible for human beings, and how one would answer it. I shall sidestep these issues here, for I shall be making comparative evaluations of motives assumed to be possible, rather than trying to determine the most useful of all causally possible motivations.
6 I am here denying, as applied to motives, what Bernard Williams rather obscurely calls the "act-adequacy premise" [A Critique of Utilitarianism," in J. J. C. Smart and Williams, *Utilitarianism, For and Against* (New York: Cambridge, 1975), pp. 119–30].
7 I believe this is the most natural reading of Sidgwick, but it may be barely possible to construe him as meaning only that the perpetual *consciousness* of such a concern would be an impediment. See *Methods*, 48f.
8 The terminology of "dominant" and "inclusive" ends was developed by W. F. R. Hardie, "The Final Good in Aristotle's Ethics," *Philosophy*, xl, 154

(October 1965): 277–95; Rawls makes use of it. J. S. Mill seems to treat the maximization of utility as an inclusive end in *Utilitarianism*, ch. 4, §§ 5–8.

9   Cf. Jan Narveson, *Morality and Utility* (Baltimore, Md.: Johns Hopkins, 1967), p. 105: "Let us begin by recalling the primary function of ethical principles: to tell us what to do, i.e., to guide action. Whatever else an ethical principle is supposed to do, it must do that, otherwise it could not (logically) be an ethical principle at all."

10 It may be thought that Sidgwick has already begun this modification, by holding that good actions ought not to be praised, nor bad ones blamed, except insofar as it is useful to praise and blame them. See *Methods*, 428 f., 493.

11 By a process similar to that by which David Lyons, in his *Forms and Limits of Utilitarianism* (New York: Oxford, 1965), has tried to show that rule utilitarianism is equivalent to act utilitarianism.

Part III

Contemporary Discussion

13

Classical Utilitarianism

John Rawls

There are many forms of utilitarianism, and the development of the theory has continued in recent years. I shall not survey these forms here, nor take account of the numerous refinements found in contemporary discussions. My aim is to work out a theory of justice that represents an alternative to utilitarian thought generally and so to all of these different versions of it. I believe that the contrast between the contract view and utilitarianism remains essentially the same in all these cases. Therefore I shall compare justice as fairness with familiar variants of intuitionism, perfectionism, and utilitarianism in order to bring out the underlying differences in the simplest way. With this end in mind, the kind of utilitarianism I shall describe here is the strict classical doctrine which receives perhaps its clearest and most accessible formulation in Sidgwick. The main idea is that society is rightly ordered, and therefore just, when its major institutions are arranged so as to achieve the greatest net balance of satisfaction summed over all the individuals belonging to it.[1]

We may note first that there is, indeed, a way of thinking of society which makes it easy to suppose that the most rational conception of justice is utilitarian. For consider: each man in realizing his own interests is certainly free to balance his own losses against his own gains. We may impose a sacrifice on ourselves now for the sake of a greater advantage later. A person quite properly acts, at least when others are not affected, to achieve his own greatest good, to advance his rational ends as far as possible. Now why should not a society act on precisely the same principle applied to the group and therefore regard that which is rational for one man as right for an association of men? Just as the well-being of

John Rawls, "Classical Utilitarianism," *A Theory of Justice* (Cambridge, MA: Harvard University Press, 1971), pp. 23–7.

a person is constructed from the series of satisfactions that are experienced at different moments in the course of his life, so in very much the same way the well-being of society is to be constructed from the fulfillment of the systems of desires of the many individuals who belong to it. Since the principle for an individual is to advance as far as possible his own welfare, his own system of desires, the principle for society is to advance as far as possible the welfare of the group, to realize to the greatest extent the comprehensive system of desire arrived at from the desires of its members. Just as an individual balances present and future gains against present and future losses, so a society may balance satisfactions and dissatisfactions between different individuals. And so by these reflections one reaches the principle of utility in a natural way: a society is properly arranged when its institutions maximize the net balance of satisfaction. The principle of choice for an association of men is interpreted as an extension of the principle of choice for one man. Social justice is the principle of rational prudence applied to an aggregative conception of the welfare of the group (§30).[2]

   This idea is made all the more attractive by a further consideration. The two main concepts of ethics are those of the right and the good; the concept of a morally worthy person is, I believe, derived from them. The structure of an ethical theory is, then, largely determined by how it defines and connects these two basic notions. Now it seems that the simplest way of relating them is taken by teleological theories: the good is defined independently from the right, and then the right is defined as that which maximizes the good.[3] More precisely, those institutions and acts are right which of the available alternatives produce the most good, or at least as much good as any of the other institutions and acts open as real possibilities (a rider needed when the maximal class is not a singleton). Teleological theories have a deep intuitive appeal since they seem to embody the idea of rationality. It is natural to think that rationality is maximizing something and that in morals it must be maximizing the good. Indeed, it is tempting to suppose that it is self-evident that things should be arranged so as to lead to the most good.

   It is essential to keep in mind that in a teleological theory the good is defined independently from the right. This means two things. First, the theory accounts for our considered judgments as to which things are good (our judgments of value) as a separate class of judgments intuitively distinguishable by common sense, and then proposes the hypothesis that the right is maximizing the good as already specified. Second, the theory enables one to judge the goodness of things without referring to what is right. For example, if pleasure is said to be the sole good, then presumably pleasures can be recognized and ranked in value by criteria that do not presuppose any standards of right, or what we would normally think of as such. Whereas if the distribution of goods is also counted as a good, perhaps a higher order one, and the theory directs us to produce the most good (including the good of distribution among others), we no longer have a teleological view in the classical sense. The problem of distribution falls under the concept of right as one intuitively understands it, and so the theory lacks an independent definition of the good. The clarity and simplicity of classical teleological theories derives largely from the fact that they factor our moral judgments into two classes, the one being characterized separately while the other is then connected with it by a maximizing principle.

Teleological doctrines differ, pretty clearly, according to how the conception of the good is specified. If it is taken as the realization of human excellence in the various forms of culture, we have what may be called perfectionism. This notion is found in Aristotle and Nietzsche, among others. If the good is defined as pleasure, we have hedonism; if as happiness, eudaimonism, and so on. I shall understand the principle of utility in its classical form as defining the good as the satisfaction of desire, or perhaps better, as the satisfaction of rational desire. This accords with the view in all essentials and provides, I believe, a fair interpretation of it. The appropriate terms of social cooperation are settled by whatever in the circumstances will achieve the greatest sum of satisfaction of the rational desires of individuals. It is impossible to deny the initial plausibility and attractiveness of this conception.

The striking feature of the utilitarian view of justice is that it does not matter, except indirectly, how this sum of satisfactions is distributed among individuals any more than it matters, except indirectly, how one man distributes his satisfactions over time. The correct distribution in either case is that which yields the maximum fulfillment. Society must allocate its means of satisfaction whatever these are, rights and duties, opportunities and privileges, and various forms of wealth, so as to achieve this maximum if it can. But in itself no distribution of satisfaction is better than another except that the more equal distribution is to be preferred to break ties.[4] It is true that certain common sense precepts of justice, particularly those which concern the protection of liberties and rights, or which express the claims of desert, seem to contradict this contention. But from a utilitarian standpoint the explanation of these precepts and of their seemingly stringent character is that they are those precepts which experience shows should be strictly respected and departed from only under exceptional circumstances if the sum of advantages is to be maximized.[5] Yet, as with all other precepts, those of justice are derivative from the one end of attaining the greatest balance of satisfaction. Thus there is no reason in principle why the greater gains of some should not compensate for the lesser losses of others; or more importantly, why the violation of the liberty of a few might not be made right by the greater good shared by many. It simply happens that under most conditions, at least in a reasonably advanced stage of civilization, the greatest sum of advantages is not attained in this way. No doubt the strictness of common sense precepts of justice has a certain usefulness in limiting men's propensities to injustice and to socially injurious actions, but the utilitarian believes that to affirm this strictness as a first principle of morals is a mistake. For just as it is rational for one man to maximize the fulfillment of his system of desires, it is right for a society to maximize the net balance of satisfaction taken over all of its members.

The most natural way, then, of arriving at utilitarianism (although not, of course, the only way of doing so) is to adopt for society as a whole the principle of rational choice for one man. Once this is recognized, the place of the impartial spectator and the emphasis on sympathy in the history of utilitarian thought is readily understood. For it is by the conception of the impartial spectator and the use of sympathetic identification in guiding our imagination that the principle for one man is applied to society. It is this spectator who is conceived as carrying out the required organization of the desires of all persons into one coherent system of desire; it is by this construction that many persons are fused into one. Endowed with ideal powers of sympathy and imagination, the impartial spectator is the perfectly rational individual who identifies with and experiences the desires of others as if these desires were his own. In this way he ascertains the intensity of these desires and assigns them their appropriate weight in the one system of desire the satisfaction of which the ideal legislator then tries to maximize by adjusting the rules of the social system. On this conception of society separate individuals are thought of as so many different lines along which rights and duties are to be assigned and scarce means of satisfaction allocated in accordance with rules so as to give the greatest fulfillment of wants. The nature of the decision made by the ideal legislator is not, therefore, materially different from that of an entrepreneur deciding how to maximize his profit by producing this or that commodity, or that of a consumer deciding how to maximize his satisfaction by the purchase of this or that collection of goods. In each case there is a single person whose system of desires determines the best allocation of limited means. The correct decision is essentially a question of efficient administration. This view of social cooperation is the consequence of extending to society the principle of choice for one man, and then, to make this extension work, conflating all persons into one through the imaginative acts of the impartial sympathetic spectator. Utilitarianism does not take seriously the distinction between persons.

Notes

1 I shall take Henry Sidgwick's *The Methods of Ethics*, 7th ed. (London, 1907), as summarizing the development of utilitarian moral theory. Book III of his *Principles of Political Economy* (London, 1883) applies this doctrine to questions of economic and social justice, and is a precursor of A. C. Pigou, *The Economics of Welfare* (London, Macmillan, 1920). Sidgwick's *Outlines of the History of Ethics*, 5th ed. (London, 1902), contains a brief history of the utilitarian tradition. We may follow him in assuming, somewhat arbitrarily, that it begins with Shaftesbury's *An Inquiry Concerning Virtue and Merit* (1711) and Hutcheson's *An Inquiry Concerning Moral Good and Evil* (1725). Hutcheson seems to have been the first to state clearly the principle of utility. He says in *Inquiry*, sec. III, §8, that "that action is best, which procures the greatest happiness for the greatest numbers; and that, worst, which, in like manner, occasions misery." Other major eighteenth century works are Hume's *A Treatise of Human Nature* (1739), and *An Enquiry Concerning the Principles of Morals* (1751); Adam Smith's *A Theory of the Moral Sentiments* (1759); and Bentham's *The Principles of Morals and Legislation* (1789). To these we must add the writings of J. S. Mill represented by *Utilitarianism* (1863) and F. Y. Edgeworth's *Mathematical Psychics* (London, 1888).

The discussion of utilitarianism has taken a different turn in recent years by focusing on what we may call the coordination problem and related questions of publicity. This development stems from the essays of R. F. Harrod, "Utilitarianism Revised," *Mind*, vol. 45 (1936); J. D. Mabbott, "Punishment," *Mind*, vol. 48 (1939); Jonathan Harrison, "Utilitarianism, Universalisation, and Our Duty to Be Just," *Proceedings of the Aristotelian Society*, vol. 53 (1952–3); and J. O. Urmson, "The Interpretation of the Philosophy of J. S. Mill," *Philosophical Quarterly*, vol. 3 (1953). See also J. J. C. Smart, "Extreme and Restricted Utilitarianism," *Philosophical Quarterly*, vol. 6 (1956), and his *An Outline of a System of Utilitarian Ethics* (Cambridge, The University Press, 1961). For an account of these matters, see David Lyons, *Forms and Limits of Utilitarianism* (Oxford, The Clarendon Press, 1965); and Allan Gibbard, "Utilitarianisms and Coordination" (dissertation, Harvard University, 1971). The problems raised by these works, as important as they are, I shall leave aside as not bearing directly on the more elementary question of distribution which I wish to discuss.

258 *John Rawls*

Finally, we should note here the essays of J. C. Harsanyi, in particular, "Cardinal Utility in Welfare Economics and in the Theory of Risk-Taking," *Journal of Political Economy*, 1953, and "Cardinal Welfare, Individualistic Ethics, and Interpersonal Comparisons of Utility," *Journal of Political Economy*, 1955; and R. B. Brandt, "Some Merits of One Form of Rule-Utilitarianism," *University of Colorado Studies* (Boulder, Colorado, 1967). See below §§27–8.

2   On this point see also D. P. Gauthier, *Practical Reasoning* (Oxford, Clarendon Press, 1963), pp. 126f. The text elaborates the suggestion found in "Constitutional Liberty and the Concept of Justice," *Nomos VI: Justice*, ed. C. J. Friedrich and J. W. Chapman (New York, Atherton Press, 1963), pp. 124f, which in turn is related to the idea of justice as a higher-order administrative decision. See "Justice as Fairness," *Philosophical Review*, 1958, pp. 185–7. For references to utilitarians who explicitly affirm this extension, see §30, note 37. That the principle of social integration is distinct from the principle of personal integration is stated by R. B. Perry, *General Theory of Value* (New York, Longmans, Green, and Company, 1926), pp. 674–7. He attributes the error of overlooking this fact to Emile Durkheim and others with similar views. Perry's conception of social integration is that brought about by a shared and dominant benevolent purpose. See below, §24.

3   Here I adopt W. K. Frankena's definition of teleological theories in *Ethics* (Englewood Cliffs, N.J., Prentice Hall, Inc., 1963), p. 13.

4   On this point see Sidgwick, *The Methods of Ethics*, pp. 416f.

5   See J. S. Mill, *Utilitarianism*, ch. V, last two pars.

14

Utilitarianism and Welfarism

Amartya Sen

"Some of the unacceptable features of utilitarianism," argues Bernard Williams, "are to be traced to its general character as a form of consequentialism."[1] In this paper I shall be concerned with those features which *cannot* be traced to consequentialism. The intention is to provide a critique of utilitarianism without disputing the acceptability of consequentialism.

The scope of such a critique will, naturally, depend on how narrowly the consequences are characterized and how broadly utility is defined. It is possible to define things in a way that makes a teleologist necessarily a utilitarian in a broad sense, as in the following statement of David Lyons: "Teleologists claim that the rightness of acts depends solely upon their utility, that is, upon their contribution towards intrinsically good states of affairs."[2] In contrast, in this paper I shall be concerned with investigating the relationship between goodness of states of affairs and the utility characteristics of those states. Utility will be taken to stand for a person's conception of his own well-being, and although this would still permit alternative interpretations in terms of "pleasure" and "desire," there is no definitional link with the "goodness of states of affairs." That link will be treated as an open moral issue.

In section I various utilitarian structures will be examined. A principle that seems to be shared by all variants of utilitarianism (such as act and rule utilitarianism) identifies the goodness of a *state of affairs* (or outcome) with the sum total of individual utilities in that state, and this will be called "outcome utilitarianism." Outcome utilitarianism will be itself factorized into more elementary requirements, which will be examined in turn in the sections that follow.

Amartya Sen, "Utilitarianism and Welfarism," *The Journal of Philosophy* 76, 9 (1979): 463–89.

Section II is concerned with "sum-ranking," i.e., with the *addition* of individual utilities as the appropriate method of aggregation. Section III will deal with "welfarism," i.e., the principle that the goodness of a state of affairs depends ultimately on the set of individual utilities in that state, and – more demandingly – can be seen as an increasing function of that set. Welfarism implies that any two states of affairs that are identical in terms of individual utility characteristics must be judged to be equally good no matter how different they are in non-utility respects, and also that any state that has more utility for someone and no less utility for anyone in comparison with another state is a better state than the other. This last characteristic is sometimes called "Paretianism."

A weak version of Paretianism requires that if one state has more utility for *everyone* than another, then it is a better state; this may be called "weak Paretianism."[3] Section IV is devoted to a critique of weak Paretianism, and it is argued that the principle deserves rejection in its general form. Since weak Paretianism is a mild version of welfarism, this consolidates the critique of welfarism.

I.   Outcome Utilitarianism and Complex Utilitarian Structures

Take act utilitarianism. This is the morality that says that, in choosing one among various alternative acts, one should choose an act that yields at least as high a sum total of utilities as any other alternative act. This assertion can be derived from combining the following two principles:

Act Consequentialism: An action α is right if and only if the state of affairs x resulting from α is at least as good as each of the alternative states of affairs that would have resulted respectively from the alternative feasible acts.

Outcome Utilitarianism: Any state of affairs x is at least as good as an alternative state of affairs y if and only if the sum total of individual utilities in x is at least as large as the sum total of individual utilities in y.

Act consequentialism establishes a correspondence between the rightness of acts and the goodness of resulting states of affairs (including the value of the performed acts).[4] Outcome utilitarianism is a method of judging the goodness of states of affairs. Act consequentialism can be easily combined with a different "outcome morality," judging goodness of states of affairs in some other way, e.g., in terms of the utility levels of the worst-off group of persons.[5] Similarly, outcome utilitarianism can be combined with consequentialism applied to instruments other than acts, e.g., rules or motives, which can differ substantially from act consequentialism.

It could be asked whether outcome utilitarianism is a *moral* principle at all. On its own it asserts nothing about rightness of actions. But, combined with some way of relating actions to states of affairs (e.g., act consequentialism or rule consequentialism), it does contribute to the moral assessment of actions.

Even on its own, outcome utilitarianism asserts something of moral interest. If it is said that the volcanic eruption in Krakatoa in 1883, which killed many and made many others homeless, was a tragedy, and that the meteorite fall in Siberia in 1908 on uninhabited land was not a tragedy, something of substance is being asserted.[6] Outcome utilitarianism provides a sufficient basis for such judgments. It is, of course, possible to translate this into *as if* choices, e.g., if one *could have* chosen not to have the Krakatoa disaster, one *should have* chosen not to, but it does not seem very helpful to interpret the tragedy of Krakatoa as "ultimately" one of rightness of action. Similarly, intertemporal comparisons of "social welfare" based on, say, real national income,[7] are primarily judgments of states of affairs and not of actions.

It is possible to combine outcome utilitarianism with nonconsequentialist moralities, but I shall not explore that avenue in this paper, since the utilitarian approach is typically combined with some variant or other of consequentialism. Act consequentialism is perhaps the simplest case of consequentialism (and is sometimes taken to be the only proper case). Outcome utilitarianism provides a way of assessing alternative "histories" of what can happen, and for a consequentialist approach of any variety, that must be the ultimate basis of evaluation. But different entities – such as acts, or rules, or motivations, or dispositions – can be varied to influence such "histories."

A utilitarian moral structure consists of the central element of outcome utilitarianism combined with some consequentialist method of translating judgments of outcomes into judgments of actions. The most comprehensive consequentialist structure would require that the *combination* of all influencing variables be so chosen that the result is the *best feasible* state of affairs according to outcome utilitarianism. However, the literature on utilitarian ethics displays a preference for dealing with one influencing variable at a time, e.g., one act from a set of acts, or one rule from a set of rules. This may be called "single-influence consequentialism," of which act utilitarianism, rule utilitarianism, etc., are special cases with the influencing variable being, respectively, an act or a rule, etc. There are various strategic issues to be considered in evaluating the efficacy of these different utilitarian moral structures, and it is easy to construct examples such that each of these limited structures fails to achieve the best outcome that could have resulted from a comprehensive structure.[8] But in this paper I shall not go into these strategic issues, since my main concern is with outcome utilitarianism as an outcome morality.

The translation from the "best outcome" to the "right action" is affected not merely by such strategic considerations, but also by qualifications about what is or is not within a person's or an agent's control. For example, it may be possible to identify which type of "personal disposition" is most effective in achieving the best state of affairs according to the chosen outcome morality (in this case, outcome utilitarianism), but this need not point immediately to a best course of action, since personal dispositions are not entirely controllable by the person in question.

This problem arises particularly sharply with what Robert Merrihew Adams has called "motive utilitarianism." There is little difficulty with his characterization of this as the theory that "one pattern of motivation is morally better than another to the extent that the former has more utility that the latter."[9] This is obtained by combining "outcome utilitarianism" with what we may call "motive consequentialism," i.e., single-influence consequentialism applied to the set of possible motivations.[10] There is, however, more difficulty with his further characterization of motive utilitarianism as the theory that "the morally perfect person, on this view, would have the most useful desires, and have them in exactly the most useful strengths; he or she would have the most useful among the patterns of motivation that are causally possible for human beings" (470). One can indeed rank *motives* as such in terms of the combination of motive consequentialism and outcome utilitarianism, but this does not in itself yield a method of ranking *persons*, or identifying "the morally perfect person."

There are indeed two separate difficulties with using motive utilitarianism to rank persons in terms of "moral perfectness." First, the choice over motivation may not be in the person's control. As Adams points out, "motive utilitarianism is not about what motives one ought to foster and promote, or *try* to have, but about what motives one ought to *have*" (474). This is indeed so, but it is by no means obvious that one must accept the moral superiority of the *person* who happens to have the best motives "without really trying" over the person who does his damnedest best to develop the best motives. Second, even if the motives are entirely within the person's control, it is arguable whether the rightness of the motive may be fully translatable into the goodness of the person. If, for example, it were to turn out that the motivation of merciless profit maximization happens, in fact, to produce the highest utility sum, though it would be clearly right in terms of motive utilitarianism to describe that as the best motivation, the judgment of the moral worth of the person capable of such ruthlessness would remain a separate issue, requiring a treatment of its own.

II. Outcome Utilitarianism and Sum-ranking

Since outcome utilitarianism is common to different varieties of utilitarianism, any criticism of outcome utilitarianism applies to all these variants.[11] I shall confine my discussion to only two types of difficulties with outcome utilitarianism, but they can be seen as applying respectively to two "weaker" requirements into which outcome utilitarianism can be factorized.

> *Welfarism*: The judgment of the relative goodness of alternative states of affairs must be based exclusively on, and taken as an increasing function of, the respective collections of individual utilities in these states.

> *Sum-ranking*: One collection of individual utilities is at least as good as another if and only if it has at least as large a sum total.

It is easily checked that welfarism and sum-ranking together are exactly equivalent to outcome utilitarianism. I am concerned with sum-ranking in this section and will go into welfarism in the next. Sum-ranking can be criticized from the moral perspective of egalitarianism, and John Rawls's "Difference Principle" was partly a response to the characteristic of utilitarianism of being "indifferent as to how a constant sum of benefits is distributed" (*A Theory of Justice*, p. 77). That sum-ranking is completely insensitive to the inequality of utilities is obvious enough. I have tried to discuss elsewhere the unpalatable implications of sum-ranking,[12] and rather than repeat that discussion I shall confine myself to a few additional remarks only.

First, it is possible to define individual utilities in such a way that the only way of aggregating them is by summation. By confining his attention to utilities defined in that way, John Harsanyi has denied the credibility of "nonlinear social welfare functions."[13] That denial holds perfectly well for the utility measures to which Harsanyi confines his attention, but has no general validity outside that limited framework.[14] Thus, sum-ranking remains an open issue to be discussed in terms of its moral merits – and in particular, our concern for equality of utilities – and cannot be "thrust upon" us on grounds of consistency.[15]

Second, if interpersonal comparisons of utility are given only norma-tive interpretations, without any independent descriptive content, then it is possible to have a "dual" representation such that in terms of one rep-resentation the utility sum is maximized while in terms of the other representation the specified conditions of "equity" are met.[16] Although this remarkable result is of very considerable analytical interest, it does not resolve the conflict between sum-ranking and equity when utility comparisons do have *descriptive* content, as is assumed by the typical utilitarian.

Third, that great utilitarian, Henry Sidgwick, was himself acutely aware of the fact that "the Utilitarian formula seems to supply no answer" to the question "whether any mode of distributing a given quantum of happiness is better than any other" (*The Method of Ethics*, 416). He declared his support for "pure equality" as "the only one which does not need a special justification" (417; see also 447). This would go against sum-ranking and also against outcome utilitarianism, but Sidgwick did not seem to entertain any possibility of trade-offs between the size of the utility sum and the equality of the utility distribution. Indeed, one gets the impression that the strict ordering of the sum total would have lexicographic priority over the consideration of equality in Sidgwick's system, which could make the violation of sum-ranking very marginal indeed. The "classical utilitarian," as Rawls observed, "appeals to equal-ity only to break ties" (77). It is not surprising that people who argue for equality don't find this good enough.

Finally, an important question on distributional equity concerns the correspondence between our attitudes toward two kinds of distribution: between different persons, and between different time-periods in the life of the same person. Utilitarians have the same attitude to both, believing (i) that equality of utility distribution between persons has no more intrin-sic value than equality of utility distribution at different points of time for the same person, and (ii) that value is negligible (used only for breaking ties, if it is used at all). Derek Parfit has forcefully argued that this utili-tarian attitude becomes more plausible – though by no means obligatory – if we reject what he calls "the simple view" about the nature of personal identity.[17] On this view, which he believes that most of us implicitly hold, personal identity is a peculiarly deep further fact, over and above the facts of bodily or psychological continuity. I accept that personal identity may be less deep than we commonly assume, and agree that the effect of realizing this is to weaken the claim that "a person's burden, while it can be morally outweighed by benefit to him, cannot ever be outweighed by mere benefits to others" (Parfit, 1973, p. 156). My difficulty with Parfit's argument that the rejection of the "simple view" provides some defense for the utilitarian unconcern with *inter*personal distribution arises partly from the belief that the moral intuitions dealing with *intra*personal distribution which are referred to in this defense depend heavily on the acceptance of the "simple view." When we reject the "simple view," the case for revising our moral beliefs on *intra*personal distribution is very strong. Thus, we could move *toward* (i) but *against* (ii). This would provide a different way, unlike that of the utilitarians, of making our attitudes to *inter*personal and *intra*personal distribution correspond closely to each other.

Even in terms of moral beliefs that can be found among people who take the "simple view," it is, in fact, not the case that no importance is attached to *intra*personal distributions. The tragedy of King Lear's fate is not thought to be effectively blunted because Lear was unusually fortunate in the earlier parts of his long life. Similarly, the typical economic judgment on the undesirability of "poverty" or "inequality" looks at a "snapshot picture" of the economy at a point of time, and the poverty of a person is not weighed up or down in terms of the deal that he has got in the past or is expected to get in the future. I am not arguing that these judgments will be fully vindicated by further moral reflection, but only that it is not true that there is a general acceptance of the moral irrelevance of *intra*personal inequality. And this is already the case even for those who take the "simple view" of personal identity which Parfit attacks. The "equilibrium" moral beliefs if we reject that view may well involve further emphasis being put on *intra*personal distribution.

III.   Welfarism as Outcome Morality

I turn now to welfarism, which is the other – and in some ways, more fundamental – element in simple utilitarianism. This can be seen as imposing an "informational constraint" in making moral judgments about alternative states of affairs.[18] If all the personal utility information about two states of affairs that can be known is known, then they can be judged without any other information about these states. This need not stop us from using non-utility information as "surrogates" for utility information when utility information is scarce (e.g., using the availability of "primary social goods" as an index of utility in one – apocryphal – interpretation of Rawls's approach), but the non-utility information then has no status of its own independent of the indications it gives of the utility picture.

A very general approach within the structure of welfarism is that of maximizing the sum of some particular concave transformation of each person's utilities. This approach has been used by James Mirrlees.[19] The kind of egalitarian considerations we discussed in the last section can be easily accommodated within the Mirrleesian approach, of which simple utilitarianism and the utility-based version of the Rawlsian difference principle will be special cases.[20] But welfarism also covers cases that are not within the Mirrleesian approach, e.g., judging the welfare of the society in terms of the utility of the "median" person in the utility ranking. This section is concerned with a critique of welfarism as such, and in the arguments to be presented nothing more will be used than the informational constraint asserting the *sufficiency* of utility information for judgments of states of affairs.

It is perhaps also worth remarking that welfarism is, in an important way, less demanding than the Aristotelian notion of "eudaimonism," which has been recently discussed by Bernard Williams and others. Eudaimonism has clear affinities with welfarism, but they are not the same, since eudaimonism is concerned with judging *actions*, whereas welfarism is an approach for judging *states of affairs*. "To say . . . that the system is *eudaimonistic* is to say that what it regards as the desirable feature of actions is that they should increase or maximize people's *happiness*" (Williams, 1973, 79). This characterization of eudaimonism is in line with Aristotle's own action-centered introduction to the subject: "let us discuss what is that which is aimed at by politics and what is the highest of all goods achievable by *action*."[21] On this characterization of eudaimonism, it corresponds to welfarism in a way similar to the correspondence between consequentialist utilitarian structures and outcome utilitarianism. But it is also clear that Aristotle was, in fact, greatly concerned with examining the claims of what we have been calling welfarism, in much the same way as someone may be concerned with outcome utilitarianism as a basis for complex utilitarian structures.

Welfarism is essentially an informational constraint for moral judgments about states of affairs. In order to scrutinize it, we may consider *two* pairs (x,y) and (a,b) of states of affairs which have *identical* utility information (x has the same as a and y has the same as b), but differ in other respects. Welfarism would require that x must be ranked vis-à-vis y in exactly the same way as a is ranked vis-à-vis b, irrespective of the non-utility descriptions.

Consider first the pair (x,y). Let there be two persons r (rich) and p (poor), and let the difference between x and y rest in the fact that in x there is no redistributive taxation, whereas in y some money obtained by taxing r has been passed on to p, even though r continues to remain richer than p. The utility values of the two persons in the two states are the following:

		states	
		x (no tax)	y (redistributive tax)
	r	10	8
utilities			
	p	4	7

Outcome utilitarianism must rank y above x. So must the utility-based variant of the Rawlsian difference principle. So must all criteria that combine considerations of *total* utility with the *equality* of utility distribution.[22] But this isn't what I am concerned with here, since my focus must be on the correspondence between the ranking of two pairs, of which (x,y) is one.

For considering states of affairs a and b, let r be a romantic dreamer and p a miserable policeman. In b the policeman tortures the dreamer; in a he does not. The dreamer has a happy disposition ("the future is ours") and also happens to be rich, in good health, and resilient, while the policeman is morose, poor, ill, and frustrated, getting his simple pleasures out of torturing. The utility values for p and r happen to be the same as in x and y.

		states	
		a (no torture)	b (torture of r by p)
	r	10	8
utilities			
	p	4	7

Welfarism leaves us free to rank a over b *or* the other way round (or as indifferent), just as it leaves us free to rank x vis-à-vis y in either way, when we consider these rankings separately. However, it requires that x and y be ranked *in exactly the same way* as a and b, respectively. That is, welfarism would insist that the state of affairs with redistributive taxation (y) is better than that without taxation (x) *if and only if* the state of affairs with the torture (b) is better than that without torture (a). Many people would, however, hold that the case involving redistributive taxation is better (i.e., *y is* better than *x*) but the case involving torture is not (i.e., *b* is not better than *a*). One is free to hold such a view only by rejecting welfarism. To discriminate between the two pairs would bring in non-utility information, which can have no role of its own under welfarism.

Before I consider the example further, I would like to point out certain claims that welfarism does *not* require us to make. It is important to emphasize the claims that are not being made if we are to avoid being influenced against welfarism through misunderstanding of its content.

First, to say that the state of affairs with torture is better than that without it, is not the same as saying that the policeman *p should* undertake this torture. That would be a judgment about actions, not about states of affairs as such, and the link between the two must depend on whether a consequentialist view is taken, and even if consequentialism were accepted, it would depend on the *version* of consequentialism to be used. To say that the state of affairs with torture is better does not even amount to asserting that the policeman would not be acting wrongly by indulging in his simple pleasures. (An act consequentialist who accepts welfarism – for brevity, an "act welfarist" – must do this translation if this torture has no other consequences, but a welfarist need not be an act consequentialist.)

Second, to say that the state of affairs with torture is better than the one without it, does not even remotely imply that the policeman is being a *good man* in torturing the romantic dreamer. Indeed, even an act consequentialist does not have to translate the judgment about states of affairs into a judgment about the goodness of the person undertaking the action in question. Indeed, an act consequentialist who supports both taxation and torture in the two cases as respectively the "right" actions, is not even obliged to accept the torture as "good action," if he characterizes "good action" as "what a good man would do, even if not right."[23]

If we find the welfarist position unacceptable, we have to make sure that this finding does not arise from a misunderstanding of it as identified with these other claims. This is particularly important if we are to avoid falling into the trap of what R. M. Hare calls "the commonest trick of the opponents of utilitarianism." Hare distinguishes between "level-1" thinking at an immediate intuitive level and "level-2" thinking at a more critical level. "Level-1" principles are for use in "practical moral thinking especially under conditions of stress," and "they have to be general enough to be impartable by education (including self-education), and to be 'of ready application in the emergency'," while "level-2 principles are what would be arrived at by leisured moral thought in completely adequate knowledge of facts, as the right answer in a specific case" (122/3).

The commonest trick of the opponents of utilitarianism is to take examples of such [level-2] thinking, usually addressed to fantastic cases, and confront them with what the ordinary man would think. It makes the utilitarian look like a moral monster. The anti-utilitarians have usually confined their own thought about moral reasoning (with fairly infrequent lapses which often go unnoticed) to what I am calling level-1, the level of everyday moral thinking of ordinary, often stressful, occasions in which information is sparse. (123)

Hare's distinction between level-1 and level-2 thinking is clearly important, and one has to be careful that in evaluating applications of utilitarianism – more generally, of welfarism – that go against one's moral intuition, one is not being caught in the trap of the roughness of level-1 immediacy rather than exercising level-2 wisdom. Hare would presumably think that that is exactly what is happening in the taxation-and-torture correspondence, since he is persuaded that "the thinking of our archangel" – uncompromisingly level-2 – will be of "a specific rule-utilitarian sort," which is "practically equivalent to universalistic act-utilitarianism"; this clearly will incorporate outcome utilitarianism. Departures from this would reflect, at best, "the thinking of ordinary people whom he [the archangel] has educated," reflecting "good general principles," which they use "in ordinary level-1 moral thinking especially in situations of stress" (124/5).

It seems a bit immodest to have to claim that one's rejection of welfarism does not reflect "the thinking of ordinary people" indulging in level-1 cogitation. But perhaps a few cautious defensive statements could be made.

First, there is little difficulty in accepting the proposition that *if* the "archangel" *were* utilitarian, he may encourage people to have a hostile attitude toward torture, since such an attitude can be an effective *means* to utilitarian ends. But that is not the same thing as saying that one's disapproval of torture arises *only* from such indirect reasons. Whether giving "equal weight to the equal interests of all the parties in a situation," to use Hare's formula (116), requires one to attach the same weight to a person's enjoyment of food or shelter or personal liberty as to his joy from torturing is surely subject to critical questioning. The utilitarian archangel, since he must accept outcome utilitarianism, has to put b (with torture) above a (without torture), even though, when it comes to choosing "general principles" for the "ordinary people," he will include a principle against torture as a good means to the utilitarian end. But an archangel who has not taken such a simple interpretation of giving "equal weight to equal interests" need not be a utilitarian, nor a welfarist. If one finds after "leisured moral thought" that one is unable to attach the same level of "urgency"[24] to utilities arising from different sources, this need not be put down as the result of some archangelic cunning in implanting moral education in pursuit of goals that do not discriminate among different sources of utility.

Second, to be of practical use, level-1 principles must be of rather simple kind, e.g., torture is always bad, or give "no weight at all or a negative weight" to such desires (see Hare, 122). Welfarism contradicts not only such straightforward rules, but also rather less simple principles; e.g., utility from torture should get less weight than utility from other sources (this weight can be positive, negative, or zero). If someone is inclined to take such a position, it is unlikely that all he is doing is to express his level-1 prejudice. Indeed one could even claim that to attach the same importance to all types of utility irrespective of source as a rough-and-ready principle has some appeal for intuitive level-1 thinking, but not at the critical level-2 when there is time and leisure to consider principles more complex than the simple welfarist rules such as the utilitarian rule.

Third, welfarism and outcome utilitarianism are directly concerned not with judging action, but with ranking *states of affairs*. This is, in a significant sense, at some distance from one's immediate intuitions on *action*, with which level-1 thinking must be primarily concerned. Since welfarism would not by itself assert – as explained earlier – in the example about taxation and torture that "policeman p will not be acting wrongly in torturing the romantic dreamer, if the redistributive taxation is justified," a denial of welfarism does not turn on this issue at all. Moral thinking about judgments on ordering states of affairs requires one to move some distance from attitudes toward actions as such, and would necessitate the use of one's critical faculty.

It is, however, possible that a person making a judgment on outcome utilitarianism or welfarism might not precisely understand what he is doing, and his revulsion at the policeman's *act* of torture at this level-1 thinking could be "infecting" his judgment in ordering the states of affairs.[25] In order to avoid this, the example can be somewhat changed so that neither party brings the situation about through some positive action. Let r be the rider of a motor cycle – joyful, rich, in good health and resilient – while p is a pedestrian – morose, poor, ill in health, and frustrated. In state m the rider gleefully goes by; in state n he falls inadvertently into a ditch, breaking his bike and getting bruised badly. The rider is worse off in n than in m, while the pedestrian, who has not caused the accident in any way, thoroughly enjoys the discomfiture and discomfort of the rider

("I could kill myself laughing looking at that crestfallen Angel!"). The utility values of r and p are the same in this case as in the earlier two cases.

		states	
		m (no accident)	n (accident)
	r	10	8
utilities			
	p	4	7

Welfarism would require us to say that if the state of affairs with taxation (y) is better than the one without it (x), then the state of affairs with the rider in the ditch (n) is better than the one without the accident (m). If on reflection one would like to deny this – as I would – maintaining that one can distinguish between sources of utility in deciding on the moral weights to be put on them, there is no danger of this judgment being due to any "infection" from a level-1 judgment about acts like torture where one person inflicts harm on another, since no such act is involved.

It is perhaps worth emphasizing that a nonwelfarist view that suggests that "m may not be ranked vis-à-vis n in exactly the same way as x is ranked vis-à-vis y" need *not* be based on attaching *zero or negative* weight to the pedestrian p's pleasure (because it arises from someone else's discomfort or discomfiture). It is adequate that the utility of poor p from more income through redistributive taxation be treated differently from the utility of p from enjoying the tragic fate of r. It is indeed possible to maintain without any inconsistency that a much larger utility gain of p or a much smaller utility loss of r from the accident might have made the state with the accident better than the state without it. All that is being denied is that a coincidence of the utility picture of (m,n) vis-à-vis (x,y) must necessitate that (m,n) be ranked in exactly the same way as (x,y).

Welfarism is an exacting demand, ruling out essential use of any non-utility information (the use of non-utility information being confined to instrumental analysis or as surrogate for utility information when the latter is incomplete). In this paper the non-utility information that has been most discussed relates to different *sources* of utility and the motivation underlying it, but similar difficulties can arise from the relevance of other kinds of non-utility information as well. An outcome morality incorporating such principles as "equal pay for equal work," or elimination of "exploitation," or priority for feeding the hungry, requires essential use of non-utility information. An outcome utilitarian (or a welfarist) who defends such principles must do so on some instrumental grounds, i.e., in terms of their favorable influence on outcomes judged rigidly in the utilitarian (or some other welfarist) scale, and this misses those discriminations which can be achieved by making these principles have some role in the outcome morality itself. The informational constraints imposed by welfarism restrict the scope of moral discrimination of outcomes very severely indeed. The limitations can be brought out by looking at correspondences between judgments in different cases that are identical on the utility space but not in terms of particular non-utility information (as in the method of argument used in this section).[26]

IV. Weak Paretianism as Outcome Morality

Welfarism asserts unconditionally the adequacy of utility information for outcome morality. Weak Paretianism asserts this adequacy conditionally, viz., for the special case in which everyone's utility ranking happens to coincide.

> *Weak Paretianism*: If state of affairs x is higher than state of affairs y in everyone's utility ranking, then x is a better state than y.

This is indeed a mild-looking component of welfarism and outcome utilitarianism, and if weak Paretianism is to be rejected, then the adequacy of utility information would be denied in what might appear to be the most straightforward case. Indeed, weak Paretianism is typically regarded as the least controversial of the criteria used in welfare economics for judging states of affairs.[27]

Does the criticism of welfarism in the last section apply to weak Paretianism? The immediate answer is no, since the cases considered involved *conflicts* in individual utility rankings (with p and r having opposite rankings). But a more probing question can be posed. Is it possible that the type of considerations that led us to question welfarism by attaching different importance to utility from different sources can also provide a case for violating even the shared utility ranking of all? If the possibility of differential importance of utility according to source is conceded, because of the relevance of non-utility considerations, is it not possible that the resulting outcome morality could go even against everyone's total utility ranking, thereby violating the weak Pareto principle?

This type of question relates closely to the issues underlying the problem of the "Paretian Libertarian" which I have analyzed elsewhere.[28]

Libertarian values require that particular importance be attached to each person's desires over pairs that are, in an obvious sense, "personal" to him, e.g., what he should read. If two states of affairs x and y differ from each other only in some such private features related to a particular person, and are in other respects identical, then the ranking of x vis-à-vis y may be thought to belong to that person's "personal domain" or "protected sphere." Libertarianism may be seen, thus, to require that that person's utility ranking should prevail in the outcome-morality ranking of such pairs in each person's "protected sphere." It can be shown that such a condition of libertarianism, *even* in the very limited form of demanding a nonempty "personal domain" for just two persons, can easily conflict with the weak Pareto principle in terms of the inter-pair consistency of outcome morality.[29]

I shall not go here into the formal aspects of this impossibility result, but refer only to an example that was used to illustrate the conflict. There is a book thought to be pornographic and disapproved of by prude P but not by lewd L. (My first presentation of the problem is clearly dated by the fact that I chose *Lady Chatterley's Lover* as the controversial book in question – a choice that may now appear puzzling.) The states of affairs p, l, and o differ from each other in the respect that in p the prude reads the book, in l the lewd reads the book, and in o nobody reads the book. The utility ranking of the prude in descending order is: o ("great escape"), p ("sad to have to read that muck"), l ("much more awful to think of that depraved lewd gloating over this terrible stuff"). The lewd's utility ranking in descending order is: p ("true delight in thinking of the discomfort of that pompous prude suffering the consequences of his absurd disposition"), l ("good fun"), o ("waste of a good book"). The orderings, thus, are:

P's utility ranking	*L's utility ranking*
o	p
p	l
l	o

The outcomes do not differ in any other respect, e.g., through the influence of one's reading on one's actions or dispositions or capacities,[30] and no indirect effects need be considered.

An outcome morality that is both libertarian and weak Paretian then faces the following dilemma. Clearly, o is better than p on libertarian grounds, since the difference between the two states consists in whether the prude has to read the book or not (the lewd is not directly involved), and the prude has no desire to read it since he suffers from reading it. Similarly, l is better than o, since the difference in this case consists in whether the lewd reads the book or not (the prude is not directly involved), and the lewd desires to read the book and gains from it. But on Paretian grounds p is better than l, since both have more utility from p than from l. *Every* state is worse than some other in this Paretian and libertarian outcome morality.

Various ways of avoiding this conflict have been proposed in the literature. Some methods, proposed by Allan Gibbard, Julian Blau, and others, preserve the Pareto principle and make the libertarian principle conditional.[31] Others, including Robert Nozick and – amidst exploring other solutions – Michael Farrell, have responded to the problem by retaining the Pareto principle in the outcome morality, resting the burden of safeguarding liberty on *nonconsequentialist* judgments of action.[32] And some have proposed relaxing the weak Pareto principle by making it conditional, retaining the libertarian principle in the outcome morality.[33] Still other avenues have been explored.[34]

I have tried to discuss elsewhere the merits of the proposed solutions,[35] and will refrain from doing this here. By varying the exact non-utility description of the conflict but retaining the same utility rankings, persuasive arguments can be produced *either* in favor of relaxing the weak Pareto principle *or* in favor of relaxing the libertarian principle. It is not my intention to deny this plurality. Rather to assert it. The plurality shows how a variation of non-utility description can precipitate different moral judgments even when the utility description is unaltered,[36] and this is, of course, contrary to the essence of welfarism. Non-utility information relating to *how* "personal" the choices are,[37] what *motivation* the persons have behind their utility rankings, whether the interdependence arises from liking or disliking the others' physical *acts* (in this case, the reading of the book) or from the *joys and sufferings* of the others, etc., may well be found to be relevant in deciding which way to resolve the conflict. If so, then the adequacy of utility information is denied. More particularly, the existence of circumstances that would lead to the moral rejection of the outcome supported by the weak Pareto principle would indicate that welfarism even in this apparently mild form can be too demanding.

Can this criticism of Paretianism be softened by invoking Richard Hare's distinction between "level-1" ("intuitive") and "level-2" ("critical") moral thinking? There is, of course, no difficulty in *conceiving* of an archangelic outcome-utilitarian (or – more generally – an archangelic welfarist, or – even more generally – an archangelic weak Paretian) supporting libertarian intuitions for day-to-day quick decisions, and even of a domesticated archangel bent on the task "to bring up his children" – sticking to the Harean analogy (Hare, 1976, p. 124) – with fostered libertarian values. But can the tension not be interpreted in exactly the opposite line to this? Paretianism does seem to have immense immediate appeal; it is very much a level-1 winner. Insofar as Paretianism is based on catering to everyone's interests – on a very simple interpretation of interests – its immediate appeal is not difficult to explain. Nor is it in general a bad quick rule to follow even from the libertarian point of view: conflicts of the kind captured in the example above (and more generally in the Pareto-libertarian impossibility theorems) may well be rare. Libertarian values, on the other hand, require rather complex distinctions to be made, e.g., between *sources* of happiness, between *domains* of personal affairs, and between different conceptions of a person's *interest*. It seems, therefore, not unplausible that an intuitive (level-1) Paretianism may go with a critical (level-2) libertarianism.

In the conversation that follows – between a libertarian outcome moralist and an outcome utilitarian – I have tried to demonstrate the plausibility of such a combination. It may seem that I have put Richard Hare on his head – exactly reversing the correspondence of utilitarian and nonutilitarian positions vis-à-vis "critical" and "intuitive" moral thoughts. But I would like to emphasize that the argument has the "Harean" feature of invoking the distinction, which seems to me to be important, between these two levels. More specifically, the general principle that is used as the main criterion is the Harean one of "giving equal weight to the equal interests of the occupants of all the roles in the situation" (116). The difference arises from the interpretation of a person's "interest," disputing its identification with utility – either as desire-fulfillment or as happiness.

I have to report that it was a little difficult to get an outcome libertarian for the dialogue, since libertarians tend to be anti-consequentialist and ferociously "deontic," but by a lucky coincidence the prude P in the example considered earlier, confessed to being an outcome libertarian. He was dispatched to talk to the utilitarian, who found (not to his surprise, since he had read his Hare) that his adversary had "usually confined" his "own thought about moral reasoning (with fairly infrequent lapses which often go unnoticed) to . . . level-1, the level of everyday moral thinking of ordinary, often stressful, occasions in which information is sparse" (123). P was himself acutely aware of his own condition, and eagerly met the utilitarian healer – Doctor U – in the latter's surgery for diagnosis and advice.

U: I understand you experience moral intuitions. When do you get them?

P: At night, doctor, and also during the day. I am much bothered by them.

U: I bet you are, but don't worry, we are here to help you.

P: Shall I tell you about my moral intuitions?

U: Yes, yes, please do so. I am resigned to hearing them; people are always telling me about their moral intuitions. But I must later explain to you that what is important is not what moral intuitions you have, but what moral intuitions you *ought* to have.

P: I am truly relieved to hear that, doctor, since I am much bothered by my immediate moral intuitions.

U: Don't worry at all; that's a good sign. I take it that your immediate moral intuitions relate to fantastic cases which make the utilitarian look like a moral monster? I know that ailment well.

P: Actually, doctor, my immediate moral intuitions are typically utilitarian, and certainly invariably Paretian.

U: So what seems to be the problem?

P: Just that when I have one of my fairly infrequent lapses into thinking critically about my Paretian and utilitarian moral intuitions, I find I cannot sustain them.

U: Obviously, you must think critically *differently*. But first tell me about this Lawrence book – which I understand you find pornographic.

P: A truly revolting book, doctor. What I have heard about it is enough. I certainly wouldn't wish to go so far as to read it.

U: Yes, but I gather that you desire that the lewd shouldn't read it either?

P: How can I desire anything else, doctor? I would suffer so immensely from the thought of his gloating over it. Imagine his face, doctor! Or worse. No, no, I desire even less that he should read that stuff.

U: I understand that he too desires that you rather than he should read the book.

P: Exactly. And so my immediate moral intuition is that it is better that I should read the book rather than he. *Must be* good, I hear myself saying when I am in a hurry, since it increases everybody's utility!

P: Have you made sure that there are no indirect effects? You must consider them too.

P: I have. There are none. No, my reading the book, stopping the lewd from reading it, will make everyone happier.

U: So what's the problem? What's wrong with you reading it rather than the lewd?

P: Simply that I *detest* the book and he *loves* it! When I think about it coolly, I ask myself: why should I have to read something I hate, while he is stopped from reading something he would so much enjoy reading?

U: But, don't you see, P, that he would *enjoy even more* your reading the book, and you would have *even more pain* from his reading the book. The net gain in utility of both is positive from your reading the book.

P: Yes, so far as the *total* utility of each is concerned. But should the lewd's pleasure in meddling in my affairs or my discomfort from my nosiness about what he does, have the same weight in the moral accounting as his own reading pleasure or my own reading discomfort?

U: Perhaps you are trying to say that it is morally wrong for you to have these nosy feelings. Perhaps you are really worried that the world would be a less happy place if everyone were nosy about others' tastes. If so, I am inclined to think that I can help you to build a more sophisticated argument involving universalization.

P: But, doctor, I haven't been able to see that it is morally wrong for me to have these nosy feelings. Indeed, I would never forgive myself if I were not revolted by the lewd's detestable reading pleasures! I am not saying that I shouldn't have these nosy feelings, but only that these nosy feelings shouldn't count in the moral weighing of what the lewd ends up reading – at least not count as much as his own feelings about his reading. The lewd has the right to enjoy reading what he likes; I have the right to feel revolted by it; and the only reason his pleasure has a different moral status from my pleasure, in this particular case, is that it is *his* reading that we are talking about.

U: And you wouldn't find it odd to recommend something that makes everyone unhappier than he need be?

P: My immediate intuitions are, of course, offended by it. But thinking about it more critically, I can see that such a recommendation must follow from agreeing that it is morally better that the lewd be able to read what he likes than that I have to read something I detest. What is at stake is our interests in the form of our ability to do with our own lives what we want. This covers our ability to read what we like and avoid reading what we don't like. Our interests are less clearly involved in the power to stop others from reading what they like or to make them read what they detest. Do you see what I am trying to say?

U: Of course, I follow your simple thoughts, but I have to tell you that you have just replaced one set of moral intuitions by another. You are still stuck at level 1, and will, I guess, stay there until your critical thinking takes you in a different direction. If you want to defend libertarian values critically, you would find better ground by introducing indirect effects, and by considering the problems posed by universalization, and you can then be a utilitarian too, I am happy to say.

P: That's a nice thought; I would have loved to be a utilitarian, since my immediate intuitions *are* rather utilitarian. But reflection reveals that in this case utilitarianism – even Paretianism – will conflict with acknowledging that it is morally better that the lewd – rather than I – should read the book he loves and I detest. And I am thus forced to reject utilitarianism – even Paretianism. The lewd also agrees with this moral judgment, as it happens.

U: He does, does he? What would you say, then, if someone suggested that you are *already* a Paretian – possibly even a utilitarian, since *both* of you think that the lewd reading the book is better. You are thus recommending what everyone desires and what is in everyone's interest.

P: I would say, quoting Hare, please "do not confuse the issue, as some do, by introducing moral considerations into this prudential question" as to "what are someone's true interests," i.e., "by alleging that becoming morally better, or worse, in itself affects a man's interests" (Hare, 118).

U: Despite your poor ability to absorb what you read, you do show good taste in your reading. But, I am afraid, you have a long way to go, and much more to read.

P: I know that, doctor. I will, in fact, read more utilitarian literature if I get the time.

U: Now, there! You have just given – at long last – a good reason why the lewd – and not you – should read that other book, which he loves and you detest. You need the time to read utilitarian literature, and that will increase everyone's utility. Good critical thinking, P, and a fine indirect utilitarian justification of your intuitive libertarian feelings!

I leave them there, and end this section with a clarificatory remark. Corresponding to the distinction between pleasure-based utilitarianism and desire-based utilitarianism, both welfarism and Paretianism can be defined in either way. It is, therefore, worth noting that the difficulties with Paretianism discussed here (and those with welfarism discussed in the last section) apply to interpretations based on desires as well as to pleasure-based interpretations. The descriptions given can be taken in either sense, or both, without eliminating the problem. In fact, both the interpretations were explicitly invoked in the dialogue.

V. Concluding Remarks

I end with a few general remarks, to put the discussion in perspective.

First, an "outcome morality" is a morality dealing with judging states of affairs. Any utilitarian moral structure, e.g., act utilitarianism, rule utilitarianism, or motive utilitarianism, is made up of such an outcome morality, viz., "outcome utilitarianism," and some version of consequentialism causally relating other entities (e.g., acts, rules, or motives) to states of affairs, which are assessed through outcome utilitarianism. Since outcome utilitarianism is common to all these structures, any limitation of it applies to these structures without exception (section I). This is independent of how we decide to assess actions, e.g., whether by contrasting one act with another, or one rule with another.

Second, outcome utilitarianism can be split into "welfarism" and "sum-ranking" (section II). Welfarism asserts that the goodness of states of affairs depends ultimately only on the personal utilities in the respective states, and sum-ranking asserts that the appropriate way of combining personal utilities to assess goodness is by addition.

Third, sum-ranking makes it difficult to accommodate egalitarian values, when personal utility measures are taken to have independent descriptive content rather than being defined in terms of the *moral* valuation of the respective individual situations. This limitation remains substantial even after what Parfit calls the "simple view" of personal identity (section III) is rejected.

Fourth, welfarism is a more limited approach than it might appear at first sight. Its limitations can be properly brought out only by considering *correspondences* between different judgments, and not by considering each such judgment on its own (section III).

Fifth, Hare's distinction between "intuitive" level-1 and "critical" level-2 thinking is both important and useful, but it is not easy to sustain the claim that intuitive difficulties with the implications of the utilitarian (and, more generally, welfarist) approaches would tend to be resolved at the critical level (section III). Indeed, the exact opposite can be the case, and an *intuitive utilitarian* (or welfarist) position may go with a *critical non-utilitarian* (or non-welfarist) position (section IV).

Sixth, considerations of liberty and rights have been viewed here as parts of the structure of outcome morality itself (sections III and IV). This contrasts with treating them as constraints on, or nonconsequentialist judgments of, actions, as in the systems proposed by, say, Nozick (Nozick, 1974). This shift is possible because of the departure from the tradition – often implicit – of identifying *consequences* with *utility consequences* (and of basing the description of states of affairs entirely on utility information regarding these states). But a tortured body, an unfed belly, a bullied person, or unequal pay for equal work, is as much a part of the state affairs as the utility and disutility occurring in that state.[38] A teleological approach can, therefore, give more than an instrumental role to rights.[39]

Seventh, the weak Pareto principle can be viewed as a mild version of welfarism. Even this mild version raises serious consistency problems with elementary considerations of personal liberty, and a case can be made for the rejection of the unconditional use of the weak Pareto principle (section IV). A critical issue relates to whether a person's "interests" are best represented by his or her utility level (interpreted either in terms of pleasure and pain, or as desire satisfaction), *irrespective* of the source of utility and the non-utility characteristics of states of affairs.

Finally, since (i) any utilitarian moral structure implies outcome utilitarianism (but not vice versa), (ii) outcome utilitarianism implies welfarism (but not vice versa), (iii) welfarism implies Paretianism (but not vice versa), and (iv) Paretianism implies weak Paretianism (but not vice versa), a rejection of weak Paretianism has rather far-reaching consequences, affecting *all* utilitarian moralities, *and* a great many others.

Notes

1   "A Critique of Utilitarianism," in Williams and J. J. C. Smart, *Utilitarianism: For and Against* (New York: Cambridge, 1973), p. 79. Williams explains that in this essay he is "particularly concerned with" the features referred to.

2 *Forms and Limits of Utilitarianism* (New York: Oxford, 1965), Preface.

3 See Kenneth J. Arrow, *Social Choice and Individual Values* (New York: Wiley, 2nd ed., 1963), p. 96.

4 Cf. "Standardly, the action will be right in virtue of its causal properties, of maximally conducing to good states of affairs . . . even a situation . . . in which the action itself possesses intrinsic value is one in which the rightness of the act is derived from the goodness of a certain state of affairs – the act is right *because* the state of affairs which consists in its being done is better than any other state of affairs accessible to the agent" (Williams, "A Critique of Utilitarianism," pp. 86/7).

5 See John Rawls, *A Theory of Justice* (Cambridge, Mass.: Harvard, 1971), pp. 76/7. It may be important to mention here that, although Rawls considers the claim of the *minimal* element of utilities as against that of *total* utility, his "Difference Principle" focuses directly on the minimal availability of "social primary goods" and not on minimal utility as such.

6 Although Sidgwick argued that "the Good investigated in Ethics is limited to Good in some degree attainable by human effort; accordingly knowledge of the end is sought in order to ascertain what actions are the right means to its attainment" [*The Method of Ethics* (London: Macmillan, 7th edition, 1907), p. 3], this is a statement on where the main interest in a principle like outcome utilitarianism would lie, and not a denial of its independent status. Indeed, Sidgwick made frequent use of outcome utilitarianism, even though he defined utilitarianism as "the ethical theory, that the conduct which under any given circumstances, is objectively right, is that which will produce the greatest amount of happiness on the whole" (411). In a different context, Sidgwick even asserted that "Bentham's dictum must be understood merely as making the conception of ultimate end precise . . . not as directly prescribing the rules of conduct by which this end will be best attained" (432).

7 Cf. my "Real National Income," *Review of Economic Studies*, XLIII, 1 (February 1976): 19–39.

8 For examples of the failure of act utilitarianism to deliver the best outcome, see Allan Gibbard, "Rule Utilitarianism: A Merely Illusory Alternative?," *Australasian Journal of Philosophy*, XLIII, 2 (August 1965): 211–19, and John Harsanyi, "Rule Utilitarianism and Decision Theory," *Erkenntnis*, XI (1977). I have tried to argue elsewhere that such failures apply not merely to act utilitarianism but to all single-influence consequentialism, including some versions of rule utilitarianism, while other versions of rule utilitarianism can lead to sub-optimal outcomes for other – clearly specifiable – reasons ("Welfare and Rights," text of Hägerström Lectures, delivered at Uppsala University in April 1978).

9 "Motive Utilitarianism," *Journal of Philosophy*, LXXIII, 14 (Aug. 12, 1976): 467–81, p. 470.

10 There is an additional issue, however, as to whether the motivation in question is that of a given person (which motivation of this person would lead to the best outcome *given* the motivations of the others?) or that of all members

of the community (which motivation, if *shared* by members of this community, would lead to the best outcome?).

11   I am not concerned in this paper with the problem of population being a variable, so that the distinction between "classical utilitarianism" and "average utilitarianism" does not arise.

12   *On Economic Inequality* (New York: Oxford, 1973), pp. 15–22.

13   "Nonlinear Social Welfare Functions: Do Welfare Economists Have a Special Exemption from Bayesian Rationality?" *Theory and Decision*, VI, 3 (August 1975): 311–32.

14   See my "Welfare Inequalities and Rawlsian Axiomatics," *Theory and Decision*, VII, 4 (October 1976): 243–62; reprinted in R. Butts and J. Hintikka, eds., *Foundational Problems in the Special Sciences* (Boston: Reidel, 1977).

15   For some moral arguments on the two sides, see Harsanyi, "Nonlinear Social Welfare Functions: A Rejoinder to Professor Sen," and my "Nonlinear Social Welfare Functions: A Reply to Professor Harsanyi," in Butts and Hintikka, eds., *Foundational Problems*. For the axiomatic structure of "utilitarianism" (in fact, of outcome utilitarianism), see C. d'Aspremont and L. Gevers, "Equity and the Informational Basis of Collective Choice," *Review of Economic Studies*, XLIV (1977); R. Deschamps and Gevers, "Leximin and Utilitarian Rules: A Joint Characterization," *Journal of Economic Theory*, XVII (1978); Eric Maskin, "A Theorem on Utilitarianism," *Review of Economic Studies*, XLV (1978); Kevin Roberts, "Interpersonal Comparability and Social Choice Theory," mimeographed, 1977, forthcoming in *Review of Economic Studies*, XLVII (1980).

16   See Peter Hammond, "Dual Interpersonal Comparisons of Utility and the Welfare Economics of Income Distribution," *Journal of Public Economics*, VII (1977).

17   "Later Selves and Moral Principles," in A. Montefiore, ed., *Philosophy and Personal Relations* (London: Routledge, 1973). See also his "Personal Identity," *Philosophical Review*, LXXX, 1 (January 1971): 3–27, and "Against Prudence," mimeographed 1977, ch. III.

18   See my "On Weights and Measures: Informational Constraints in Social Welfare Analysis," *Econometrica*, XLV (1977). "Welfarism" is defined there a bit less demandingly, viz., moral goodness of states being a function just of the n-tuple of individual utilities but not *necessarily* an *increasing* function. The informational constraint operates nevertheless.

19   "An Exploration in the Theory of Optimal Income Taxation," *Review of Economic Studies*, XXXVIII (1971). See also A. B. Atkinson, "On the Measurement of Inequality," *Journal of Economic Theory*, II (1970).

20   See also Arrow's "Some Ordinalist-Utilitarian Notes on Rawls's Theory of Justice," *Journal of Philosophy*, LXX, 9 (May 10, 1973): 245–63, and 13: 422; in which this entire approach is called "utilitarian." Arrow is, thus, led to the view that the Rawlsian maximin is a "limiting case" of utilitarianism. For the cardinal utility framework underlying the use of utilitarianism, this is, strictly speaking, inaccurate, since the strictly concave *exponential* transformations

considered by Arrow are not permissible. Arrow's statement applies, thus, to the class of additive social-welfare functions rather than to utilitarianism as such. On the particular form of the limiting case (i.e., whether pure maximin *or* lexicographic maximin should prevail as the degree concavity is taken to the limit), see Hammond, "A Note on Extreme Inequality Aversion," *Journal of Economic Theory*, xi (1975).

21 *The Nichomachean Ethics*, translated by H. G. Apostle (Dordrecht: Reidel, 1975), p. 3.

22 A class of such synthetic criteria have been investigated by C. Blackorby and D. Donaldson, "Utility vs. Equity: Some Plausible Quasi-orderings," *Journal of Public Economics*, vi (1977).

23 R. M. Hare, "Ethical Theory and Utilitarianism," in H. D. Lewis, ed., *Contemporary British Philosophy*, iv (London: Allen & Unwin, 1976), p. 126.

24 See T. M. Scanlon, "Preference and Urgency," *Journal of Philosophy*, lxxii, 19 (Nov. 6, 1975): 655–69. Note also that Rawls's specification of "the measurement of benefit" being in terms of "an index of social primary goods," including "rights, liberties and opportunities, income and wealth, and the social bases of self-respect," uses a notion of "urgency" that differs from intensities of utilities. The "difference principle" under this interpretation has the advantage of not being tied to welfarism (as the utility-based difference principle must be), and can discriminate between the cases of taxation (x,y) and torture (a,b). This is particularly important if one rejects the "priority" of Rawls's "principle of liberty" over his "difference principle" as untenable, since that priority is another way of distinguishing the two cases. For a powerful critique of that "priority" argument, see H. L. A. Hart, "Rawls on Liberty and Its Priority," *University of Chicago Law Review*, xl (1973); reprinted in Norman Daniels, ed., *Reading Rawls* (Oxford: Blackwell, 1975).

25 I am grateful to Derek Parfit for drawing my attention to this possibility. The example that follows, which tries to avoid any scope of such an "infection," owes much to my discussions with him.

26 For some indirect implications of welfarism and related conditions, see my "On Weights and Measures." The impossibility theorems of the type pioneered by Arrow (*Social Choice and Individual Values*) can also be shown to result from combining welfarism with *poor* utility information.

27 See Paul Samuelson, *Foundations of Economic Analysis* (Cambridge, Mass.: Harvard, 1947), ch. 8; J. de V. Graaff, *Theoretical Welfare Economics* (New York: Cambridge, 1957), pp. 9/10; I. M. D. Little, *A Critique of Welfare Economics* (New York: Oxford, 1957), pp. 84/5.

28 *Collective Choice and Social Welfare* (San Francisco: Holden-Day, 1970), ch. 6, and "Liberty, Unanimity and Rights," *Economica*, xliii (1976).

29 *Collective Choice and Social Welfare*, Theorems 6*1, 6*2, and 6*3. There are also related problems of internal consistency of libertarian values, on which see Gibbard, "A Pareto-consistent Libertarian Claim," *Journal of Economic Theory*, vii (1974); M. J. Farrell, "Liberalism in the Theory of Social Choice," *Review*

of Economic Studies, xliii (1976); Sen, "Liberty, Unanimity and Rights," pp. 234/5 and 243/4; Kotaro Suzumura, "On the Consistency of Libertarian Claims," *Review of Economic Studies*, xlv (1978).

30   Cf. "An adolescent ploughs through D. H. Lawrence in pursuit of pornographic matter and comes to acquire a taste for writing that is more passionate, original and imaginative than the works of Ian Fleming," Anthony Quinton, *Utilitarian Ethics* (London: Macmillan, 1973), p. 57.

31   Gibbard, "A Pareto-consistent Libertarian Claim"; Blau, "Liberal Values and Independence," *Review of Economic Studies*, xlii (1975); P. Bernholz, "Is a Paretian Liberal Really Impossible?" *Public Choice*, xix (1974); Christian Seidl, "On Liberal Values," *Zeitschrift für Nationalökonomie*, xxxv (1975); Jerry Kelly, "Rights-exercising and a Pareto-consistent Libertarian Claim," *Journal of Economic Theory*, xiii (1976); John A. Ferejohn, "The Distribution of Rights in Society," in H. W. Gottinger and W. Leinfellner, *Decision Theory and Social Ethics: Issues in Social Choice* (Boston: Reidel, 1978); Wulf Gaertner and Lorenz Kruger, "From Hand-cuffed Paretians to Self-consistent Libertarians: A New Possibility Theorem," forthcoming in *Economica*; Edi Karni, "Collective Rationality, Unanimity and Liberal Ethics," *Review of Economic Studies*, xlv (1978).

32   Nozick, *Anarchy, State and Utopia* (Oxford: Blackwell, 1974), pp. 164/5; Farrell, "Liberalism in the Theory of Social Choice," pp. 9/10; C. R. Perelli-Minetti, "Nozick on Sen: A Misunderstanding," *Theory and Decision*, viii, 4 (October 1977): 387–93.

33   Farrell, "Liberalism in the Theory of Social Choice," pp. 3–8; Sen, "Liberty, Unanimity and Rights," pp. 235–7 and 243/4; and Suzumura, "On the Consistency of Libertarian Claims," pp. 330–4. This line was examined also in my original presentation of the problem in *Collective Choice and Social Welfare*, pp. 83–5.

34   The scope of solving the problem by taking a nonbinary approach to social evaluation has been investigated by R. N. Batra and P. K. Pattanaik, "On Some Suggestions for Having Non-binary Social Choice Functions," *Theory and Decision*, iii, 1 (October 1972): 1–11, establishing that the problem reappears in the nonbinary context. The scope of "domain restriction" was explored by Blau, "Liberal Values and Independence," and also by F. Breyer, "The Liberal Paradox, Decisiveness over Issues, and Domain Restrictions," *Zeitschrift für Nationalökonomie*, xxxvii (1977). Other aspects of the problem have been studied in some other contributions, e.g., James Buchanan, "An Ambiguity in Sen's Alleged Proof of the Impossibility of the Paretian Libertarian," mimeographed paper, Virginia Polytechnic, 1976.

35   "Liberty, Unanimity and Rights," and also "Personal Utilities and Public Judgements: Or What's Wrong with Welfare Economics?," *Economic Journal*, lxxxix (1979). The latter also evaluates another line of reasoning that has been advocated, which seeks a "solution" to the problem by arguing that the "libertarian" outcome of the lewd reading the book cannot be an "equilibrium,"

since both parties would gain from passing on the book to the prude on condition that he read it. Thus the libertarian outcome is "unfeasible," and the chosen position must be Pareto optimal. This overlooks the possibility that the lewd or the prude, if libertarian, would not offer such a contract, and the assumption that each *must* do whatever maximizes his personal utility simply abstracts from the moral issue that is under discussion. The absence of an "equilibrium" with the "libertarian" outcome *if* everyone *were* to behave in a way that maximizes his personal utility provides no "solution" to the problem at hand. (It is also the case that such a contract may not be offered by the lewd on the prudential – rather than moral – ground that he may not be able to ensure that the prude will, in fact, read the book once it has been handed over to him.)

36 Contrast the two descriptions of the "Edwin-Angelina" case given respectively in Gibbard's "A Pareto-consistent Libertarian Claim," pp. 398/9, and in my "Liberty, Unanimity and Rights," pp. 225/6.

37 Cf. Ronald Dworkin's distinction between "personal" and "external" preferences, in *Taking Rights Seriously* (London: Duckworth, 1978), pp. 234–8.

38 I have tried to argue elsewhere that certain moral problems, e.g., the responsibility of person 1 when strong-armed 2 beats up person 3, can be much more easily analyzed in a system that incorporates rights in the outcome morality itself rather than just in nonconsequentialist evaluation of, or constraints on, actions ("Liberty, Unanimity and Rights," pp. 229–31, and more extensively in my Hägerström Lectures, "Welfare and Rights").

39 It may also be worth remarking that there is no reason why a nonwelfarist outcome morality (incorporating rights) cannot be combined with assessing actions in a non-fully-consequentialist way (incorporating rights in some way not captured by the first route). The status of rights in both these methods will be, in an important sense, more primitive than the instrumental status that rights enjoy in a consequentialist and welfarist moral structure (e.g., under act or rule utilitarianism).

Index